Ending the Siege of Leningrad

Acknowledgements: *Pablo Sagarra Renedo, Juan Negreira Parets, Lucas Molina Franco, Daniel Burguete, Lorenzo Fernandez-Navarro de los Paños, José Enrique Usunariz Mocoroa, Miguel Sanz, the Andrés Family, Galera Family, Hernanz Family, Marí Family, Prieto Family, Antonio Sánchez Pascuala and the Ysasi Family.*

Ending the Siege
of Leningrad

German and Spanish Artillery at the Battle of Krasny Bor

CARLOS CABALLERO JURADO

Translated by
Steve Turpin White

Pen & Sword
MILITARY

AN IMPRINT OF PEN & SWORD BOOKS LTD.
YORKSHIRE - PHILADELPHIA

First published in 2015 by Galland Books as *El Cerco de Leningrado*

First published in Great Britain in 2020 by
Pen & Sword Military
An imprint of
Pen & Sword Books Ltd
Yorkshire - Philadelphia

ISBN 978 1 52674 102 8

Typeset by Aura Technology and Software Services, India.
Printed and bound in England
By TJ International Ltd.

Pen & Sword Books Ltd incorporates the Imprints of Pen & Sword Archaeology, Atlas, Aviation, Battleground, Discovery, Family History, History, Maritime, Military, Naval, Politics, Railways, Select, Transport, True Crime, Fiction, Frontline Books, Leo Cooper, Praetorian Press, Seaforth Publishing, Wharncliffe and White Owl.

For a complete list of Pen & Sword titles please contact

PEN & SWORD BOOKS LIMITED
47 Church Street, Barnsley, South Yorkshire, S70 2AS, England
E-mail: enquiries@pen-and-sword.co.uk
Website: www.pen-and-sword.co.uk

or

PEN AND SWORD BOOKS
1950 Lawrence Rd, Havertown, PA 19083, USA
E-mail: uspen-and-sword@casematepublishers.com
Website: www.penandswordbooks.com

Contents

I

Introduction: The Overlooked Protagonists

"Artillery conquers the ground, infantry occupies it." With this proud phrase artillerymen have for ever been underlining the decisive role their weaponry plays in modern warfare. *"Infantry is the* [chess] *queen of battles"* the infantry have replied, with no less pride. The deep-rooted *esprit de corps* residing in military institutions produces – in the eyes of the layman – the strange effect that soldiers in the same army but in different corps may see the same battle in two different ways, and it is not unusual for the men from corps "X" to blame a good percentage of their misfortunes not on the enemy but on corps "Y" of the same army.

Until now the Battle of Krasny Bor, about which we have a more comprehensive knowledge with every passing day, has been described mainly from the perspective of the infantry. Some years ago I made my own contribution to the bibliography on the subject,[1] but – as will become apparent on reading this book – while I tried hard to analyse the role of artillery in that battle, I fell short of the mark. This is something I intend to put right, now I have had access to more information, which prompted me to revisit the subject in greater depth.

I would like to give very special thanks to Fernando Ceán-Bermúdez Pérez for pointing me towards a large number of German documents.[2] It was due to studying those documents that I was encouraged to delve deeper into the subject, leading me to consult Spanish sources that I had not previously used. As I set to work, several friends came to my aid with their advice, in particular Daniel Burguete Garcia, without a doubt the best informed researcher of the biographies of Spanish artillerymen on the Russian campaign, who opened up his archive to me. Other friends, Blue Division scholars with a wealth of knowledge on the subject, such as Alfredo Campello Llobregat, José Manuel Estévez Payeras, Lorenzo Fernández-Navarro de los Paños y Álvarez de Miranda, Miguel García Díaz, and Pablo Lope Sagarra Renedo, either provided me with documentation they had access to, or read the manuscripts of this book at various stages of its writing, making interesting and insightful observations on its content which benefited the final version. I was thus able to reach new conclusions, which I shall attempt to present here.

In the latest great contribution to our knowledge of this battle, General Fontenla's work,[3] artillery is conspicuously absent, although while describing the fighting the author provides very precise information about the participation of the Spanish batteries at various times, this information always comes from dispatches written by infantry units. And among the impressive wealth of documentation that Fontenla succeeds in rescuing from oblivion in what is a sensational book, there was unfortunately no original documentation from the artillery units *per se*.

Finally, it should also be noted that when the Battle of Krasny Bor is studied on the basis of collections of testimonies from veterans, we also find a clear predominance of contributions from the infantry.[4] Books of memoirs written by Blue Division artillerymen are few and far between, although in the case of the Battle of Krasny Bor we do have those written by Captain De Andrés, Lieutenant De La Vega, and Gunner Blanch Sabench.[5] Blue Division gunner Arturo Espinosa's comprehensive work is of no use to us in this instance, since his battery was entirely uninvolved in this battle.[6]

However, it is also true that the Blue Division artillery is beginning to be the subject of historiographical studies, as evidenced by the work of Artillery Colonel José Mª Manrique, providing us with a thorough study of all the types of artillery pieces (accompanying, field, and anti-tank) used by our expeditionary force in Russia.[7]

As a result of his constant research into the Battle of Krasny Bor, Fontenla has provided us with another historical scoop; the hitherto unpublished memoirs of a gunner of the 9th Battery. This is a document of great importance insofar as the 9th Battery was the last Spanish unit to withdraw from the battlefield of Krasny Bor, something of which we had previously been unaware.[8]

The reasons behind the little importance given to the artillery in the battle are twofold. The most deep-rooted reason is that the historical-military narrative has always given precedence to the infantry viewpoint, while in this particular case another reason is that, sadly, the documentation relating to the 250th Artillery Regiment, i.e. the Blue Division's artillery regiment, has been poorly and incompletely preserved.[9] This is why, until I was able to study more documents relating to the battle, especially German ones, I had not been in a position to correct certain mistakes I had made in my publication on this battle. I hope to do that now.

With this book I aim to place readers at the scene of the Battle of Krasny Bor with the perspective of a gunner, seeing the battle essentially as a duel between the Soviet and the Hispano-German artilleries. And to avoid any possible offence, I should start by assuring you that nothing is further from my intention than to underestimate the role of infantry in any way. It is simply that on this occasion we are going to look at the battle from the artillery observation posts rather than from the trenches.

But perhaps the first thing I should stress – leaving aside clichés and any misunderstood *esprit de corps* – is that Spanish artillerymen in general, and of course those of the Blue Division in particular, always saw themselves as an arm at the service of the infantry. The expeditionary force had not yet left Spain when they received General Instruction no. 2 of the Division, issued on 7 July 1941 under the title "*General Instruction of Troops*". It stated:

"*III. Artillery (...)*

"*For the Artillery, liaison with the Infantry, which is essential for the correct execution of any action, is a matter to which all else must be subordinate. The gunner must see the events of the battle through the eyes of an infantryman and will make it a matter of honour never to leave without supporting the units which have been entrusted to him. All commanders of both arms must get to know one another personally and the officers of the accompanying units must billet with their infantry counterparts, since this bond is the basis of liaison".*[10]

These basic ideas were complemented by other, later instructions that were heavily influenced by German regulations (inevitably so, since the Spanish were going to be operating alongside them). This can be seen in General Instruction no. 3, published by the 3rd Section (Operations) of the Divisionary Staff on the same day as the previous one, with the title *"Artillery-Infantry and Artillery-Armoured Forces Cooperation. Notes on German Regulations"*. This document meticulously describes the way in which such cooperation, which was expected to be really close, should be implemented. A little later – while the Division was still in Madrid – on 11 July, Divisional Artillery Command released another document entitled *"Special Instruction no. 1 for Artillery. Notes on the use of artillery. Extract from German Regulations"*, with detailed information about a plethora of aspects, from the type of weapons and munitions and the kind of fire which could be used, to the duties of regimental and group commands.

At Grafenwöhr, and during the march to the front, this process of providing the Spanish artillerymen with the information they would need on the typical German artillery procedures continued, This is evidenced by, for example, General Instruction 3007 on *"Use of Artillery Units"*, dated 6 August; General Instruction 3019 on *"Use of an Artillery Group in manoeuvre warfare and against organized positions"*, dated 16 August; and General Instruction 4017 on *"Munitions Service"*.[11] The last of the three was dated 1 October 1941 when the Blue Division was close to the front; they would join the line just twelve days later.

II

The Siege of Leningrad: Two Artilleries, Head to Head

In 1941, during the attacking phase of Operation Barbarossa, the Germans thought that Leningrad would fall into their hands like ripe fruit as a result of what they assumed would be the rapid collapse of the USSR. When this failed to happen, they thought that it would be enough to subject the city to a tight encirclement; a city of that size could not resist long without large amounts of supplies and would soon capitulate. Although the artillery of the German divisions laying siege to the city could, in some cases, reach the city, at the beginning few heavy artillery units were sent to Leningrad; they were being used on more active fronts. The lack of any plan to launch an assault on Leningrad was another reason why concentrating artillery was unnecessary.

By early 1942 those pipedreams had evaporated and the Germans had realized that it would take a long siege to capture the city. And as in every siege situation, artillery would be decisive.[1] The Soviets accumulated an impressive mass of artillery to defend the city, which had once been the capital of Russia and the cradle of the Bolshevik revolution. As for the Germans, while the strength of the Wehrmacht infantry taking part in the encirclement would not increase by any substantial amount, the artillery was – proportionally – heavily reinforced.

The Germans became increasingly aware that they could not continue to use such a significant number of troops at Leningrad as the siege required. It was necessary to attack the city once and for all, which would free up a substantial infantry force to be used on other fronts. So in the summer of 1942, after having captured the city-fortress of Sevastopol, Marshal von Manstein, with the General Staff of his 11th Army, was sent from Crimea to Leningrad with orders to take command of the troops there and assault the city. On the journey there the famous marshal was accompanied by a handful of infantry, but more importantly by a significant collection of heavy and superheavy artillery pieces: the Wehrmacht's siege train.

The Spanish troops who arrived at the Leningrad Front in late August 1942 were most impressed by the artillery they could see amassed in the German rear, ready to be used in the attack on the city.[2] On 31 August, the Spanish artillery officers in command of batteries and groups attended a meeting of commanders during which the artillery commander of LIV Corps, which the Spanish officers had just joined, told them of his experience regarding the role of artillery in the siege of Sevastopol and informed them in broad terms of what was expected of them in what was assumed to be the imminent assault on Leningrad. After the long months of hard fighting on the Volkhov Front, the Blue Division's artillery had left there with significant shortages of materiel. In early August 1942 they were missing four 150 mm and six 105 mm guns, lost for various reasons during the previous months, the complement of draught horses was incomplete, and radio resources, vital to artillery, had suffered serious attrition. On the Spaniards' arrival at the new deployment area the German logistics services set about covering all those shortfalls with remarkable speed. The Spanish artillery had to be in perfect shape for the planned attack.

The Soviets, meanwhile, had an impressive mass of artillery with which to defend Leningrad. The concentration of heavy artillery pieces was spectacular. In 1941, counting only heavy artillery, the Red Army had deployed there thirty-seven 122 mm guns, ninety 152 mm guns, and nine 220 mm guns from reserve units, while reinforcing the lighter calibre divisional artillery pieces used in the city's defence.

And there were still more guns: Leningrad, and more specifically Kronstadt, were the main Soviet navy bases, and since their units were virtually bottled up there, a fair number of Russian ships were able to use their gigantic guns against land targets. In some cases, naval cannons were removed from ships to be used on land. All Soviet coastal artillery in the area was placed under the orders of the Red Army to be used against land targets. In total the navy transferred to the Red Army the use and control of 360 guns of over 130 mm.

It was no accident that the Red Army entrusted to the defence of Leningrad an officer with a long track record in artillery: Leonid Aleksandrovich Govorov. He had trained as an artillery officer in the Czarist Army, but during the Russian Civil War he had switched to the Red Army. His entire career had been in the artillery; he was an instructor of tactics in the Artillery Academy and served with distinction in several important military operations. Marshal Zhukov was one of his sponsors. In April 1942 he was finally sent to besieged Leningrad, where a gigantic artillery battle took place. Nobody could have been better suited for the job.

Returning to the Germans, an unusually large number of artillery units began to concentrate on Leningrad. Until the spring of 1942 the German divisions in the sector basically had their organic complement of artillery; i.e. one artillery regiment per division. Each artillery regiment consisted of four groups, three light and one heavy. The regular gun for the three light groups was the *10.5 cm leichte Feldhaubitze 18* (type 18, 10.5 cm light field howitzer) while for the fourth group it was the *15 cm schwere Feldhaubitze 18* (type 18, 15 cm heavy field howitzer).[3]

Originally each group had three batteries and each battery had four guns. The various groups of the regiments were designated by Roman numerals separated by a slash from the number of the regiment; this latter number was generally the same as that of the division which the battery served (in the case of the Blue Division, from I/250th to IV/250th). The batteries were numbered in a single sequence from the 1st to the 12th, and their designation also included the regimental number (in the case of the Blue Division, from the 1st/250th to the 12th/250). Although in principle the first three batteries belonged to the first group, the next three to the second group, etc., in practice, once deployed on the front, the battery type units could be tactically incorporated in groups different from those to which they theoretically belonged. In addition to these gun batteries, each group had its own staff battery, but these were not numbered.

For readers less familiar with artillery organization[4] I should explain that a unit at group level is usually commanded by an officer with the rank of major, aided by a staff which would include a number of officers directly under his orders (his adjutant – always an artilleryman –, a medical officer, a veterinary officer, a military chaplain, etc.). Meanwhile the staff battery enables the group commander to direct his batteries' fire, and includes topographic, observation, transmission and other services. Officers from other corps would also form part of a staff battery, such as quartermasters who are responsible for supplies, pay, etc.

Batteries are normally commanded by officers with the rank of captain and usually each one would have three junior officers (lieutenants or second lieutenants) under him.

In the case of gun batteries, which are what most interest us here, one of those junior officers would command a gun line, the key component of a battery, and the others would be responsible for various duties, aided by the most veteran NCOs: advanced observation posts, topographical services, battery transmission services, organization of the second echelon (livestock care, kitchen, etc.)

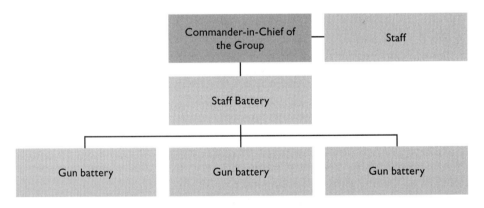

But let us return to the Leningrad Front as spring was arriving in 1942. The artillery regiments of the German divisions deployed in the encirclement of Leningrad began to receive large numbers of two types of guns from the huge haul of guns captured from the French, known to the Germans as *schwere Feldhaubitze 414 (f)* and *22 cm Mörser 531 (f)* respectively; the Germans assigned their own designations to war booty materiel. These designations included the type of weapon, a number and, between brackets, a letter identifying its country of origin. The "(f)" stood for *französisch* or French.

Among the extraordinary number of 155 mm war booty guns captured by the Germans in France there was a huge variety of different types, which meant a large number of designations. The German artillery catalogued these versions for subsequent use:

French designation	German designation
Canon de 155 C mle. 1917 Schneider	Schwere Feldhaubitze 414 (f)
Canon de 155 C mle. 15 St. Chamond	Schwere Feldhaubitze 415 (f)
Canon de 155 L mle. 1917 Schneider	Kanone 416 (f)
Canon de 155 GPF-CA	Kanone 417 (f)
Canon de 155 GPF	Kanone 418 (f)
Canon de 155 GPF-T	Kanone 419 (f)
Canon de 155 L mle. 16 St. Chamond	Kanone 420 (f)
Canon de 155 mle. 1877-1914 Schneider	Kanone 422 (f)
Canon de 155 L mle. 1918 Schneider	Kanone 425 (f)

There were also two French 220 mm guns that the Germans incorporated into their artillery:

French designation	German designation
Mortier de 220 mle. Schneider	22 cm *Mörser* 531 (f)
Canon de 220 L mle. 1917 Schneider	22 cm Kanone 532 (f)

It should be mentioned at this point that the Germans classified as a *Kanone* (cannon) any gun that fired at a low angle (up to 45 degrees of elevation), *Mörser* (heavy mortar or heavy howitzer), one that fired at a high angle (over 45 degrees), and *Haubitze* (howitzer), a gun that could fire at either angle. What we would generally call a mortar, the Germans called a *Granatenwerfer (grenade launcher)*.

A problem of nomenclature arises here. If we refer to the guns that the Germans call *Mörser* as "mortars", readers will inevitably think of the light portable mortars used by the infantry. Therefore, although it may seem pedantic, in this book we will always refer to these heavy howitzers as *Mörser*.

*Beute*Gerätbatterien (batteries of captured guns) or simply *Gerätbatterien* (gun batteries) were created using guns of the two aforementioned French types, the *schwere Feldhaubitze 414 (f)* and the *22 cm Mörser 531 (f)*. They were assigned to the various line units and it was up to the artillery regiments who received them to provide the men to operate them.[5]

On the Leningrad Front the batteries equipped with 155 mm guns[6] used geographic names (for example, "Hannover", "Schlesien", "Mecklenburg", or "Pommern"). Those equipped with 220 mm guns were given the names of important characters in German military history ("Wallenstein", "Blücher", "Moltke", "Ludendorff", etc.). Later, in order to differentiate the two types of batteries more clearly, the latter type were given a purely numerical designation, in the 5,000 series (for example, the "Ludendorff" Battery became *Gerätbatterie* 5021).

By way of example, the 121st Infantry Division, which the Blue Division was to relieve when the time came to deploy in front of Leningrad, had the Schlieffen

Battery (named after the German general who designed the war plan against France used in the First World War), with three 220mm guns (which in fact were distributed among three of its artillery groups, one per group); and the Hessen Battery (named after a region of central Germany), originally equipped with five 155 mm guns. By the time the Spanish took charge of the sector the Schlieffen Battery had ceased to exist and – as we shall see – the number of 220 mm guns which were assigned to the Spaniards was higher than this unit had originally been equipped with. With regard to the last mentioned battery, the Hessen, the Spanish were the third users of these captured guns, since they had originally been operated by men from the Artillery Regiment of the 5th Mountain Division, also deployed in the encirclement of Leningrad. By that time the battery had been reduced to just three guns.

The type of materiel with which the two types of batteries were equipped naturally created logistical problems; the lack of replacements meant guns spent long periods under repair, which normally involved cannibalizing some guns to provide components for others. The composition of these batteries would therefore vary from month to month; every so often one battery would be dissolved and what was left of its equipment would be distributed among the remaining batteries. For the same reason, a battery would sometimes be kept in existence with just a few guns (even with just one) in the knowledge that it was only a matter of time before it would receive materiel from other batteries. It was also normal for the divisions which had been assigned these 155 or 220 mm batteries to choose to distribute their guns among the different groups of their respective artillery regiments. Because another problem of these guns was that they were delivered without any means of transport of their own. Conversely, when these guns were kept together and organized into batteries, the normal thing was for such units to be attached *de facto* to the heavy regimental groups.

In the course of 1942 other types of reinforcements arrived; no longer gun batteries without men assigned to divisional artillery regiments, but instead complete artillery units. Part of these units were formations belonging to the army's coastal artillery. In Germany it was traditionally the navy which was responsible for coastal defence. But after March 1941 the huge length of the coastline of occupied Europe forced the German land army, the *Heer*, to cooperate in the defence of the shoreline by organizing artillery groups and independent batteries for coastal defence. These units were designated *Heeres-Küsten-Artillerie-Abteilungen* (HKAA, or army coastal artillery groups) and *Heeres-Küstenbatterien* (HKB, or army coastal batteries) and were equipped with a motley arsenal of captured guns. A "division of labour" arose. The *Kriegsmarine* would take charge of the artillery defence of ports and naval bases while the *Heer* would cover the coasts where amphibious actions might occur.

With the Soviet fleet bottled up in its base at Kronstadt, it was correctly assumed that there would be no need for all the coastal artillery batteries and groups sent to the Baltic by the *Heer* to be deployed along the coast. So Baltic Navy Command

(*Marine Befehlshaber Ostland*) handed them over to the *Heer*, which made them available to the 18th Army (the large unit of Army Group North which would occupy the seaward flank), under the assumption that a handful of naval coastal artillery units would be enough to protect the region's main ports. It would be this same 18th Army which would reach Leningrad itself, so it was reasonable to expect that they would be up against the ships of the Soviet navy based at Kronstadt and with the coastal artillery defending that base. Who better to face up to them than the men and guns of the army's coastal artillery?

Thus as early as June 1941 three coastal groups were transferred to the 18th Army, and in June 1942 it received four more groups and five independent batteries, also coastal. By January 1943 the 18th Army had a total of eight groups and six independent batteries of coastal artillery for use in ground combat. This long explanation was necessary because later we will see that several of these coastal groups were deployed alongside the Blue Division's artillery, a fact which readers may initially find surprising.

The *Heer*, like armies all over the world, also had autonomous artillery units, separate from divisions. They belonged to the type known as *Heerestruppen* (the equivalent of troops of the Army General Reserve in Spain). They used guns of higher calibres and/or ranges than those of divisional artillery and although most of these units were classified as heavy, some of them were classified as *schwersten*, or superheavy.[7] These units were either battery strength or, more normally, group strength. In either case they were designated using sequences of Arabic numerals. In some cases these groups were numbered as part of a regiment, although the regiment in question had no staff unit to coordinate the two groups and therefore they were in fact completely independent of each other. Unlike the divisional artillery groups, which in the vast majority were horse-drawn, these independent groups were motorized. At the start of the war the *Heer* had 74 of these groups in the *Heerestruppen*, and by May 1940 the figure had risen to 117.[8] The figure would continue to rise in the following years.

Since in this book we shall be talking a great deal about these independent units of long-range heavy artillery, so often completely neglected in works of military history, which focus only on army corps, divisions, etc., it would be a good idea to take a look at their distribution and assess their importance. In June 1941 the units deployed for the attack on the USSR were distributed as follows:

Heavy and long-range groups, and railway batteries, classified according to the type of armament used, as deployed for the attack on the USSR, June 1941.									Totals (Groups plus Rlwy. Batts.)
Army Group	Kanone 10,5 cm	Kanone 15 cm	Schwere Feldhaubitze	Mixed	*Mörser* 21 cm	Haubitze 24 cm	Heavy curved trajectory	Heavy flat trajectory	Railway batteries	
"North"	6	2	11	2	4	-	-	1	2	28
"Centre"	15	3	16	5	17	-	3	2	5	66
"South"	6	2	10	5	8	2	-	1	2	36
Totals	27	7	37	12	29	2	3	4	9	130

For an army the size of the *Heer* these were really quite low figures. In June 1941, Army Group North could field 26 heavy groups (plus two railway batteries), of which the 18th Army had direct control over six, although it is true that it had been assigned the two railway batteries and the aforementioned three Coastal Artillery Groups (the rest of the heavy groups were divided between those assigned to the 16th Army or the 4th Panzer Group, and those under direct control of the Army Group). Significantly, by June 1942 the 18th Army alone had 16 heavy groups (plus the two railway batteries and the coastal groups and batteries mentioned earlier).

As the campaign progressed these artillery resources had been distributed in several different manners. The 18th Army had used what had been assigned to them in their "hot" sectors, which in general had been those close to the River Volkhov, as a result of the German attempt to capture the territory to the east of that river, or the need to block the enemy's attempts to approach encircled Leningrad by crossing the river.

Only a minority of units, the superheavy ones (for example, the II/84th Group or 768th Group), had been used against the city of Leningrad. With the arrival of Marshal von Manstein and the artillery units which had laid siege to Sevastopol these *Heerestruppen* heavy artillery units were reinforced. Among the recently arrived units were, for example, the I/814th and II/814th Groups, and the 458th and 459th Batteries. The superheavy groups originally had only two batteries, or exceptionally three. Along with these "normal" units some artillery railway units arrived with their guns, also of superheavy calibres.

Meanwhile, many of the *Heerestruppen* artillery units assigned to the 18th Army were sent to positions in the corridor reaching as far as the southern tip of Lake Ladoga, a narrow passage which the Soviets hoped to capture in order to gain access to the encircled city. On 1 January 1943, in addition to the aforementioned coastal artillery units, the 18th Army had 17 heavy groups and seven independent heavy batteries under its orders, not to mention five railway batteries.[9]

These artillery units (heavy groups, railway batteries and, in the case which concerns us, coastal groups) could remain under the direct control of army-type units or be temporarily incorporated into divisions, but the normal thing was for

Evolution of the number of *Heerestruppen* artillery units assigned to the 18th Army

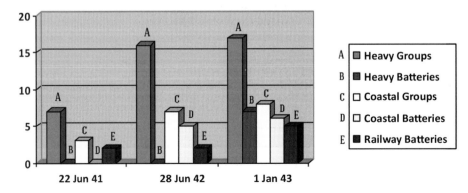

A	◻ Heavy Groups
B	◼ Heavy Batteries
C	☐ Coastal Groups
D	☐ Coastal Batteries
E	◼ Railway Batteries

them to be assigned to the army corps. These army corps controlled and led them through artillery commanders, each called an *Artillerie-Kommandeur*, normally abbreviated to *Arko*. Under their command each *Arko* had a staff comprising – according to standard staffing tables – ten officers, seven NCOs and twenty soldiers. At the start of the Russian campaign each Army Corps would usually be assigned two *Arkos*, a luxury that would soon disappear.

Normally each *Arko* only had one subordinate unit of his own; an artillery observation and range finding unit (*Beobachtungs Abteilung*), but when *Heerestruppen* units were assigned to an army corps, these units came under command of the army corps, as we have just explained. In the case of a few units these could be commanded directly, but if there were a large number of them they had pre-existing regimental staffs (*Artillerie-Regiment Stab*) which were numbered, or they improvised staffs of this type, allocating the job to personnel of one of the artillery groups under their command. *Arkos* also had to coordinate the artillery of army corps' divisions, and if the situation so demanded, they could "bypass" divisional commanders and take direct tactical control of the batteries of the divisional regiments. At this point it should be remembered that the general headquarters of the army-level units had a similar type of artillery commander, in this case called a *Höherer Artillerie-Kommandeur*, normally abbreviated to *Höh. Arko* or even *Harko*. Originally this type of commander had only existed in the armoured groups (*Panzergruppen*, later redesignated as *Panzerarmeen* or Panzer Armies), but the name eventually spread to all army-scale units. Many *Höh. Arkos* were promoted former *Arkos*. The 18th Army's *Höh. Arko* was number 303. As a general rule, an *Arko* would usually hold the rank of colonel and a *Höh. Arko* would be major-general (*Generalleutnant* in the German ranking system of the time).

Artillery observation and target location groups were highly specialized units. They were equipped and trained to detect the location of enemy batteries by various methods: there were batteries which located targets by sound (*Schallmessbatterie*, sound ranging battery), by flashes (*Lichtmessbatterie*, flash ranging battery), by captive balloons (*Ballonbatterie*), and also specialized observers who flew over battlefields and aerial photography analysts.[10]

Having looked at the *Heerestruppen* artillery units distributed among army groups at the start of the Russian campaign, let us now take a look at the distribution of these artillery commands and observation and location units at the same date:

Artillery unit and location group commands, June 1941				
Army Group	Höherer Artillerie-Kommandeur	Artillerie-Kommandeur	Artillerie-Regiment Stab	Observation and Location Groups
"North"	-	13	9	9
"Centre"	1	22	17	14
"South"	1	16	9	11
Totals	2	51	35	34

In this table, as in the previous one, we can see that in June 1941 Army Group North was the least well equipped in terms of artillery formations in comparison with Army Groups Centre and South. However, the hard fighting at the siege of Leningrad completely changed this distribution and by January 1943 the 18th Army alone had as many as seven observation groups deployed.

It is now time to take a look at the Soviet artillery. When analysing its organization we need to take into account the particularities of the Leningrad sector. As a rule the official staffing tables were not followed to the letter anywhere, but at encircled Leningrad the deviation from the regulation establishment could be considerable.[11] For this reason it is advisable to refer only to the documentation specific to this sector. The artillery was grouped into two echelons, divisional artillery and army artillery. Despite what the name suggests, a Soviet army was the equivalent of a German army corps.

The armies' artillery units were assigned by the General Reserve and therefore the volume of units they received very much depended on how the army was faring at the time. Although there were cases of armies which had three regiments of heavy field artillery, it was more normal for each army to have a single regiment of this type. Each regiment tended to have two groups, each with three batteries. Normally they would be equipped with 122 mm guns, but they might also use 107 mm and 152 mm pieces. Units with higher calibres (203, 210, 280 mm, etc.) did exist, but they were controlled by what the Russians called "fronts", normally considered to be the equivalent of German army strength units).

Apart from these field artillery regiments, the artillery units of an army would normally include a regiment of anti-tank cannons, a regiment of anti-aircraft artillery, and a mörser regiment, which would consist of four batteries of 80 mm mortars and another four of 120 mm mortars.

There were also multiple rocket launcher units, incorporated into units called "Mortars of the Guard", which in other parts of the eastern theatre of operations were large enough to be grouped into regiments. However, at this time and on this front it was unusual for them to act in concert as large units; when operating as part of specific missions it was normal for them to be assigned in smaller units, even of just one or two rocket launchers, to the sector where an attack was to be made.

In the case of Soviet divisions, they had one artillery regiment organized into three groups, each with three batteries (although one of the groups would often only have two). The batteries normally had four guns each. The equipment in each group usually consisted of two batteries equipped with the ubiquitous and reliable 76.2 mm guns, and a third battery with 122 mm guns. In the case of the two battery groups, each battery had one of the two above mentioned calibres. Each artillery regiment could therefore field eight or nine batteries, but every infantry regiment also had its own cannon company, equivalent to one battery, usually equipped with four 76.2 mm guns.

A layman in the matter of artillery may imagine that the German 105 mm guns must necessarily have been superior to the Soviet 76.2 mm pieces, and the German 150 mm guns must have been better than the Soviet 122 mm weapons, on the basis of their larger calibres. Nothing could be further from the truth; the Soviet 76.2 and 122 guns (and those of other calibres too) were surprisingly good and effective and, as the Germans would soon learn to their dismay, in many cases they were actually superior to their own guns.

Without question it would be the 76.2 mm guns which would fire most at the Spanish throughout the Russian campaign, and Krasny Bor was no exception. Until the early 1930s the Red Army had been using artillery inherited from the old Czarist Army. But then new ideas started to be developed, giving rise to the Model 1936 gun – so called because that was the year of its introduction –, the first in a series of 76.2 mm pieces. A number of improvements led to the Model 1939 and these two versions made up the bulk of the Red Army's field artillery at the start of the Russian campaign. The next step was to develop a new version which would be effective not only as a field gun but as an anti-tank cannon: the Model 1942. I mention this because for the sake of convenience I refer always to the "Russian 76.2 mm gun" in this book, when in fact there were a number of different versions.

III

The Two Blue Division Artillery Regiments

As mentioned earlier, the fact that the preserved documentation relating to the 250th Artillery Regiment is flawed and incomplete has caused more than one historian to make mistakes regarding its composition and structure.[1]

It is a German source, the Table of Organization and Equipment (TOE) of the Blue Division, entered in the War Diary of the 18th Army's L Corps when the Spanish unit joined it in late January 1943, which provides us with a true idea of the artillery force of this unit at the Battle of Krasny Bor.

This table[2] shows not only the units forming part of the Spanish artillery regiment but also other units under the orders of Corps Artillery Command deployed in the Spanish sector. A first glance paints an entirely different picture from the one we previously imagined; the 250th Spanish Regiment had four groups, plus one attached German group (Group Werner), and the additional German units deployed in the Spanish sector totalled three heavy groups, one superheavy railway battery, and one location group.

That is to say that instead of what we had traditionally been assuming – that the Spanish sector was covered by the four Blue Division artillery groups – the fact is that there were also five German artillery groups (four of guns and one target location group), and one superheavy battery. Two of the gun groups were coastal artillery groups. Hence the heading at the start of this section; in practical terms the Blue Division had not one but two artillery regiments, its own and a German one.

Similarly, among the documents of L Corps there are Orders of Battle for the L Corps artillery for various dates. The documents corresponding to 26 January and 14 February are of particular interest to us since the Battle of Krasny Bor was fought between those two dates.[3]

The aforementioned TOE provides us with highly significant information. The I/250th, II/250th and III/250th Light Groups are shown as being equipped with German 105 mm guns[4] and had full complements, meaning that each fielded three batteries and a total of 12 guns. The IV/250th Heavy Group however had less than a full complement of 150 mm guns since there were only three in each of the three batteries of the unit. The Order of Battle for 26 January slightly amends these figures, since one of the Spanish 105 mm batteries had been reduced to three guns.

The shortfall of three 150 mm guns would however be offset by the French war booty guns assigned to the Spanish once they were deployed in the Leningrad area. They were basically 220 mm guns, the *22 cm Mörser 531 (f)*. According to the TOE they were assigned to the various groups, where they formed independent sections: two for I Group, another two for II Group, one for III Group, and two for IV Group, the heavy one. A total of seven guns in all.

The Order of Battle for L Corps Artillery for 26 January, however, reduces the total of this type of gun in the Spanish groups to five, one in each group except for II Group which continued with two of these guns. From other documents we know that the second gun of IV Group was not definitively out of commission and was being repaired at the division's workshops, but the second gun of I Group had been put out of action definitively, so was awaiting a replacement. This was the endemic problem of war booty materiel, for which it was hard to find spare parts quickly, leading to their available number varying frequently. However, the situation regarding war booty guns had improved since the Blue Division had deployed in front of Leningrad, since four guns of this type were assigned to the Spanish on 16 September 1942.

German documentation was very precise regarding the availability of this captured materiel assigned to divisions and therefore provides highly detailed information about the Blue Division:

Captured materiel in the 250th Artillery Regiment						
Unit	Calibre	Complement as at 28 Dec. 1942	Complement as at 28 Jan. 1943	Operational as at 28 Jan. 1943	Being repaired at units	Being repaired at workshops in the rear
1st Battery/ Werner	220	3	3	3	-	-
2nd Battery/ Werner	220	3	3	2	-	1
Group I/250	220	1	1	1	-	-
Group II/250	220	2	2	2	-	-
Group III/250	220	1	1	1	-	-
Group IV 250	220	2	1	1	1	-
Hessen Battery (in IV/250)	155	2	1	1	-	1

According to both the TOE and the Order of Battle, IV Group also had a Hessen Battery about which we have spoken earlier and which at the time had a single French war booty 155 mm gun, a *schwere Feldhaubitze 414 (f)*. Another identical gun belonging to this battery had been sent to the 18th Army's armoury for repair. It would not be back until 3 April 1943 (the original complement of the battery when the Spanish took it over in September 1942 had been three guns).

In the documentation of the 250th Artillery Regiment, and also in some of the books published on the Blue Division, there are confusing references to this Hessen Battery. As we see, it was a gun battery of the type set out above,[5] which was now manned by Spanish gunners. But as evidence of just how incomplete this documentation is, we do not know for certain who commanded the battery, although everything points to Captain José Luis Piñeyro Caramés having been its first commander.[6]

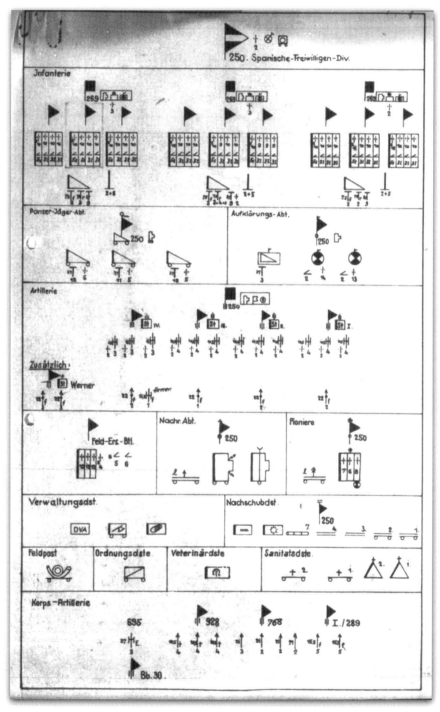

TOE of the Blue Division, 25 January 1943.

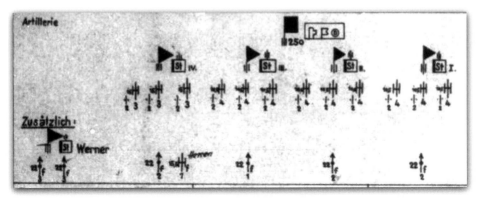

Detail of the TOE of the Blue Division, 25 January 1943: composition of the 250th Artillery Regiment.

Detail of the TOE of the Blue Division, 25 January 1943: composition of the Army Corps artillery deployed in the Blue Division sector.

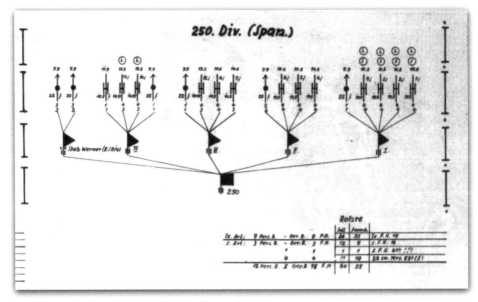

Detail of the Order of Battle of the artillery of L Army Corps, 26 January 1943: composition of the 250th Artillery Regiment.

All the batteries mentioned up to now were manned by Spanish gunners and officers. But, in addition to their own four groups, attached to the 250th Artillery Regiment there was a heavy German group, known as Group Werner, with two batteries, each with three captured French 220 mm guns (although in the Order of Battle for 26 January we see that one of them was out of service and we know that it had in fact been sent to the 18th Army's armoury for repair).

The unit was named after the surname of the German officer who commanded it, Captain Werner. He had been transferred to serve with the Blue Division on 3 November 1942 and his two batteries were deployed, one close to the Izhora (the 1st Battery) and the other halfway between Pushkin and Slutsk (the 2nd Battery).

Unless I am mistaken, the Blue Division bibliography has never mentioned this German group attached to the Blue Division. And it only appears in the Division's war diary in a very limited and oblique manner, being named sometimes when it opened fire, or when recording a casualty among its men, but never mentioning that despite being a German group it was under Spanish orders. German documentation tells us that the group was under the orders of the 250th Artillery Regiment until 18 March 1943 when it was placed under the orders of *Arko* L Corps.

It should be noted that Group Werner is also referred to as II/814th Group.[7] This group was equipped with typical siege artillery pieces; the *24 cm Haubitze 39 (t)* (Czech 24 cm Mod. 39 Howitzer). As these powerful siege guns were not being used and were held in reserve, the II/814th was stationed in the rear, but part of the group's gunners were used to operate 220 mm guns and it was these men who formed Group Werner.

This was the situation of the 250th Artillery Regiment as at 26 January, and almost certainly as at 10 February 1943 as well.

Artillery pieces of the 250th Artillery regiment, as at 26 January 1943					
Organic artillery			Attached materiel		
Calibre (mm)	Theoretical complement	Actual complement	Calibre (mm)	Theoretical complement	Actual complement
105	36 guns	35 guns	155	2 guns	1 guns
150	12 guns	9 guns	220	13 guns	10 guns
Total	48	44	Total	15	11

Therefore, and to sum up, although in late January 1943 the 250th Regiment was 4 guns short of its organic complement, its firepower had been increased with the incorporation of larger calibre guns. Under normal conditions, the Regiment should have had 48 artillery pieces. In fact, when it transferred to L Corps on paper it had 63, and on 26 January, the last date for which we have reliable data, 55 of them were operational.

L Corps also incorporated the German 215th Infantry Division and the multinational 2nd SS Infantry Brigade, in which Dutch, Flemish, Norwegians, Latvians and Germans served. For comparative purposes, let us now take a look at the artillery situation of these two units.

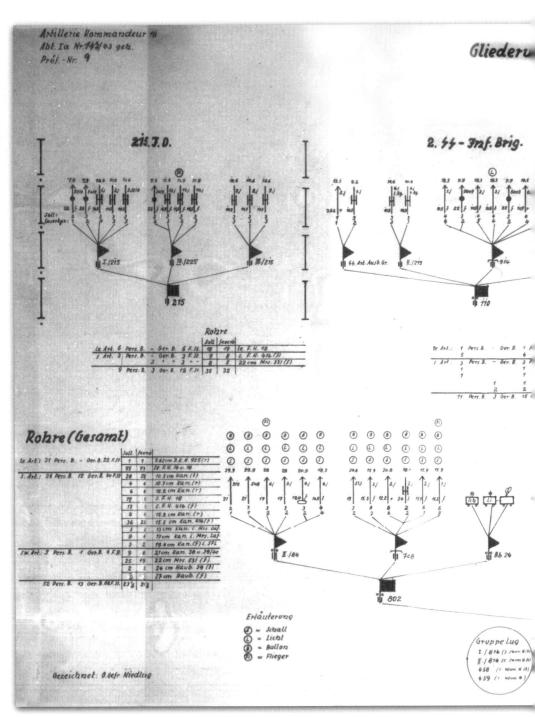

Order of battle of the artillery of the L Army Corps, 26 January 1943.

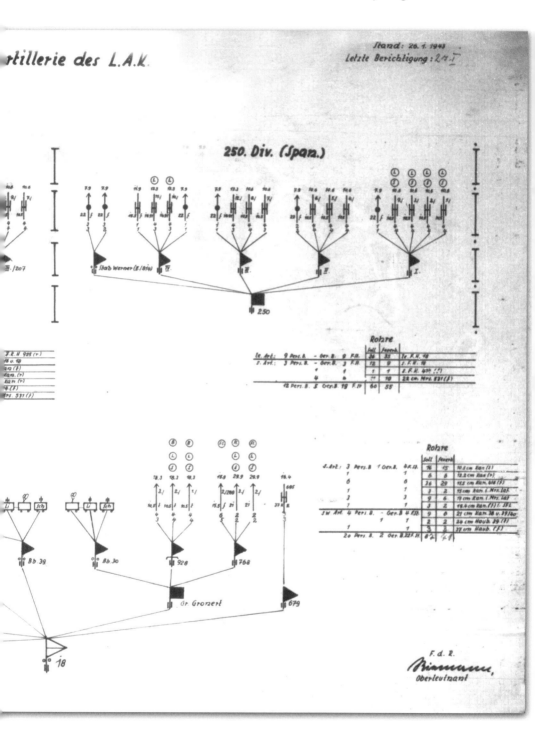

rtillerie des L.A.K.

Stand: 26.1.1943
Letzte Berichtigung: 27.1.

250. Div. (Span.)

Situation of artillery units in the Krasny Bor area

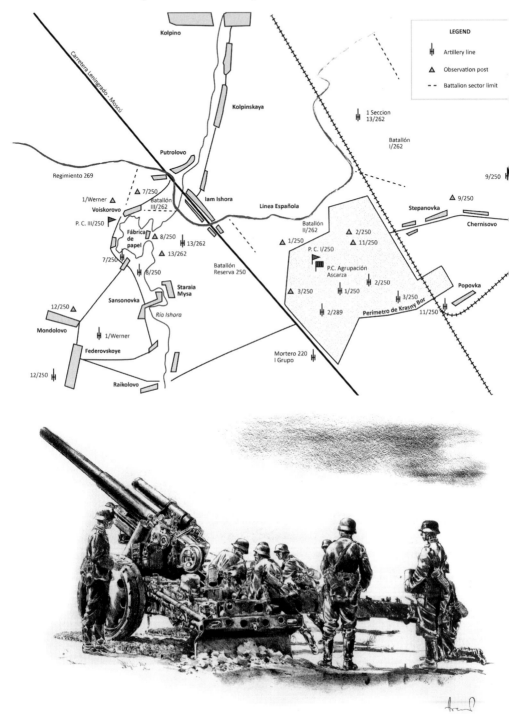

Situation of artillery units at Krasny Bor on 10 February 1943

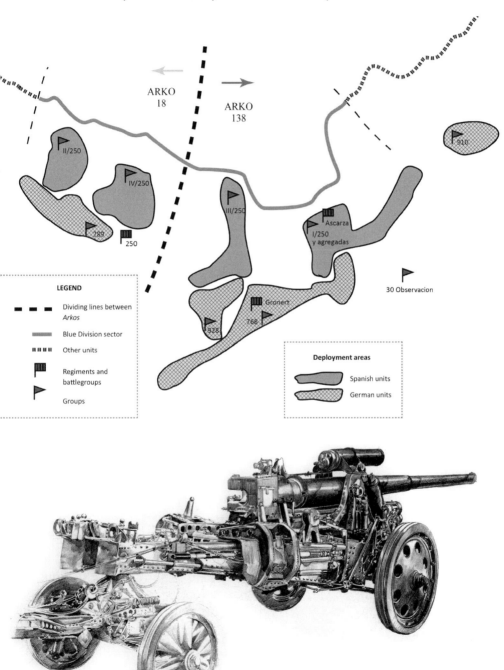

LEGEND

- ▬ ▬ ▬ Dividing lines between *Arkos*
- ▬▬▬ Blue Division sector
- ▪▪▪▪ Other units
- Regiments and battlegroups
- Groups

Deployment areas

- Spanish units
- German units

A reconnaissance aircraft flies over an artillery column. The *Luftwaffe*'s close reconnaissance squadrons mostly flew observation missions for the artillery.

Camouflage netting over German artillery pieces. On a front such as Leningrad, where artillery duels were constant, it was necessary to make use of more complex methods to conceal artillery.

Due to the complexity of their weapons, the training of gunners is much more sophisticated than that of their infantry counterparts.

Above, below and previous below: One of the unusual features of the *15 cm schwere Feldhaubitze 18* was that the barrel was removed from the gun carriage and was transported separately. In the first photo we see the barrel on its carrier, while the other two photos show the barrel carrier without the barrel.

Above and below: The unsung and untold work of topographic units was of immense importance to artillery units.

Above and below: Job done. The crew of a *15 cm schwere Feldhaubitze 18* has completed the process of positioning their gun, and a little later comes the time for a much more informal photo, one for the album.

Above and below: With their field training now completed, the men of a battery of heavy 150 mm howitzers show what they have learned. The barrel will be mounted on the gun carriage.

Above and below: With the gun now in position, all the crew go to their firing positions. In the foreground, kneeling, we see the gunners responsible for taking ammunition to the gun. Once the gun has been loaded, the gunner responsible for closing the breech will fire the gun.

Above, below and overleaf: This set of photos is not of a tug-of-war competition in a German barracks, but shows the complex manoeuvre required to break the *15 cm schwere Feldhaubitze 18* down into its two constituent parts. It is hardly surprising that in difficult tactical situations these guns had to be abandoned on the battlefield due to the impossibility of dismantling and transporting them.

A battery of *15 cm schwere Feldhaubitze 18* showing off their guns. Each German divisional artillery regiment had a group of three batteries of these 150 mm guns. In Spain divisional artillery had no guns as heavy as that.

Above: Stables in perfect order. German artillery was essentially horse-drawn, so they paid the utmost attention to their horses, on which their mobility depended.

Opposite: The *10.5 cm leichte Feldhaubitze 18* was the most used field gun in the German Army. It could hit targets at a range of just over 10 km.

Preparing to fire.

In late January 1943 the 215th Artillery Regiment had only three groups, one heavy[8] and two light. The light batteries were equipped with German 105 mm guns, but the heavy battery had French war booty 155 mm guns. The groups were also reinforced by the incorporation of three batteries equipped with French 220 mm captured guns (these were 5015th, 5016th and 5017th *Gerätbatterien*).

The case of the 2nd SS Brigade was much more unusual. This type of unit had no organic artillery,[9] so the Army Corps had assigned it one of its regimental staff units, the *Artillerie-Regiment Stab 110* (the 110th Regimental Artillery Staff), to direct the fire of the following units (as at 26 January 1943):

One light group of the neighbouring 215th Division (II/215th), with a battery that was strengthened but divided operationally into two sections.[10]

Another light group (III/207th) from the 207th Security Division which operated in the rear and which had no need for artillery in its fight against partisans. In addition to its 105 mm batteries it had the "Schlesien" Battery of French 155 mm guns as part of its artillery complement, although at the time none of them were operational.

A training unit of the *Waffen SS* (*SS Artillerie Ausbildungs Gruppe*), with obsolete German 105 mm guns and Russian 76.2 mm guns. This cannot be considered as a combat unit since its mission at the time was to train the Latvians in the brigade, who were soon to form a Latvian brigade of the *Waffen SS*.

And, finally, the 914th Coastal Artillery Group,[11] to which had been attached two independent heavy batteries equipped with Russian war booty materiel (629th and 639th Batteries) and the 5003rd and 5009th *Gerätbatterien*.

The above information should give us a good idea of the situation of the Blue Division's artillery at that time.

Artillery (own and attached) of the three major units of L Corps as at 26 January 1943				
Official German designation of the gun types (in brackets, country of origin of the guns, if not German).	Calibre (mm)	215th Division	2nd SS Brigade	Blue Division
Feldkanone 295 (r) (Russia)	76,2	-	1	-
Leichte Feldhaubitze 16	105	-	2	-
Leichte Feldhaubitze 18	105	19	17	35
10,5 Kanone(t) (Czechoslovakia)	105	-	13	-
10,7 Kanone 352 (r) (Russia)	107	-	4	-
Schwere Feldhaubitze 18	150	-	-	9
15,2 Kanonenhaubitze 433 (r) (Russia)	152	-	4	-
Schwere Feldhautize 414 (f) (France)	155	8	-	1
Mörser 531 (f) (France)	220	5	4	10
German guns		19	19	44

Official German designation of the gun types (in brackets, country of origin of the guns, if not German).	Calibre (mm)	215th Division	2nd SS Brigade	Blue Division
Captured guns		13	26	11
Total artillery pieces		32	45	55
Number of batteries		12	14	15
Number of groups		3	4	5

In both literature and historiographic output the story of the Blue Division has been told against a backdrop of rumours suggesting that the host army did not properly equip the Spanish, going so far as to imply that the Germans basically considered them as nothing more than cannon fodder. As we can see, the facts suggest something entirely different. The Blue Division was as well or better equipped than the other units of their Army Corps. Not only did they have more guns than the other two units, but their guns were standard German equipment with very few exceptions. But neither was this as a result of favourable treatment. The Blue Division simply covered a longer sector than the other two units, so they were given more guns to do the job. What is most striking is the fact that they had proportionally fewer captured guns, an important advantage when it came to obtaining spares and ammunition.

The Army Corps had assigned part of its own artillery resources to the 2nd SS Brigade and, to a lesser extent, to the Blue Division. But it still had the resources to coordinate two masses of fire on the front line controlled by its *Artillerie-Kommandeur*, at the time *Arko 18*, through its regimental staffs.

The left wing was commanded by the 802nd Artillery Staff which directed the fire of the II/84th Heavy Group[12] and the 708th Coastal Group.[13]

Both units had been reinforced with the attachment of three independent coastal batteries (the 508th and 515th joined II/84th; the 513th joined the 708th). The batteries of this 802nd Artillery Staff were deployed behind the 215th Division. But their mission was not so much to support this division as to attack the city of Leningrad. Due to their location and the range of their guns the units of the 802nd Artillery Staff were well suited to the task.

The right wing was commanded by Artillery Staff Gronert, named after its commander. It comprised:

The staff and half the batteries of the 768th Heavy Group.[14]

The 928th Coastal Group.[15]

The 679th Heavy Railway Artillery Group. However only part of the 695th Railway Battery of this unit was operational.

Another coastal group, the 289th,[16] was under the direct orders of *Arko 18*. However, one of its batteries was attached to the 768th Group, so the 503rd Coastal Battery had been attached to the group.

All the groups and batteries of the Gronert Staff and the 289th Coastal Group were deployed in the sector covered by the Blue Division, which is evidenced both by the maps of L Corps Staff and the TOE of the Blue Division referred to earlier.

Due to the type of guns and their emplacement, this artillery mass did not yet have the capacity to hit the city of Leningrad. However, it was perfectly capable of reaching the large town of Kolpino, near Leningrad, and also the positions of the major Soviet artillery groups defending Leningrad from any German attempt to storm the city.

Now is the time to compare the composition of the two wings into which *Arko 18* had distributed its guns. For this purpose, given its location, we shall consider the 289th Coastal Group to be part of the Gronert Staff. The breakdown of this line of fire controlled by *Arko 18* is as follows:

Operational artillery under the direct orders of *Arko 18* as at 26 January 1943			
Official German designation of the gun types (in brackets, country of origin of the guns, if not German)	Calibre (mm)	Left wing. Staff of 802nd (rearguard of the 215th Division)	Right wing. Gronert Staff (rearguard of the Blue Division)
10,5 Kanone (t) (Czechoslovakia)	105	4	11
12,2 Kanone (r) (Russia)	122	6	-
15 Kanone in *Mörser-Lafette*	150	2	-
Schwere Feldhautize 416 (f) (France)	155	15	14
17 Kanone in Mörser-Lafette	170	4	2
19,4 Kanone (f) Sfl (self-propelled)	194	2	-
21 Kanone 38/39 and 40	210	2	4
24 Haubitze 39 (t)	240	2	-
37 Haubitze – Eisenbahn (f)	370	-	3
Total artillery pieces		37	34
Number of batteries		12	10
Number of groups		2	3

By combining the information of these last two tables, we can see that in the segment of front covered by the Spanish Blue Division there were a total of eight artillery groups (four Spanish and four Germans) with 25 batteries (13 manned by Spanish gunners and the rest by Germans), and a sum total of 89 operational artillery pieces as at 26 January. This is almost double the complement of artillery guns of an infantry division such as the Blue Division, which had four groups of three batteries with 4 guns each,[17] a total of 48 artillery pieces. To put it another way, and as I have said before, for practical purposes the Blue Division had not one but two artillery regiments to provide support.

In late January 1943 L Corps' three division-scale units had 132 artillery pieces (of a theoretical complement of 146) and the *Arko 18* units interspersed between the groups serving the divisions totalled a further 71 guns (of a theoretical complement of 87). The telling fact should be noted that this total included 16 different types of guns.

Of the 203 artillery pieces deployed in the L Corps sector (this figure includes railway guns) which were operational in late January 1943, 89 or 44 per cent of the guns were in the Spanish sector. However, I repeat that Spanish historiography and the memoirs of the Spanish veterans of the Battle of Krasny Bor give the impression that the Spaniards were not properly protected by artillery.

This impression stemmed from the fact that the number of batteries and guns was indeed insufficient to match the firepower that the Red Army could bring to bear, but it is absolutely wrong to imagine (as many have done) that the Germans had left the Spanish without artillery protection. They assigned all the artillery they could to the Blue Division, even though it was not enough to match the enemy's firepower.

Arko 18 held its siege gun batteries in reserve[18] in a group known as *Gruppe Lug*, which despite its name was actually of battlegroup size,[19] comprising the I/814th and II/814th Superheavy Groups, and the 458th and 459th Superheavy Batteries.[20] And although at this time they were under the direct command of the 18th Army and not of the Corps, they were near most of the batteries of the 679th Railway Group[21] and so should be considered as a reserve for the sector. The aforementioned group comprised the 688th and 693rd Batteries and half the 686th Battery (the other half, and half the 695th Battery were seconded to another group about which we shall be speaking later, Group Hilpert).

No less important was *Arko 18*'s large observation and location force: three *Beobachtungs Abteilungen*. *Arko 18* had direct operational control over the 39th Observation and Location Group, the 24th operated under the orders of the 802nd Artillery Staff, and the 30th was at the disposal of the Gronert Staff. Other smaller units under the orders of *Arko 18* were a meteorological platoon (*Wetterpeilzug 516*) and a calibration troop (*Velocitäts Messzug 518*).

These observation and location groups could detach part of their elements to the units they were supporting as their forward eyes and ears. It is noteworthy that, with regard to the Blue Division artillery as at 24 January, only a few observation and location elements had been detached; in the case of the 215th Division to one of the batteries of the IV/225th, and in the case of the 2nd SS Brigade to the 914th Coastal Group. However, from the Order of Battle for late January we know that the German observation groups now had men attached to two of the batteries of the Spanish IV/250th and to all four batteries which at that time made up I/250th. By this time there were already signs building up of an imminent Soviet attack on this sector, hence the detachment of these elements to support the Spanish front line units.

Regiments of front line units and the groups (highlighted borders indicate heavy units)											
215th Division				2nd SS Brigade			Blue Division				
215th Art. Reg.				110th Reg. Staff			250th Art. Reg.				
I/215th	III/215th	IV/225th	SS Instruc.	II/215th	III/207th	914th Coast.	I/250th	II/250th	III/250th	IV/250th	Werner
Artillery units of *Arko 18*											
802nd Reg. Staff				Direct control			Reg. "Gronert" Staff				
24th Observ. Gr.				39th Observ. Gr.			30th Observ. Gr.				
II/84th Gr.	708th Coastal Gr.			289th Coastal Gr.		928th Coast. Gr.	768th Heavy Gr. (part)		695th Rlwy Batt. (part)		
Gruppe Lug (in reserve)						679th Railway Group (in reserve)					
I/814th Gr.	II/814th Gr.		458th Batt.		459th Batt.	686th Batt. (part)	688th Batt.		693rd Batt.		695th Batt. (rest)

The detailed composition of each of these artillery units at this time is to be found in Appendix 2.

Another noteworthy feature of the 250th Artillery Regiment was its excellent complement of men. When the initial contingent of the Blue Division was recruited in June-July 1941, it was done in a great hurry. The personnel – commanders and troops – were excellent and very highly motivated, but a number of mistakes were made, such as sending to Russia a large number of young provisional 2nd lieutenants and lieutenants who still needed to attend the so called Transformation Academy with the result that, having just arrived at the front, a large number of these young artillery officers had to be sent home and replaced by officers who had passed out of the Transformation Academy.

After the first months of fierce fighting on the Volkhov Front, it had been finally decided in Spain to replace the initial contingent with another one, with the idea of carrying out a mass relief of the expeditionary force. The Minister of the Army, General Varela, ordered General Esteban-Infantes to organize this "Second Division". And the methodical general set about doing so, first carefully selecting his commanders.

Things did not turn out as planned; the "Second Division" did not relieve the "First Division", far from it. As the march battalions arrived in Russia their men were dispersed among already formed units, since it was thought to be absurd to replace all the veterans by newly arrived troops. First the complements were brought up to full strength and only later did they start actually relieving men. As a result, the Spanish units were almost at full complement, a situation that was highly unusual on the Eastern Front.

None of the volunteers who set out from Spain in July 1941 are among the men mentioned in this book (in chapters or appendices). Among those who are mentioned in this book, who arrived in the contingent that left Spain in late September 1941 to relieve the men who had to return to the Academy, are Lieutenants Argamasilla, Campuzano, Cardona, Michelena, Ocaña, Torres, Valenzuela and Villareal. In late January and February 1942 small contingents of officers and troops left Spain to urgently cover casualties, including some artillery officers mentioned in this book: Captains Agut Morales and Álvarez Lasarte, and Lieutenant Ferrer González.

Most of the officers who would take part in the Battle of Krasny Bor crossed the Franco-Spanish border bound for the Russian Front in the spring or summer of 1942. In April Captains López Alarcia, and Muñoz Acera, and Lieutenants Colorado, Docampo, Farge, Hernanz, Iturzaeta and Muro all crossed the border, while in May it was the turn of Lieutenant Colonel Santos Ascarza, Major Vázquez, and Lieutenant Lisarrague. June was the month when most of the Spanish artillerymen involved in the battle crossed the border into France: Colonel Bandín, Major Reinlein, Captains Andrada, De Andrés, Butler, Gómez Díaz-Miranda, Mateos del Corral, and Villalobos; Lieutenants Álvarez Montes, Arenas, Carretero, Gutiérrez de Osuna, López Orive, Martínez Viamonte, Montojo, Retenaga, and Sánchez Domingo; and 2nd Lieutenants Álvarez and Pita.

In the summer there was less movement, although in August Captain Moreno Aznar and Lieutenants De La Vega, Gómez-Trenor, and Sieiro all crossed the Franco-Spanish border, and in September it was the turn of Captain Castro and Lieutenants Hernández Miranda, Garzón, and Ibaibarriaga.

In the case of NCOs and gunners, the process was very similar. The men who manned the batteries involved in the Battle of Krasny Bor mostly formed part of the contingents that had arrived in 1942, although there were still some veterans left from the first contingent, since due to their number, gunners were more difficult to relieve.

A not inconsiderable number of "urban legends" surround the Blue Division, one of them being that in 1941 there were enough volunteers, but that in 1942 the men arriving in Russia in the march battalions – including officers – had been more or less forced or "pressed" into going. If that had been the case, which it certainly was not, they would never have performed so magnificently at the Battle of Krasny Bor.

Furthermore, the 250th Artillery Regiment had already accumulated considerable experience, especially as a result of its cooperation with German artillery units. This is a fact that tends to be neglected in the historiography of the Blue Division. In October 1941, when the Blue Division had only just arrived at the front, a German artillery group, the II/207th Artillery Regiment, strengthened by a battery from another unit (the 9th Battery of the 18th Artillery Regiment), was made available for operations at the Volkhov Bridgehead.

This close collaboration would become even closer during the cycle of operations we know as the "Battle of the Volkhov Pocket". As is well known, a number of Spanish battalions took part at various times. Much less known is that Spanish artillery was involved in this battle to a greater extent than Spanish infantry in proportional terms. By way of example, in mid-May 1942, the Artillery Commander assigned to XXXVIII Corps – to which belonged the Blue Division and the units attacking the pocket from the south – was *Artillerie-Kommandeur 2*. Under his direct orders were:

- Seven light and three heavy batteries of the 158th Artillery regiment (belonging to the 58th Infantry Division, a unit which had arrived from Leningrad to lead the assault on the Pocket from the south).
- What remained of the 126th Infantry Division's artillery, the unit whose front had been breached by the Red Army allowing it to penetrate west of the Volkhov in January 1942: two light and three heavy batteries.
- Two light batteries of the 207th Artillery Regiment (belonging to a Security Division deployed in the rear, which did not really require artillery firepower in the course of its duties).
- Four heavy batteries from one of the heavy groups of the *Heerestruppen*, the II/58th (which despite its designation had no organic relationship with the 58th Division).
- And, finally, as a contribution from the Spanish, five light batteries (1st, 2nd, 3rd, 6th and 8th) and two heavy batteries (10th and 12th) of the 250th Artillery Regiment; that is to say, the bulk of the Spanish unit which, as we have seen, had a total of 12 batteries.

So, either because German units had been attached to Blue Division's artillery, or because Spanish batteries had been under the direct tactical orders of German artillery units, the fact is that, by the time that concerns us, Hispano-German artillery cooperation was a well-oiled machine that had already been put to the test on a number of occasions.

I shall give an example as a case in point. Captain Álvarez Lasarte, who, as we will see later, would play a decisive role in the Battle of Krasny Bor, had left Spain bound for Russia in early February 1942, reaching the front late that same month. After a period of adaptation, in April he took command of the Staff Battery of IV Group before being sent to command the 12th Battery in June. When you look through his service record[22] for the months of June and July, the most frequently written expression used to describe the actions in which he took part is *"in collaboration with the Germans"*. In fact, with the exception of the times when he was laying down barrage fire on predetermined points, in all his other operations we see that his battery was working in close collaboration with German observation and location teams. This was not, of course, an isolated case and it must be said that the Blue Division's artillerymen had achieved an excellent level of coordination with their German comrades.

And the cooperation between the Spanish artillery and infantry was even closer. The gruelling positional war centred on Leningrad, with its constant attacks and counter-attacks, had raised their level of collaboration to near perfection. Thus, the "Divisional General Order" for 3 February 1943 contained the following words of praise:

> *"The brilliant actions that the infantry units of this division have been constantly carrying out demonstrate not just the rapport but the true bond of brotherhood that there is between these units and the gunners who support them and provide them with highly effective assistance.*
>
> *"To these gunners, who every day carry out their duties without a trace of ostentation under the difficult conditions of which we are all aware, and in doing so demonstrate not only their courage but also their refined tactical awareness, I would like to publicly express my gratitude and that of their comrades-in-arms."*

Although the signatory was the Blue Division's Chief of Staff, he signed "by Order of His Excellency"; that is to say it was an accolade penned by General Esteban-Infantes himself. Barely a week later the Spanish gunners would show just how felicitous the general's opinion of them was.

IV

The Storm Closes In

Without intending to give a detailed description of the strategic situation of Army Group North in general and the 18th Army in particular, which readers will either already know or can find in other works, I do need to provide a brief overview so readers will understand the role of the artillery at the Battle of Krasny Bor.

We need to go back at least as far as 12 January 1943 when, in a renewed attempt to break out of the siege which was squeezing Leningrad, the Soviets launched a major offensive to the south of Lake Ladoga, both from inside the encircled area and from the River Volkhov. After some very hard fighting, the Soviet pincers dislodged the German troops holding the southern bank of the lake, forcing them to withdraw southwards and opening up what was still a narrow corridor to Leningrad. It was the start of a series of battles which the Germans refer to as the "Second Battle of Ladoga". The "First Battle of Ladoga" had been fought late the previous summer with the Russians carrying out practically the same manoeuvre but on that occasion the Germans had managed to repulse the Soviet incursions, albeit with great difficulty, and the lines had returned to their original positions. The Soviet offensive had been a total tactical failure, but strategically it had succeeded in delaying German plans to attack Leningrad by using up the reserves set aside for that purpose.

Without entering into further details, suffice it to say that as a result of the Russian offensive initiated on 12 January, the German positions were no longer lining a corridor stretching to the southernmost banks of Lake Ladoga; now they extended southwards in a deep bulge with Mga at its centre. For the Soviets the elimination of this bulge was vital because the corridor to Leningrad that they had opened up was very narrow and still perfectly in range of German artillery. And for the Germans it was essential that they held those positions or, even better, push the Russians back to the southernmost shores of Lake Ladoga, because otherwise the encirclement of Leningrad would be breached.

We have already seen that when the Red Army launched an attack against the Spanish positions at Krasny Bor on 10 February, the Blue Division had powerful artillery support, the like of which it had never enjoyed before. But those guns had not always been there, and if they had been moved to those positions it was because after the middle ten days of January there was a growing fear that an attack would be launched on the Spanish sector. The reason was that the Spanish were deployed in an area that we might describe as the left hand base of the Mga bulge. And nothing could be more tempting for the Soviets than to cut off that bulge at its base with a fresh two-pronged offensive, with one force from Leningrad and the other from the Volkhov.

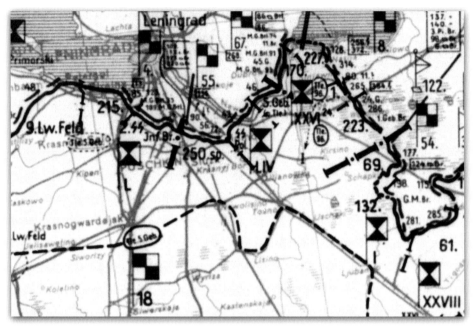

Deployment of the German Army in the Leningrad sector as at 31 December 1942.

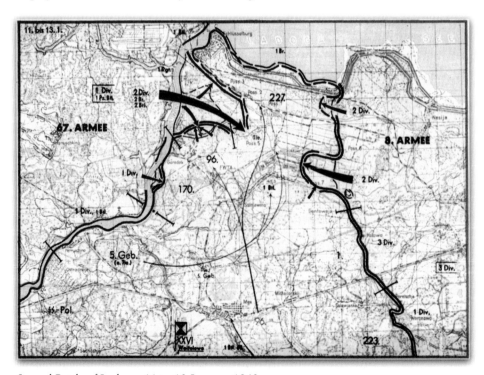

Second Battle of Ladoga, 11 to 13 January 1943.

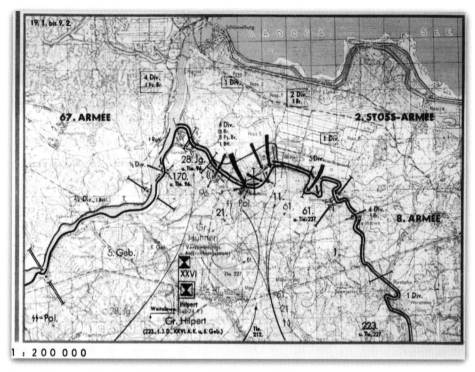

Second Battle of Ladoga, 19 January to 9 February 1943.

It was on 20 January 1943 when the 18th Army ordered the LIV Corps (the unit to which the Blue Division still belonged) to be reinforced by assigning it more artillery; the 289th, 708th and 928th Coastal Groups and part of the 768th Heavy Group were transferred to the Corps. But the most important orders of that day addressed the urgent needs created by the battle at the Mga bulge.

In order to manage all the German units deployed there, a temporary command called Group Hilpert had been set up, named after its commanding officer. This temporary battlegroup was somewhat larger in scale than an Army Corps but smaller than an Army. Basically it consisted of LIV Corps plus what remained of XXVI Corps, the Corps that had occupied the corridor to Lake Ladoga and which had suffered terrible losses. The 18th Army assigned its own artillery command to Group Hilpert, and so it was that *Höh. Arko 303,* under the leadership of its commander, Major-General Hans Kratzert, commanded all the artillery in the "Second Battle of Ladoga". The artillery units which had hitherto been under the direct command of *Höh. Arko 303* were transferred to the Army Corps and Kratzert concentrated on the operations at the Mga bulge. In order to be able to manage his artillery resources properly, Kratzert assigned the coordination of the fire from each of the faces of the bulge to a different *Arko. Arko 123* (Colonel Gotthard Fischer) would direct the batteries on the eastern face, *Arko 113* (Colonel Hans-Joachim Fouquet) those of the northern face, and *Arko 18* (Colonel Karl Koske) – previously assigned to L Corps – would command those of the western face. Kratzert held another *Arko*, *Arko 138* (Colonel Walter Wissmath), in reserve.

On 22 January, Kratzert's decision to concentrate on the tricky battle at the Mga salient made it necessary for *Höh. Arko 303* to transfer to L Corps control over the "jewel of the crown", the most important of the guns able to hit Leningrad due to their long ranges. Another reason for the change of control was their proximity, since they were deployed to the rear of the 215th Division. These guns had previously been under the direct command of 18th Army Artillery Command. This group of long-range guns included the 508th, 513th, and 515th Coastal Batteries, the II/84th Superheavy Group, the 708th Heavy Group, and the 679th Railway Group, all under the command of the 802nd Staff. A large percentage of these units' guns had ranges of 30 km or even more. That same day was when the Blue Division was ordered to transfer from LIV Corps to L Corps, an order which also applied to the aforementioned heavy groups which had deployed alongside the Spanish batteries.

As it was clear that all this firepower required proper management, on the 23rd of the month *Arko 18*, under the command of Colonel Koske as we have just seen and traditionally linked to L Corps, returned to that corps after his fleeting attachment to Group Hilpert. This fact shows that the German command was aware of the dangerous situation of the area covered by L Corps. And, as we have seen, quite some time before the Battle of Krasny Bor the German artillery was in no doubt as to the threat hanging over the L Corps sector in general and the Blue Division – now forming part of that corps – in particular.

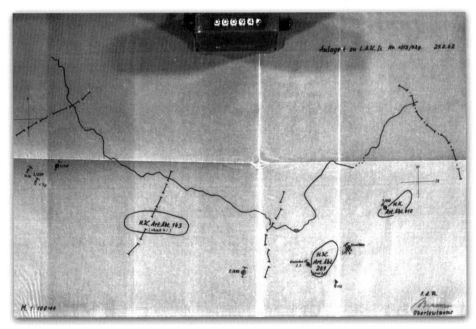

Deployment of *Heerestruppen* artillery units under the orders of L Corps in August 1942.

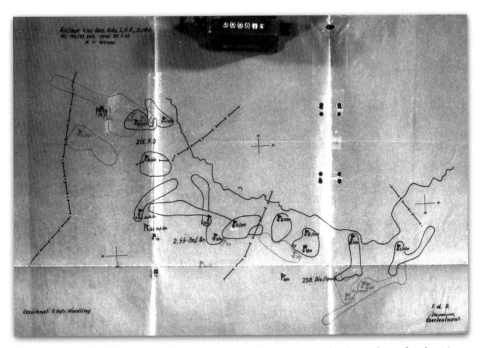

Deployment of divisional and *Heerestruppen* artillery units under the orders of *Arko* 18, as at 29 January 1943.

Spanish infantry deployments also reflect the new tactical situation created by the Soviets' opening up of the corridor to the south of Lake Ladoga. The unit deployed to its left, the 4th SS-Police Division,[1] was urgently sent to the Mga area, and on 14 January the I/262nd Battalion was sent to relieve part of its infantry previously deployed on the Leningrad-Moscow railway embankment (the rest of the SS unit's sector became the responsibility of its eastern neighbour, the 5th Mountain Light Infantry Division). On the 17th, the II/269th Battalion, the most prestigious of all the Spanish infantry battalions, came under the command of the 18th Army; it was sent to Sablino and held there in reserve, to be sent to the Mga area as soon as it was needed there. At first it was thought that this Spanish battalion would be accompanied by a Spanish battery, and the 9th/250th had been chosen for the purpose. But since it was also necessary to strengthen the Spanish sector with more artillery, eventually it was decided not to send that battery to Mga but instead use it within the Blue Division.

Up until now, only two Spanish batteries of I Group had been deployed in the Spanish-held Krasny Bor sector between the River Izhora and the aforementioned railway line. But on 17 January the 2nd Battery took its place alongside them, meaning that the Group was now at full complement in that sector. Meanwhile the 9th Battery (belonging to III Group) also received orders to join them, and was duly emplaced on the 18th of the month; the Spanish had just doubled their firepower to the east of the Izhora. That same day Colonel Bandín, commander of the Spanish artillery regiment, and one of his most competent officers, Captain Álvarez Lasarte, paid a visit to the Army Corps *Arko* at Sablino to receive instructions regarding the use of field artillery in the event of a major attack with tanks.

On 25 January the commander-in-chief of Army Group North, Marshal von Küchler, gave his subordinates his analysis of the situation. The Red Army would soon launch major new offensives against the Mga salient, in which they would make massive use of artillery. Based on that analysis his orders were to strengthen their own artillery and ready it for massive use, stockpiling all necessary munitions. That same day the *Arko* of the Army Corps informed the Artillery Regiment of the Blue Division for the first time of the high probability of an enemy attack on the sector it was manning.

Four days later, Colonel Koske sent L Corps command the regulation ten-day report (which in this case was for 19 to 29 January) on his unit, *Arko 18*, and the other forces under his orders. Its content reveals that he viewed the future with a certain degree of optimism. He reported that with the incorporation of the Blue Division and the addition of the artillery transferred from *Höh. Arko 303* the Corps had changed considerably.

- It now had nine more light batteries (those belonging to the Spanish Groups I, II and III/250th).
- At the same time the number of heavy batteries had increased by eight (those of the Spanish Group IV/250th and the 928th and 289th Coastal Artillery Groups).
- It had two superheavy batteries (2nd and 3rd of the 768th Group).
- And five *Gerätbatterien* with French 220 mm guns.
- The subordination to the Corps of the group of forces which had previously been under the direct orders of the 18th Army for the long-range bombardment of Leningrad had placed seven heavy and two superheavy batteries, plus one superheavy railway battery, under the orders of *Arko 18*.
- As a reserve force the Corps had the *Gruppe Lug* with 240 mm and 420 mm superheavy guns and the remainder of the 679th Railway Group.

The artillery under the orders of *Arko* 18 can be broken down as follows:

Maximum gun range	215th Division sector	2nd SS Brigade sector	Blue Division sector
Between 10 and 13 km	32 guns	24 guns	55 guns
Between 13 and 20 km	21 guns	21 guns	14 guns
Over 20 km	16 guns	-	17 guns

Each major unit in each sector was well covered by short-range artillery able to do battle with the forces of the opposing enemy divisions. The 215th Division and the 2nd SS Brigade accounted for the medium-range guns; in the first case because they were close enough to Leningrad to be able to pound the city, and in the second, to provide counterbattery fire on the large enemy artillery group deployed around Pulkovo. Meanwhile the longer range guns had been grouped behind the 215th in order to bombard Leningrad, and behind the Blue Division, in this case because they were able to lay down artillery fire on Kolpino, the obvious base for any attack on Krasny Bor. In this sector, a significant number of medium-range guns were able to fire on enemy artillery facing the Spanish troops. Koske's report therefore did offer reasons for optimism.

However, it is also true that L Corps had had to send artillery reinforcements to the Mga salient. Three of the batteries numbered in the 5000 series which had until not long ago formed part of the Corps, the 5001st, 5007th and 5014th,[2] had been handed over to the units operating in the salient, not only to make up for losses but also due to the need to create an artillery mass able to pound the corridor that the Soviets had opened up on the shores of Lake Ladoga until it was rendered impassable. In order to move these guns, the Germans had small motorized units tasked with the job of towing the cannons and their magazines because, as we have seen, these batteries had no permanent complement and had to be manned by gunners drawn from the unit to which they had been attached.[3]

And the fighting around the Mga salient, especially in the Sinyavino Heights area, was so fierce that entire units – especially infantry units – seemed to be swallowed up by the earth. As we have just seen, the Spanish II/269th Battalion had been stationed at Sablino as a reserve of the 18th Army. A little later it was sent to the eastern sector of the Sinyavino Heights. There, between 21 and 23 January, the battalion fought horrific engagements, which in Spanish military history are known as the Battle of Poselok. When the remnants of the battalion returned to the Blue Division a short time later, the divisional commanders were stunned to see that of an initial contingent of over 500 men, only one officer and 20 soldiers came back unscathed.

This dramatic outcome was due to the Russians' clear superiority in artillery. A report dated 1 February from General Kratzert, *Höh. Arko 303*, stated that since the offensive began on 12 January, enemy artillery had bombarded the battlegrounds with more than twice the amount of ordnance than the Germans had and – what was even more alarming – the Russians had three times as many guns.

Army Group North tried to use its diminished forces to contain the enemy attacks already under way and the threats on the horizon. On 2 February it was decided to pull the 212th Infantry Division from the Volkhov Front and deploy it at the Mga salient, a move that the unit had to carry out in stages. Meanwhile, the 4th SS-Police Division was to leave the Mga salient and return to the right flank of the Blue Division. As we shall see, these two troop movements would have an impact on the Battle of Krasny Bor. The fact that the 4th SS-Police Division returned to the sector which it had previously been defending is very revealing; the Army Group was clearly expecting an imminent attack on the Krasny Bor sector and surrounding area as part of an enemy offensive to cut off the Mga salient at its base. So this veteran and seasoned SS Division would begin to abandon the apex of the salient and return to the banks of the River Neva.

Given the scale of the imminent offensive against the Spanish sector it was impossible to conceal the preparations being made. At all levels – Blue Division, Army Group, L Army Corps and 18th Army – steps were being taken to counter the threat.

On 6 February L Corps ordered the Blue Division to reinforce its eastern sector, the Krasny Bor sector, as much as possible, since it seemed clear that the enemy would launch their attack between the Izhora and the Tosna rivers. In response to this order, the Blue Division Spanish unit concentrated its 250th Exploration Group, 250th Ski Company, 250th Anti-Tank Group, and practically the entire 250th Sapper Battalion on an area east of the Izhora

In the case of the artillery, the 11th Battery, which had hitherto been deployed as part of IV Group, also moved to east of the Izhora, which meant that there were now five batteries deployed there (the three from I Group, the 9th Light, and the recently sent 11th Heavy).

But we should not forget that to the east of the Izhora, very close to the river itself and therefore fully able to bring fire to bear on Krasny Bor, were the two remaining light batteries of III Group (7th and 8th) and the 12th Heavy Battery, which had been attached to III Group for some months. Spanish command had therefore obeyed to the letter the orders from above; they had deployed five of the nine light batteries and two of the three heavy batteries of their organic complement of artillery ready to defend the threatened sector.

The resulting artillery unit was dubbed the Ascarza Battlegroup, named after the commander appointed to lead it, Lieutenant Colonel José Santos Ascarza. As mentioned earlier, Santos had left Spain in May of the previous year, so he was already quite a veteran at the front, where he had served for longer than any other artillery commander taking part in this battle. He held the position of Second-in-Command of the 250th Artillery Regiment. Since his group had such a fleeting existence, and Santos himself was to die in battle, there has been a certain amount of confusion as to what batteries were under his direct command, and in general it was assumed that he commanded the batteries deployed to the east of the Izhora. However, an analysis of the available documentation, among which is that emanating from Captain Álvarez Lasarte,[4] commander of III Group, leaves no room for doubt: the Ascarza Battlegroup included III Group, with three batteries on the western bank of the Izhora, and I Group, reinforced by two additional batteries, to the east of the same river.

In the previous Soviet attack on the Krasny Bor sector, in the summer of 1942, when it was still defended by the 4th SS Division, the enemy's main focus of effort had been along the Leningrad-Moscow road. For this reason this sector was the one that the Spanish reinforced most heavily. The deployment of the three batteries in III Group (7th, 8th, and 12th) and the three organic batteries of I Group was enough to cover that main point of attack, and only the recently arrived 9th and 11th Batteries were emplaced further to the east, specifically to support the I/262nd Battalion, which had just relieved the Germans on the railway embankment.

Another order from L Corps that same day placed the *Kanonier Kompanie* of the Gronert Regimental Staff unit under Spanish operational control. As we know, this Staff controlled the 768th Heavy Group and the 928th Coastal Groups, and the *Kanonier Kompanie* (literally: Gunner Company) was what the Spanish would have called a *"batería pie a tierra"*; in other words, a unit made up of gunners fighting as infantrymen. The usual task of a *Kanonier Kompanie* was to protect the battery emplacements, but due to the imminence of the attack they were given a more active role. The Spanish placed the unit behind the 5th Company of the 262nd Regiment, in a kind of second line that would have another two "pockets of resistance", occupied by two sapper companies. But not much could be expected of the *Kanonier* unit since, despite its denomination of *Kompanie*, it was only 40 men strong.

More important was the Corps' order to *Arko 18* to the effect that from the night of the 6th an intense harassment barrage was to be put down by all units of the 250th Artillery Regiment, the two groups controlled by Gronert Staff, and the 289th Coastal Group (which was under the direct command of *Arko 18*) on any enemy movement or concentration detected to the south of Kolpino and also on all roads and routes that the enemy normally used in that area. To ensure the maximum level of coordination and effectiveness, *Arko 18* would have direct control over this bombardment.

At 18th Army level another important decision was taken that same day. Given the strong likelihood of an enemy attack between the rivers Tosna and Izhora, *Arko 138* (held as a reserve of *Höh. Arko 303*) was to take charge of that sector when the attack became imminent. Although the normal practice was for each corps to have a single *Artillerie-Kommandeur* under its command, when tactical circumstances demanded, a sector of the area covered by a corps could be entrusted to another *Artillerie-Kommandeur*. This would be the case here; it was assumed that the enemy was about to launch a major artillery offensive, and the sector covered by L Corps was very long, since it extended westward as far as the Baltic. Therefore, to ensure the efficient command of the artillery to be employed in the battle that was expected at the eastern end of the Corps' sector, it was necessary to assign a specific artillery command, the aforementioned *Arko 138*, led by the previously mentioned Colonel Wissmat.

The creation of the Ascarza Battlegroup by the Spanish was actually a consequence of this division of responsibilities; it grouped together all the Spanish artillery which was to be placed under the command of *Arko 138*.

Other orders given that day by the 18th Army worth mentioning were those received by the 563rd Tank Destroyer Group and III *Luftwaffe* Field Corps. The former, an independent tank destroyer unit, with two companies of self-propelled anti-tank cannons and a third company equipped with guns towed by motorized vehicles, was attached at the time to Group Hilpert. It needed to assemble men and equipment and prepare for a move to the L Corps sector. In total the 563rd Group had nine 75 mm self-propelled guns and ten towed guns (seven 37 mm and three 75 mm French war booty guns adapted to anti-tank use), so it was by no means a very imposing force. As for III *Luftwaffe* Corps, its divisions had small detachments of *Sturmgeschütz III* assault guns, which

L Corps also asked to be made available to it. It should be remembered that although this unit was under the command of the Army, it was nevertheless a *Luftwaffe* unit[5] and so the request had to be made through Air Fleet 1, the major *Luftwaffe* unit in the north sector of the Eastern Front. This effectively slowed down the process of making these weapons available and only four guns were eventually able to be transferred.

Finally, and still referring to 6 February, we know that the Army Group, which was closely monitoring what was happening in the sector, ordered the armoured and artillery units that were under the orders of Group Hilpert at the Mga salient to prepare for a move to Krasny Bor.

In all cases the assembly point was Sablino, a settlement located a few kilometres to the south of Krasny Bor, which had a railway station suitable for the offloading of men and materiel. The same destination was assigned to the 390th Infantry Regiment, a unit belonging to the 215th Division. It had been taken out of its sector (the division had been manning the westernmost segment of L Corps' sector, close to the Baltic Sea) and was to take up a new position in the area of the Mga salient, where the build-up of men continued at a hectic pace. Given the likelihood of an enemy attack on Krasny Bor, the 309th was ordered to stay at Sablino on standby. Incidentally, this regiment had set out for Mga accompanied by one of the artillery batteries from its division, the 6th of the 215th Regiment, a unit that would also be involved in the Battle of Krasny Bor, as we shall see later.

No similar order was given to the 212th Division, whose various units were in transit around these dates from the Volkhov to the Mga salient, a march which took all of them through Sablino.

On the 7th, following instructions from the Army Group, the 18th Army ordered the 502nd Heavy Tank Battalion and the 226th Assault Gun Group, hitherto under the orders of Group Hilpert, to place themselves under the orders of L Corps, whereupon liaison officers were immediately sent to the Corps HQ. We must be careful not to be confused by the designations. The Heavy Tank Battalion had no more than one company, with four heavy Panzer VI *Tiger* tanks and another three light Panzer IIIs which acted as escort tanks. The Assault Gun Group had only its 3rd Battery operational, with four *Sturmgeschütz III*; this was the unit which was to be sent to cooperate with the batteries sent by the *Luftwaffe* Field Corps. The "massed armour" that Army Group North hoped to assemble could scarcely be more modest: seven tanks and eight assault guns.

This being the case, it comes as no surprise that greater faith was placed in the artillery, and on that same day, the 7th, the 18th Army gave the order for *Arko 138* to report to L Corps and take charge of the Krasny Bor sector as from 24:00 in order to direct the battlegroup's fire. This group was given the name Group Sablino, and would comprise the two aforementioned units, plus the 768th Heavy Group and the 928th Coastal Group, both deployed to the South of Krasny Bor, and the 910th Coastal Group,[6] emplaced to the east of Krasny Bor.

As a result of this change of structure the Gronert Regimental Staff came to be designated the Wenner Regimental Staff, due to having changed commander.

As we have already mentioned, the recently created Spanish Ascarza Battlegroup was under the direct orders of *Arko 138*.

Since the German artillery units I have just mentioned were to be decisive at the Battle of Krasny Bor and have so far been ignored in this book, it is time to take a detailed look at them.

The 768th Heavy Group was a *rara avis* since it was a motorized unit. At that time it consisted of two of the group's batteries and had another one attached from the 289th Coastal Group. Its own two batteries were equipped with exceptional 210 mm calibre guns. The German company Krupp had designed and manufactured the *21 cm Kanone 38*, which it produced in very small numbers. But the Czech company Skoda had designed a similar weapon, which the Germans ordered them to continue producing when they occupied Bohemia-Moravia, including them in their arsenal with the designation *21 cm Kanone 39/40*. Their shell weight and range meant that these 210 mm guns were very serious weapons indeed. The attached battery with French 155 mm guns did not use the same type of barrel as the one assigned to divisions; instead they used the 155 mm long barrel and were used for flat trajectory fire, as *Kannon*, to make maximum use of their range.

768th Heavy Group				
Battery	No. of guns	Calibre (mm)	Range (km)	Official designation
2nd/768th	2	210	33.9	21 cm Kanone 38 and 39/40
3rd/768	2			
2nd/289	5	155	17.3	15,5 Kanone 416 (f)

The 928th Coastal Group used another excellent weapon that the Germans had incorporated into its arsenal after the occupation of Bohemia-Moravia: Czech 105 mm cannons.

928th Coastal Group				
Battery	No. of guns	Calibre (mm)	Range (km)	Official designation
1st/928th	4	105	18.3	10,5 Kanone (t)
2nd/928th	4			
3rd/928th	3			

Spanish documentation makes a vague reference to the arrival of "*a group of 21 [cm] and a battery of 10.5 [cm]*" on the 30th of the month (these were the aforementioned 768th and 928th Groups) as Army Corps artillery elements, placing them "*to the south of Federovskoye*".

As for the 910th Coastal Group, it had four batteries with a varying number of guns operational at any time, although in theory each had four artillery pieces. In this case, the group did not need to move from its emplacement, since it could fire on the sector under threat from where it was.

910th Coastal Group				
Battery	No. of guns	Calibre (mm)	Range (km)	Official designation
1st/910th	4			
2nd/910th	4	155	15.9	15,5 Kanone 416 (f)
3rd/910th	2			
4th/910th	3			

Arko 138 was also responsible for the tactical control of the part of the 695th Railway Battery operating from Sablino station, which was equipped with three French 370 mm guns. It was also given control over other heavy units, such as the 744th Battery and Groups I/814th and II/814th. As already mentioned, part of the men and the Staff of the II/814th had been provisionally organized as Group Werner and attached to the Spanish Blue Division. It was now time to make use of the rest of that group's men and materiel, since the group was equipped with fearsome 240 mm Czech *Haubitzen*. The men of the II/814th who were not already serving in Group Werner joined one of the group's batteries (the 4th/814th) and, along with the Staff and one of the batteries of the I/814th (the 1st/814th), they moved from the rear to take up a position between Federovskoye and Sablino, specifically around Chornaya Rechka, from where Kolpino was in effective range, since it was clear that the enemy attack would be launched from there. Thus, four more formidable guns could be brought to bear on the battlefield.

We must also remember the aforementioned 744th Heavy Battery, which was sited more to the east than the other guns referred to in the previous paragraph. It was placed in position on 9 February, and although it was not in the greatest of shape, with only one gun operational of its theoretical complement of four, that one gun is worth mentioning as it was a 280 mm howitzer.

Moving these heavy guns to forward positions, such as those at Chornaya Rechka, was a major risk when it was known that the enemy was about to launch a heavy attack, due to the difficulty of moving them from their emplacements. Given that these heavy guns were highly valuable materiel, precautions were taken so that if they were in danger of being captured, infantry forces would be sent to protect them. I shall be returning to this matter later.

To sum up, by 8 February the Germans had prepared a total of fourteen batteries to be used specifically in the Krasny Bor sector under the command of *Arko 138*, with:

- Eleven 105 mm guns
- Eighteen 155 mm guns
- Four 210 mm guns
- Four 240 mm guns
- One 280 mm gun
- Three 370 mm railway guns

In support of these batteries *Arko 138* was assigned the 30th Observation and Location Group.

There can be no doubt that this artillery was a decisive, fundamental reinforcement of the five light and two heavy batteries of the 250th Spanish artillery regiment deployed in the same sector, which were further strengthened by the 1st Battery of Group Werner, deployed very close to the River Izhora.

In the first report on the Battle of Krasny Bor sent to Spain it was said that the Spanish artillery was at a total disadvantage, and reference was made only to the five Spanish batteries deployed to the east of the Izhora. This statement, that only five batteries were facing the Soviet attack, has been repeated time and time again since then.

In previous works of mine mentioned earlier I have tried to correct the injustice of omitting the three batteries in the Spanish III Group, which played a very active part in the Battle of Krasny Bor. I also tried to draw attention to the presence of German artillery units, although up until now I had only been able to reliably identify the 2nd/289th Battery and the 928th Group. Now it is possible not only to identify all of them accurately but also to know what materiel these German units were equipped with, in the certain knowledge, I repeat, that 14 German batteries were to reinforce the eight Spanish batteries at Krasny Bor.

And the situation was expected to improve with the arrival of the 4th SS-Police Division, which on 8 February began to take up positions to the right of the Spaniards, relieving the 5th Mountain Light Infantry Division. As this unit's infantry was very weakened by the hard fighting it had been involved in, the 4th SS-Police Division occupied only a narrow sector of the front, from the eastern end of the Spanish lines at the embankment of the Leningrad-Moscow railway line to where the River Tosna empties into the River Neva.

While the SS Division's infantry was understrength, its artillery regiment was largely intact. As at 8 February it consisted of:

- I Group: Three batteries, with a total of seven German 105 mm guns, plus two additional pieces, one a Russian 122 mm and the other a Czech 155 mm.
- II Group: Three batteries, with a total of nine German 105 mm guns.
- III Group: Three batteries, also with a total of nine German 105 mm guns.
- IV Group: Three batteries with a total of eight German 150 mm guns, one Russian 122 mm gun, and three French 220 mm pieces.

The SS Division – and all its artillery – was expected to be in position before the enemy launched their attack. As this artillery would have been able to pound the attackers it would have been a valuable reinforcement had it been battle ready in the early hours of the 10th. Unfortunately it was not.

As is to be expected, between *Arko 18* and *Arko 138* there was a separating line dividing the two artillery commands; starting at Antropschino in the German rear, it ran through the front line at Slutsk, and ended in the enemy's rear at Moskovskaya Slavyanka. This meant that in the case of the 250th Spanish Artillery Regiment, its Groups II and IV, plus the 2nd Battery of the attached German Group Werner, and the 289th Coastal Group – which was deployed behind the Spanish lines – would be controlled by *Arko 18*, while the Ascarza Battlegroup, and the 1st Battery of Group Werner would fall under the command of *Arko 138* together with the German units described previously.

The orders issued by L Corps for *Arko 138* and *Arko 18* were the same. Both artillery commands were immediately to prepare joint firing plans to be used by their forces and those of their subordinate divisions. Both the artillery units under the direct command of the two *Arkos* and the divisional units were to immediately practice opening fire on all places where the enemy might conceivably concentrate. Once these orders had been received, the artillery units were to react very actively to any threat, sparing no ammunition.

Where any enemy movements were detected, and in areas where there were known to be ammunition and supply stockpiles, harassing fire (*Störungsfeuer*) was to be laid down. The purpose of this type of fire was to cause the maximum possible disruption to the enemy. Depending on such variables as available ammunition, the tactical situation, etc., this was achieved by firing intermittently and randomly using either entire batteries or individual guns.

It was assumed that when the enemy launched their offensive it would be preceded by an intense artillery attack of the type which the Germans called *Trommelfeuer* (sustained fire, although the literal translation would be "drumfire"). As soon as this began, the order for *Arko 18* and *Arko 138* was to respond immediately and with every gun at their disposal with *Vernichtungsfeuer* (annihilating fire) of their own on all infantry concentration areas and enemy artillery emplacements. The name of this type of fire leaves no doubt as to its intended effect. However for it to achieve its objective it is necessary for an effective observation system to be deployed in order to direct the fire accurately onto the targets, and for the guns themselves to have an ample supply of ammunition, since annihilating fire requires a high consumption of shells.

As a result of the experience being gained during this "Second Battle of Ladoga", in order to be 100 per cent sure of being able to continue operating once the battle had started, each unit of group size was ordered to set up a reserve of forward observers equipped with the required transmission equipment, capable of replacing existing forward observation points in the event of their destruction. Also, to prevent the Soviets from capturing abandoned guns, something that had been happening in the past, all guns had to be equipped with the means for blowing them up before abandoning them. Additionally it was established that *Arko 18* and *Arko 138* should work closely together and, since it was feared that in the event of an enemy breakthrough Group Hilpert would be encircled, *Arko 138* was also to be in close contact with *Höh. Arko 303*.

New orders to strengthen the sector were issued on 9 February. Among those affecting the artillery was the order to prepare a rocket launcher group to send to the Krasny Bor area. No less interesting was the fact that on that day the 182nd *Luftwaffe* Artillery Anti-Aircraft Regiment[7] reported that they were finally in a position to carry out the order they had received to form three anti-aircraft sections to be sent to the Krasny Bor sector. These *Flakkampftruppen* were each composed of two 88 mm guns and three 20 mm guns, and they were to be used against tanks rather than against aircraft. The 88 mm guns were devastating against tanks, while the 20 mm cannons were to protect the 88s and could be used very effectively in support of infantry. The rocket launcher group was to be in position by the night of the 9th, as indeed was the case, in between the 269th Regiment and the 262nd Regiment, both Spanish units. The *Flakkampftruppen* 51 and 53 would not be arriving at the Sablino area until the 10th and from there they were to go to Krasny Bor (which they duly did).

Strangely, official Spanish reports never mentioned the participation of these small German *Flak* units in the battle, although today we have no doubt that they were in the battle area, something which has been verified by a number of veterans in their campaign memoirs. Since there were only three *Flakkampftruppen*, their contribution can scarcely be considered to be decisive. But as these units were very effective against enemy tanks, neither can we ignore them. The fact that in order to fight they needed to be protected by infantry, which in this case were Spanish, was what made it possible for this part of the story to reach us, because such diminutive units leave very little trace in any documentation.[8]

Although this book focuses on field artillery, we need to take a brief look at the Blue Division's anti-tank guns, insofar as these flat trajectory weapons could also be used – and indeed were used – to support infantry.

The anti-tank cannons were distributed among the regimental anti-tank companies (the 14th of each regiment), a section of the Exploration Group, and the Anti-Tank Group. Although the basic equipment was the German 37 mm *PaK*, a gun that was totally obsolete as an anti-tank weapon but useful for other purposes, the Blue Division also had more respectable guns, such as 45 mm *PaK* guns captured from the Russians, and other war-booty materiel adapted for anti-tank use, such as those designated by the Germans as *PaK 7,5 cm (f) 97/38* and *PaK 7,62 cm (r)*. The former was the gun barrel of a French artillery piece to which a number of modifications were made before it was mounted on the carriage of a *PaK 38*. The latter was an adaptation to anti-tank use of the Russian 76.2 mm field gun.

While their calibres were considerably larger than that of the by now totally obsolete *PaK 37*, they were not however the panacea, since they were ultimately "bodge" solutions, there were not very many of them, and the few there were had no towing vehicles so were completely static.

Anti-Tank cannons of the Blue Division. Breakdown as at 26 January 1943						
Type of gun (German designation)	263 Reg.	269 Reg.	262 Reg.	ATT Gr.	Expl. Gr.	Totals
PaK 37	9	9	9	35	3	65
PaK 4,5 cm (r)	4	-	-	-	-	4
PaK 7,5 cm (f) 97/38	2	2	2	-	-	6
PaK 7,62 cm (r)	2	3	2	-	-	7

In an effort to strengthen the Spanish 262nd Regiment's sector covering the Krasny Bor area, the neighbouring 2nd SS Brigade was ordered to send three 75 mm anti-tank guns manned by Norwegian volunteers over there. The order was duly carried out, although the role they would play in the subsequent battle was not entirely successful. Meanwhile it should be remembered that as early as the 2nd of the month Army Corps command had ordered the Blue Division to reserve one gun from its batteries sited to the east of the Izhora for anti-tank duties. This was to have an emplacement different from the remaining guns and be allocated a separate supply of suitable ammunition.

Since we have mentioned anti-tank artillery, we need to make at least a passing reference to the guns of the 13th company of each regiment. These infantry cannon companies each had a complement of six *7,5 cm leichtes Infanteriegeschütz 18* guns and two *15 cm schweres Infanteriegeschütz 33* pieces. The 75 mm guns were probably one of the worst weapons of the German arsenal; they were complicated, hard to manoeuvre and not very effective. The 150 mm guns were much better, but their excessive weight and their bulkiness rendered them unsuitable for front line use. Despite the Germans' great enthusiasm for this type of guns the fact is that infantry cannons had already been surpassed by mortars by a long way. And the Soviets were fortunate to possess a large number of different mortars.

The 13th Company of the 262nd was of course present at the Battle of Krasny Bor. The courage and spirit of sacrifice with which its men fought is beyond any doubt, as is also the fact that, unfortunately, their sacrifice had no bearing whatsoever on the course of the battle, since their weapons – as mentioned earlier – were ineffectual in the case of the 75 mm guns or highly vulnerable in the case of the 150 mm pieces. Also, the unit was deployed in response to how it was assumed the enemy would attack. The two 150 mm and four of the 75 mm guns were sited in the Leningrad-Moscow road sector and only one section of two 75 mm guns had been emplaced behind the I/262nd Battalion.

The day of the 9th was one of tense waiting. The 18th Army informed Army Group North of the imminence of a Soviet attack, which was likely to have two scenarios; the forces in Leningrad would attack at Krasny Bor and there would no doubt be another attack from the big bulge the Soviets had in the Pogostye area. At the Mga salient, the situation was also complicated, since it was very likely that the enemy would also attack there and Group Hilpert only had in reserve one regiment of the 212th Division (which had already arrived) and one group of heavy artillery. In the Krasny Bor area the Blue Division had assembled its own reserves. A little further to the east, the 4th SS-Police Division was continuing to carry out the recently ordered relief of the 5th Mountain Light Infantry Division.

For the L Corps sector the 18th Army had the 390th Infantry Regiment as its only reserve at Sablino. But it was actually a diminutive force. Not only because it was one of the German regiments that had had its complement reduced to two battalions, but also because of the puniness of the remaining two battalions. Since much has been written about this 390th Regiment in the literature about Krasny Bor, perhaps we should take a closer, more detailed look at it. Its headcount was so low that a training unit was added to it to make up numbers. This was the Sapper School Battalion of the 18th Army whose job was to train sapper NCOs from all the Army's units in anti-tank warfare.

Readers will almost certainly be surprised to see what the Germans dignified with the term battalion and company (when in the best of cases they actually had the strength of mere companies and sections). With the attached Sapper Battalion, the 390th Regiment had these strengths as at 10 February:

Unit	Composition and equipment	Men
II/390th	3 companies of riflemen, each with 6 machine guns and 2 mortars; and 1 heavy company, with 10 machine guns and 6 mortars.	260
III/390th	3 companies of riflemen, with a total of 10 machine guns.	60
Sapper School Battalion	3 companies of riflemen, with a total of 8 machine guns; and 1 heavy company, with 6 machine guns and 4 mortars.	330
13th/390th	Four 75 mm infantry cannons.	145
14th/390th	Four 37 mm anti-tank cannons, plus one 50 mm and one 75 mm.	

To provide readers less familiar with the structure of the various units with some frame of reference, we should explain that, at that time, each of the Spanish 262nd Regiment's battalions deployed on the front line had three companies of riflemen with 10 machine guns and 6 mortars each, and one heavy company with between 10 and 12 machine guns and 5 mortars; a total of 40 machine guns and over 20 mortars, manned by nearly 600 men. For practical purposes the so-called 390th Regiment (just over 50 machine guns and fewer than 20 mortars) was really the equivalent of a battalion and therefore its effectiveness in the battle that was about to unfold was questionable.

During 9 February it is therefore unsurprising that the Army Group, acutely aware of the imminence of the attack, should pay special attention to readying the artillery, ordering all units in the threatened sectors to concentrate their firepower on a *Feuerschwerpunkte*.[9] Group Hilpert had to be ready to send part of their heavy artillery and rocket launcher units to L Corps' sector (in the Krasny Bor area) and possibly XXVIII Corps' sector (in the Pogostye area). The 18th Army asked the Army Group to call on Air Fleet 1, to be used in particular against Kolpino, the neuralgic centre of the coming attack. The 18th Army were asking for an attack to be launched with *Stukas* in the evening of the 9th while on the following day they wanted the *Luftwaffe* to try to gain air superiority over the sector.

The Stuka attack never happened, so the only thing to be done was to use L Corps' artillery on a large scale. In his book quoted earlier, after a comprehensive, in-depth analysis of Spanish documentation, General Fontenla states that on the 9th the Spanish artillery fired 691 shots while "only" 270 shots were recorded from the enemy against the Spanish lines. An analysis of the Divisional War Diary reveals that for a number of days, while the enemy kept up a limited artillery pressure spread out along the entire length of the sector occupied by the Spanish, thereby concealing where their main effort was to be, the Spanish gunners concentrated on Kolpino and the surrounding areas, such as the areas around Moskovskaya Slavyanka and Yam Izhora.

In order to make the following paragraphs easier to understand, the table below shows the deployment of the Blue Division's artillery:

Deployment areas and batteries in each sector			
263rd Regiment and western sector of the 269th	Joint action over the entire divisionary sector	262nd Regiment and eastern sector of the 269th	262nd Regiment
		West of the Izhora	East of the Izhora
II Group	IV Group	Ascarza Battlegroup	
		III Group	I Group
4th(*), 5th and 6th Batteries Heavy mortar section (2 guns)	10th Battery (heavy) Heavy mortar section (1 gun) Hessen Battery	7th and 8th Batteries (light) Battery 12th (heavy) Heavy mortar section (1 gun)	1st, 2nd and 3rd Batteries 9th Battery (light) 11th Battery (heavy) Heavy mortar section (1 gun)
	2nd Battery of Group Werner	1st Battery of Group Werner	
(*) On 10 February the 4th Battery would be attached to IV Group.			

5 February:

> "(...) Artillery: The enemy directed mortar and small calibre artillery fire on our front line positions and on our rear, with centres of gravity at Voyskorovo [in a meander of the Izhora, to the rear of the III/262nd Battalion] and Pushkin [to the rear of the 263rd Regiment]. Our own artillery directed counterbattery, correction and harassment fire on various enemy targets, including troops in the area of Yam Izhora, concentrations of forces to the north of the Krasny Bor sector, workers working on fortification works in the "El Trincherón" triangle to the north of Krasny Bor, and train traffic at Kolpino".

6 February:

> "(...) Artillery: The enemy directed more intense harassment fire than usual on our front line and our rear using medium and large calibre mortars and cannons. The centres of gravity were Pushkin and Slutsk Park [to the rear of the 269th Regiment] yesterday afternoon, and Krasny Bor this morning. Our own artillery directed counterbattery, correction and harassment fire on

troops, vehicles and various other targets. (…) two anti-tank cannons towed by trucks were destroyed by our fire. We also fired on vehicles to the south of Kolpino and on a group of 140 men who were joining the front line opposite the position of the 6th Coy of the 262nd Regiment".

7 February:

"(…) Artillery: Normal enemy activity with anti-tank and medium and large calibre artillery; harassment fire on our front line and our rear with the centre of gravity at Pushkin. Our own artillery directed harassment fire on various enemy targets (…) and positions to the north of the Krasny Bor sector; anti-tank ditch and south Yam Izhora sector. Also, concentrated fire was directed on troops at various points; on a bunker on the Moscow to Leningrad road and on vehicles to the west of Moskovskaya Slavyana. (…) Yesterday continuous movements from the enemy front to the Krasny Bor sector. Today visibility was poor as a result of a storm. However we could see that troop traffic was more intense than usual, especially in the south to north direction. At 14:05 we saw an apparently enemy tethered balloon shot down, without being able to see where it fell".

8 February:

"(…) Artillery: The enemy directed harassment fire with mortars, anti-tank and medium and large calibre artillery on our front line and on our rear, with centres of gravity at Pushkin, Voyskorovo and Krasny Bor. Our own artillery directed counterbattery and harassment fire on various enemy targets; trucks on the main Moscow-Leningrad road to the north of Moskovskaya Slavyanka, troops, and trucks near the Kolpino stadium, (…) on the road called "tank highway", [which] went through Mokkolowo, [and along] the River Izhora [arriving at the] cemetery and chapel at Yam Izhora. (…) Opposite the Krasny Bor sector we observed troop and vehicle traffic heading towards the front line, mostly towards Yam Izhora (…). We also saw the destruction of 6 trucks by our own artillery fire to the east of "El Trincherón" and to the north of Krasny Bor".

9 February:

"(…) The enemy harassed our front line and our rear with mortar, anti-tank, and medium and large artillery calibre fire, more intense than usual and with centres of gravity at Pushkin (III Batt. of the 263rd), Voyskorovo and Krasny Bor. Our own artillery directed counterbattery and harassment fire on various enemy targets: groups of troops, (…) chapels at Yam Izhora, Moskovskaya Slavyanka, and Kusmino; the main Moscow-Leningrad road; groups of cyclists at Kolpinskaja (…)".

In fact we can reconstruct the confrontation between the Spanish and Soviet gunners in the hours prior to the battle in great detail, based on the reports received by the duty officer of the Blue Division Staff.[10] The first report of interest is the one timed at 03:00 of the 9th which includes all activity in the 12 preceding hours. Between 15:00 and 16:00 the enemy had fired mortar shots on Voyskorovo, to the rear of the III/262nd Battalion, which was the one that liaised with the 269th Regiment, as mentioned earlier, and on the main Leningrad-Moscow road, and also 42 medium calibre shots on various sectors; half had been shots from individual guns (in order to check ranges, etc.), and the other half fell on Krasny Bor. IV Group had responded to this artillery activity with 18 shots of counterbattery fire from its 10th Battery, while III Group's 8th Battery fired on enemy troops in the Yam Izhora area (14 rounds) and its 12th Battery fired 34 shots on the road out of Kolpino in the area of Kolpinskaja, along which enemy troops and equipment were moving towards Krasny Bor.

Between 16:00 and 17:00 the enemy once again fired on the rear of the 269th (29 shots), and also on the rear of the 263rd (12 shots on the Pushkin area) while in the 262nd's sector only a few anti-tank gun shots on front line Spanish positions were reported. Once again the 10th Heavy Battery was active, with 39 shots on enemy troop movements, as were the batteries of II Group (the 4th, with 16 shots and the 6th with 12 shots). But I Group was responsible for the bulk of artillery activity; its 1st and 3rd Batteries fired 68 rounds on enemy targets to the north of Krasny Bor; and the 8th Battery pounded the enemy again in the Yam Izhora area, this time with 50 shots.

After 20:00 enemy activity was minimal, as was to be expected after nightfall; 19 shots from a medium calibre battery were heard, but it was impossible to know where the shells had landed, while a single gun fired another three shots on the Spanish rear, presumably for aim correction purposes. The Spanish gunners were more active. The 10th Battery fired on traffic on the road between Moskovskaya Slavyanka and Kolpino, while the 1st and 2nd Batteries attacked targets to the north of Krasny Bor with 49 further shots. In the first minutes of the 9th the Soviets fired nine rounds from a heavy gun but once again the Spanish spotters could not tell where they fell.

The pattern of this artillery activity is quite clear. Enemy batteries fired on sectors other than Krasny Bor in an attempt to conceal their intentions, while they used single shots, not only from field guns, but also from mortars and anti-tank guns, to check and adjust their aim and range for the firing plans they had established for the imminent offensive. But it is clear that the Spanish were not taken in; all their activity was aimed at disrupting enemy movement in the Kolpino area (the base for the expected attack) and to the north of the Spanish positions at Krasny Bor.

The next information we have corresponds to the report received at 15:00 on the 9th. For reasons already explained, only the enemy opened fire in the early hours of that day. Between 06:00 and 07:00 there was light mortar fire on the Leningrad-Moscow road, 23 shots from large calibre guns, whose shells landed on unknown locations, and 12 shots from medium calibre guns.

However, between 07:00 and 08:00 the Spanish called the shots. From their positions to the east of the Izhora the three batteries of I Group fired 70 shots on enemy infantry positions at the request of the 262nd Regiment whose forward positions had seen suspicious movements. From their positions to the west of the Izhora the two light batteries forming part of III Group (7th and 8th) joined in with a further 24, while the heavy battery (the 12th) fired sparingly on Kolpino (5 rounds). Later, the very active 8th Battery concentrated its firing once again on Yam Izhora (20 shots on troops) and on the track that led to it from Kolpinskaja (14 shots on trucks).

Between 08:00 and 09:00 the enemy once again fired a large number of shots, the point of impact of which the Spanish were unable to ascertain. On several occasions they were from individual guns, other times they were from entire batteries. Sometimes large calibre guns were used, other times medium calibre. In total 84 shots were fired, of which only 10 were known to have fallen in the area covered by Battalion III/262nd while 13 fell near Federovskoye, no doubt aiming at the German heavy battery emplacement there. In the same period of time the Spanish fired 53 rounds on trucks in the Kolpinskaja area.

The Soviets continued to keep a low profile for the rest of the morning until midday with a total of 74 shots, of which in only 33 cases was the point of impact identified, always to the rear of the 269th Regiment.

The young volunteer Santiago Aranda Serrano served as a gunner in the Blue Division. He was cited as "Distinguished" at the Battle of Krasny Bor. This book is dedicated to him and to all the anonymous artillery heroes of that battle. (Archive of Daniel Burguete)

Left: A volunteer artillery corporal of the first contingent of the Blue Division. The blue Falangist shirt showing above his collar is what gives the unit its name.

Below: In the arms of these Spanish gunners, these 220 mm *Mörser* rounds reveal their impressive size.

Above: Transporting ammunition for heavy 220 mm guns.

Right: Condemned to immobility by the lack of towing vehicles, the 220 mm *Mörser* were protected by emplacing them in well-constructed fortifications.

Left: A round is primed and loaded into a 22 cm *Mörser*.

Below: The calibre (22 cm) of the round is perfectly visible on the base cover.

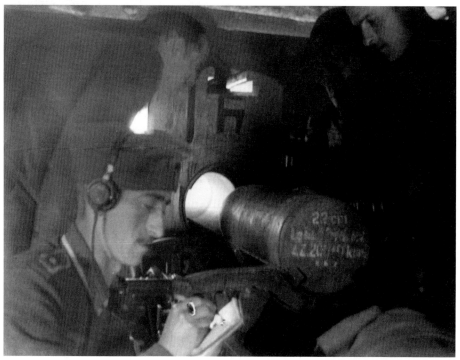

Gunners in charge of loading a round into a gun. The weight of the round made mechanical assistance necessary.

Right: The 220 mm *Mörser* were assigned at a ratio of one or two guns per Spanish artillery group.

Below: A Spanish 220 mm *Mörser* at the time of Krasny Bor. The Spanish were very fond of this materiel, since Schneider type guns were common in Spain.

Above left: Daniel Burguete wearing his Spanish gunner's uniform before leaving for Russia with one of the marching battalions. He would serve in the 8th Battery under the orders of Captain Castro at the Battle of Krasny Bor. (Archive of Daniel Burguete)

Above right: Invited by his German artillery counterparts, this Spanish officer is ready to experience an ascent in an observation balloon. The experience was no doubt interesting but it was no walk in the park since the enemy were always taking pot-shots at these balloons.

The *10,5 cm leichte Feldhaubitze 18* equipped three of the four groups of each Blue Division artillery regiment. This Spanish crew is posing for the photo. The time for some real action would come later.

Above: A group of Spanish anti-tankers pose around an example of the Germans' capacity for cobbling together weapons; it is a French field gun adapted for anti-tank use, mounted on the carriage of a German *PaK*.

Right: Before Krasny Bor the Spanish supplied their field batteries with as much ammunition as possible. Even so, once the battle started they soon ran out of rounds due to the amazing rate of fire that they kept up.

Soviet prisoners of war working for the Blue Division unloading artillery ammunition from a recently arrived train. In 1943 the German war industry was already incapable of supplying all the ammunition that was needed at the front.

This photo may well have been taken a few days before the battle: Captain Álvarez Lasarte (second from the right) with his officers. (Archive of Daniel Burguete)

Above left: In this photo we can clearly see how many men it took to man a *15 cm schwere Feldhaubitze 18*.

Above right: Captain José Fernando Álvarez Lasarte, accidental commander of III Group at the Battle of Krasny Bor. (Archive of Daniel Burguete)

Above left: Even if they could only fire a few shots, when the gigantic German railway artillery guns took part in a battle the effect on the enemy was devastating. The Battle of Krasny Bor was one of the occasions they were used.

Above right: A Spanish officer prepares the aiming mechanism of a *10.5 cm leichte Feldhaubitze 18*. The high number of casualties among artillery commanders at the Battle of Krasny Bor is eloquent proof of their spirit of sacrifice.

Right: In a German infantry division all artillery was horse-drawn. A well-known photo, often used in propaganda material, in which we see two 10.5 cm guns manned by Spanish gunners.

Above left: This photo is in striking contrast to the one following; a field mortar is set up in the open. Their light weight meant that these mortars could follow advancing infantry very closely.

Above right: In this photo we can see how this Spanish mortar is perfectly positioned in a well-constructed emplacement. The battle for Leningrad was a positional war.

Below: Captain José Luis Gómez Díaz-Miranda (first on the right, lighting a cigarette) enjoying a relaxing moment. He was one of the great artillery heroes of the Battle of Krasny Bor. Inexplicably he was turned down for the award of an Individual Military Medal. (Archive of Lorenzo Fernández Navarro de los Paños)

General view of a *15 cm schwere Feldhaubitze 18* of the Blue Division. The Infantry Divisions of the Spanish Army had no guns of such a large calibre.

Gómez Díaz-Miranda (second from the left) took command of the artillery company of the 262nd Regiment on 10 July 1942. Six months later he would meet a heroic death in battle. (Archive of Lorenzo Fernández Navarro de los Paños)

Captain Gómez Díaz-Miranda's corpse was one of the few that the Spanish succeeded in recovering. He was buried in a military cemetery in Spain. The vast majority of those that died on that day were unable to receive a proper Christian burial. (Archive of Lorenzo Fernández Navarro de los Paños)

A Spanish artillery NCO proudly poses by the breach of a *15 cm schwere Feldhaubitze 18*. Professionals such as this soldier knew the value of having guns of this category.

Above left: The *15 cm schweres Infanteriegeschütz 33* used by infantry cannon companies were excellent weapons but their size and lack of mobility made them very awkward to use on the front line.

Above right: Overhead view of a *28 cm kurze Bruno-Kanone* German railway gun, of which the Germans produced just eight units. This one formed part of the 695th Battery.

A *28 cm Kanone 5 (Eisenbahn)* railway gun. This was a sophisticated gun of which the Germans built a total of 25 units; it is without a doubt one of the most famous guns of this type used in the Second World War. The 686th Battery had two such guns, although only one of them was at Krasny Bor.

In his observation post a Spanish artillery officer uses rabbit-ear binoculars to scan enemy positions. Observation posts were the artillery's neuralgic centres and they were therefore the enemy artillery's favourite choice of target.

A Spanish crew poses in front of a *10.5 cm leichte Feldhaubitze 18*; it was the workhorse of the Blue Division's artillery units.

A Spanish sergeant gun chief drapes an arm over the barrel of his 105 mm field howitzer. Each of the Blue Division's battery had a complement of 30 NCOs while in the Spanish Army there were only three.

A group of Spanish artillery officers belonging to IV Artillery Group in a typical group photo. For many Spanish gunners the Russian experience was a fundamental part of their military career.

A 150 mm howitzer in action. It had a maximum range of over 13 km.

Above left and right: Two photos of the then 2nd Lieutenants Miguel Sánz (first image) and José Enrique Usunáriz (second image), one taken in the field in training and the other taken in a studio. Thanks to the presence of these men on the Russian campaign, the Spanish army could monitor the progress made in the field of artillery.

A great handicap of German artillery, and therefore also of the Blue Division's artillery, was its dependence on horses for traction. It limited mobility and the possibility of concentrating firepower, and tied up a large quantity of human resources in the handling and care of the horses.

In the same time period the Spanish 1st, 3rd and 7th Batteries in the Krasny Bor sector fired a total of 47 shots, aiming always at very specific, properly identified targets (gun emplacements, troop movements, etc.), while at the other end of the deployment, II Group fired 74 times on enemy targets in its area, and IV Group fired 43 times, always in the Moskovskaya Slavyanka area, where enemy troop movements towards the Krasny Bor continued to be detected along the Leningrad-Moscow road.

Artillery activity, both enemy and Spanish, in the afternoon, evening and night of 9 February is detailed in the report drawn up at 03:00 on the 10th. Between 13:00 and 15:00 there was harassing mortar fire against the entire Spanish front line in the Krasny Bor sector, but the artillery activity reported by Spanish observation posts was surprisingly light and very scattered; 21 shots in the Pushkin sector and another 34 along the entire Blue Division front. The Spanish artillery was much more active; during that same period the Spanish guns were firing constantly. At the western end of the deployment the 4th Battery fired 28 rounds, the 5th another 31, and the 6th, the most active, 80 rounds, making a total of 139 for II Group. Meanwhile, IV Group brought its only heavy *Mörser* into action, which fired 30 times against enemy fortifications. From the western bank of the Izhora, III Group opened fire 160 times; 44 rounds were fired by the 12th Heavy Battery and the rest by the two light batteries. But the heaviest fire came from the batteries deployed to the east of the Izhora. In battery level actions, the 1st Battery fired 76 times, the 2nd 101 times, the 3rd launched a record 160 mortar rounds, and even the hitherto inactive 9th fired 21 mortar rounds. But in addition to these actions at battery level there were two moments when the entire I Group opened fire simultaneously, consuming 32 rounds on the first occasion and 72 on the second. Thus the Ascarza Battlegroup as a whole fired a total of 462 105 mm rounds at the enemy from emplacements to the east of the Izhora together with the aforementioned 160 rounds from emplacements to the west of the river. It cannot be said that the Spanish gunners had stood by idly awaiting the enemy attack. Since by the time information had to be compiled for the next report the great Russian offensive had started and the reporting system had collapsed; there is no report for the next period to refer to, but we know for a fact that during the night of the 9th to the 10th the Spanish artillery remained active.

Other documents evidence this intense activity. This is the case, for example, of the service record of Captain Álvarez Lasarte, acting commander of III Group, in which we read:

> "On 1 February [1943] I reported to the colonel [of the Blue Division Artillery Regiment] that the enemy was correcting [aim] on our positions and unusual movements could be seen in enemy territory.
>
> "On the 6th I sought a new emplacement for one gun of the 7th and another of the 8th [batteries] with the idea of repelling tank attacks.
>
> "On the 7th the Group directed interdiction fire on the main communication routes, continuing on the 8th the same as the day before.

"On the 9th the Group continued firing throughout the day on troop concentrations and communication routes.

"In the early hours of the 10th, with an attack now certain, the Group fired a large number of shots on probable sites of enemy concentration."

The moment of truth was drawing near. In preparation the supplies of ammunition had been increased to unusually high levels. From the dispatch issued by the Spanish command shortly after the battle we know, for example, that each of the four Spanish light batteries to the east of the Izhora had stockpiled 1,500 rounds, although the 11th Heavy Battery had received considerably less ammunition. Without a shadow of a doubt the three batteries belonging to III Group to the west of the Izhora were also munitioned to the hilt since, as we have just seen earlier, in the hours before the battle they were firing almost as often as the batteries to the east of the river.

And the sector's munitions dump had also been given a boost. The previously existing one had been the responsibility of Infantry Second Lieutenant Enrique Riera Solanas of the Staff of the 262nd Regiment. In order to strengthen it, Artillery Lieutenant Enrique De La Vega Viguera was transferred there, with a contingent formed by a master artificer, a sergeant and 20 soldiers, whose specific task was that of supplying the Ascarza Artillery Battlegroup. From 5 February munitions were being sent to the sector. On the 8th an additional truck was allocated to the munitions dump to speed up the ammunition supply process, and an extra load was delivered, mainly comprising the two types of ammunition that were expected to be consumed at an especially high rate; 105 mm shells for the artillery and hand grenades for the infantry. Artillery Captain Abel Barahona Garrido, head of the Blue Division's munitions service, personally headed the convoy of trucks making such an important delivery.[11]

These figures alone may not mean much to the reader. For them to be fully meaningful readers should know that the normal allocation of ammunition to a German divisional artillery regiment was 8,100 105 mm rounds and 1,800 150 mm rounds. In "normal" conditions a light battery had no more than 400 rounds immediately available, to which a further 500 could be supplied by its regiment if required.[12]

The various *Arkos* were obliged to deliver ten-day reports on the activity in their sector to their superior officers. As chance would have it, *Arko 18's* ten-day report was due on 9 February.

It covered the entire L Corps sector which, as we have seen, had just been taken over by *Arko 138*. At that time the enemy had a clear superiority in terms of artillery since, according to that report, the Red Army was able to deploy 84 light batteries and 109 heavy batteries compared to the Germans' 22 light batteries and 43 heavy and superheavy batteries. In overall terms the Russians could field 193 batteries versus the Germans' 65; a manifest imbalance in favour of the Soviets.

Another very important fact emerged from reports; the lack of mobility of the German batteries. Due to the fact that they were horse-drawn units, the mobility of the four Spanish groups' batteries was rated at between 25 and 50 per cent; i.e. they could only move simultaneously between a quarter and half their guns and crews. The situation of the coastal artillery groups (289th and 928th) which were deployed alongside the Spanish batteries was even worse, with mobility rated at below 25 per cent. Only the 768th Heavy Group, which was motorized, had a mobility rating higher than 75 per cent. If the enemy were to break through the lines and approach the Hispano-German positions during the battle it would be impossible to move the artillery back to less exposed positions.

For the Spanish commanders, already uneasy due to the imminent battle, the fact that *Arko 138* would have *de facto* control over all the artillery of

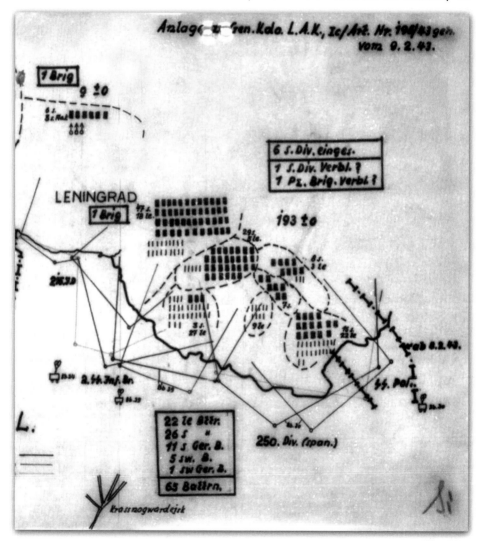

Deployment and strength of Soviet artillery according to the report from *Arko* 18 to L Corps dated 9 February 1943.

the attacked sector, including the Spanish batteries, was seriously bad news since – they claimed – it would only create confusion. The rest of the Spanish batteries were to end up in a similar situation, albeit under the control of *Arko 18*.

Many years later, when writing his history of the Blue Division, General Esteban-Infantes still complained[13] – somewhat bitterly – that the Spanish batteries, *"jointly with other German batteries, were subordinate to Army Corps Artillery Command (A.R.C.O.) [sic], without being able to maintain their natural chain of command without prior authorization from a higher echelon"*.

Seen in perspective, it would not seem to be so obviously a negative decision. In fact (in all the world's armies) such a centralized control of artillery fire under the army's own commanders tends to be the norm with a view to managing resources as efficiently and effectively as possible.

Captain De Andrés, in command of the Spanish 1st Battery, could never forget the night of 9 to 10 February, 1943 which he spent at the observation post of his battery, which he shared with the captain of one of the anti-tank companies, Teófilo Felipe Cueco.

Many years later he would describe the night as follows:[14]

"The last night before the balloon went up the Russian zone was like a rowdy village fête: shouting and noise, anarchical order, singing, lights, and a possible abundance of vodka was the order of that long night. Nobody doubted what was about to hit us. At the observation post, nobody slept. And at the guns, even less; [Lieutenant Justo] Torres [gun line officer], well aware of the situation, told me that everything was ready and the men were cheerful and in good spirits, ready to fight for the prestige of the 1st Battery, not just as a result of some amorphous collaboration. Captain Felipe, who I share this post with, commented on the situation to me and we both expected all hell to break loose. I had the rabbit-ear binoculars in the house in whose basement our bunker was (...) Which is where I was at dawn; a premature dawn, brought forward by our keenness to know and see what was happening. With the first light of day, perhaps aided by the whiteness of the nights on the steppe, through the rabbit-ear binoculars I saw the immense, barbaric Russian deployment.

"We saw hundreds of shapes looming on the front line, which we imagined were tanks; they, or at least some of them, turned out to be "Stalin's organs",[15] better known by us as "dameros malditos" (double crostics). Masses of people, some in movement and others as if waiting for the procession to start, and across the entire wide front as far as Kolpino, vehicles coming and going".

Now let us take a look at the Spanish artillery units which were going to take part in the battle, in particular their commanders. This information has been "reconstructed" by Daniel Burguete.

250th Artillery Regiment: Colonel Bandín			
	Krasny Bor Battlegroup: Lieutenant Colonel Santos Ascarza		
IV Group: Major Vázquez	III Group: Captain Álvarez Lasarte	I Group: Major Reinlein	9th Battery: Captain Andrada
4th Battery: Captain Agut	7th Battery: Captain Muñoz	1st Battery: Captain De Andrés	11th Battery: Captain López Alarcia
10th Battery: Captain Villalobos	8th Battery: Captain Castro	2nd Battery: Captain Butler	
Under the orders of *Arko 18*	12th Battery: Lieutenant Argamasilla	3rd Battery: Captain Mateos	
	Under the orders of *Arko 138*		

COMMANDERS OF THE REGIMENT AND OF THE BATTLEGROUP

REGIMENT

Colonel **Francisco Bandín Delgado** took command of the 250th Artillery Regiment on 2 July 1942 and stood down on 3 August 1943.

BATTLEGROUP

Lieutenant Colonel **José Santos Ascarza** was Second-in-Command of the Artillery Regiment from 30 June 1942 and was appointed Battlegroup Commander, being one of those killed at Krasny Bor on 10 February 1943. His Staff was ad hoc.

STAFF

Captain **Pedro Lavín del Río**, from the Staff Battery of I Group. Killed at the Battle of Krasny Bor.

Captain **Luis Cámara Molina**, previously in command of the 12th Battery. Wounded.

Lieutenant **Arturo Seguí Tomás**, from the Regimental Staff. Killed at the Battle of Krasny Bor.

Lieutenant **Enrique De La Vega Viguera**, of the Munitions, Armament and Materiel Service of the Artillery Regiment.

UNITS DEPLOYED TO THE EAST OF THE ISORA

I GROUP

1st BATTERY

Captain **Antonio De Andrés and Andrés** commanded the battery from 9 August 1942. His command ended on 2 November 1943 due to the dissolution of the Division.

Under his orders at the Battle of Krasny Bor were:

Lieutenant **Justo Torres**

Lieutenant **José Luis Sánchez Domingo**

Lieutenant **Miguel Quintana Alarcia**

Captain De Andrés and Lieutenant Torres were wounded during the battle.

2nd BATTERY

Captain **Eduardo Butler Pastor** took command of this battery on 19 July 1942 and remained in command until 16 February 1943 he took command of I Group in place of **Reinlein**.

His officers on the day of the battle were:

Lieutenant **Pablo Arenas y de Reinoso** (In July he was promoted to Captain)

Lieutenant **Mariano Martínez Viamonte** (In March he was promoted to Captain)

Lieutenant **Luis Enrique Villareal Miranda**

The three lieutenants were wounded on the day of the battle.

COMMANDER

Major **Guillermo Reinlein Calzada** took command of I Group on 19 July 1942, standing down 16 February 1943 when he became Adjutant to General Esteban-Infantes. He was promoted to Lieutenant Colonel on 14 April 1943.

STAFF

The artillery officers of his Staff (that is, with the exception of medical, veterinary, pay, etc. staff) were:

Lieutenant **Gregorio Retenaga Valerdi**

Lieutenant **Enrique Gómez-Trenor Fos**

2nd Lieut. **Eugenio De Andrés del Castillo**

The only artillery pieces that did not take part in the Battle of Krasny Bor were those of II Group (Major **Benito López López**), which at that time consisted only of the 5th Battery (Captain **Carlos Figuerola-Ferreti Peña**) and the 6th (Captain **Fernando Gil Ossorio**).

CANNON COMPANY OF THE 262nd REGIMENT

The 13th Infantry cannon company of the 262nd Regiment cannot go without mention here. All its men belonged to the artillery arm. The company was led by Captain **José Luis Gómez Díez-Miranda**, who had taken command of the unit on 10 July 1942 and would be one of those killed in the battle.

Since the unit operated in four independent sections, he had four officers under him:

Lieutenant **Luis Iturzaeta García-Ortega**	Lieutenant **Ramón Montojo Martínez de Hervás**	Lieutenant **José Rodríguez-Mondelo Añino**	2nd Lieut. **Jorge Álvarez Conti**

3rd BATTERY

Captain **Alejandro Mateos del Corral** took command of the battery in September 1942 – possibly on the 17th – and held the post until being repatriated on 29 October 1943.

His officers were:

Lieutenant **Máximo Carretero Gil** (Killed at Krasny Bor)	Lieutenant **Guillermo Gutiérrez de Salamanca y Ossuna** (Tends to appear as Guillermo Gutiérrez de Osuna)	Lieutenant **Antonio Barrios Pavía**

HEAVY MÖRSER

This unit was attached to the group under the command of Lieutenant **José María Michelena Castañeda.**

VARIOUS

Another officer belonging to the Group and apparently to the 2nd Battery was Lieutenant **Tomás Beltrán Montoya** (who joined the 2nd Battery in May 1942) but we know nothing about his role in this battle.

Also to the east of the Izhora were the 9th and 11th Batteries, forming part of the Battlegroup but separate from I Group.

9th BATTERY

Captain **José María de Andrada-Vanderwilde and de Barraute** from 9 July 1942 to 14 July 1943.

His officers that day were:

Lieutenant **Francisco Álvarez Montes** (killed at Krasny Bor)	Lieutenart **Manuel Valenzuela** Peralta	Lieutenant **Manuel Sieiro** Vilar

11th BATTERY

Captain **Manuel López Alarcia** took command of the battery in May 1942 – possibly on the 11th) and would remain in that position until he was repatriated on 3 April 1943.

The following officers served on his battery:

Lieutenant **Guillermo Hernánz Blanco** (killed at Krasny Bor)	Lieutenant **César Muro Durán**	Lieutenant **José Felix Berdugo de Acuña**

In addition to the officer killed, the other two officers serving on this battery were wounded at the Battle of Krasny Bor.

UNITS DEPLOYED TO THE WEST OF THE IZHORA

III GROUP

COMMANDER

Captain **José Fernando Álvarez Lasarte** took command of III Group after its incumbent commander fell ill and had to be relieved. He led III Group between 23 December 1942 and 2 March 1943.

STAFF

Captain **Salvador Moreno Aznar**	Lieutenant **Emilio Docampo Pascual**	Lieutenant **Fernando Hernández Miranda** (died on 14 February as a result of wounds received in this battle)

7th BATTERY

Captain **Fernando Muñoz Acera** took command on 9 July 1942 and stood down on 6 March 1943.

The following served under him on the day of the battle:

Lieutenant **Julio Farge Lázaro** (would be promoted to Captain in May 1943)

Lieutenant **Jesús Garzón Luis**

Another two Lieutenants (*Diosdado Ayuso Heredero* and *Fernando Méndez-Vigo and Rodríguez Toro*) are recorded as belonging to this battery at the time, but there are no precise details as to their role in this battle, if any.

8th BATTERY

Captain **Víctor María Castro Sanmartín** was in command of this battery from 2 November 1942 to 2 August 1943 when he was transferred to the Regimental Staff.

The following served under him at the Battle of Krasny Bor:

Lieutenant **Luis Colorado Guitián**	Lieutenant **Juan Cardona Rodríguez**	Lieutenant **Salvador Ocaña Fábregas**

12th BATTERY

This battery was attached to the group during the battle. It was led by Lieutenant **Pedro Javier Argamasilla de la Cerda Elío** who took command just a few days before the battle when Captain **Luis Cámara** moved to the "Ascarza Battlegroup".

The following served under him at Krasny Bor:

Lieutenant **José Nieto Tejedor**

Lieutenant **Rafael Ferrer González**

IV GROUP

Although further away from the combat zone, the two batteries of which IV Group then consisted also took part in the day's events. There is not the slightest doubt that the batteries actually did take part because otherwise it would be impossible for a number of their officers, NCOs and gunners to have been listed as "distinguished" in battle.

COMMAND

Major **Camilo Vázquez de Goldaraz** took command of IV Group on 30 September 1942, a position he held until 15 June of the following year.

STAFF

Lieutenant **Jesús Ibaibarriaga Suso**	Lieutenant **José María Lisarrague Novóa**	Lieutenant **José Antonio Campuzano del Hoyo**

4th BATTERY

Captain **Severiano Agut Morales** had taken command of this battery in August 1942 and remained in command until he was repatriated on 15 April 1943. This battery formed part of IV Group at the Battle of Krasny Bor.

The following officers served under him:

Lieutenant **José Luis López Orive** (he would later be promoted to captain)	Lieutenant **Baltasar Redrado Fraga**	Lieutenant **Jorge Uribesalgo Zalona**

10th BATTERY

Led by Captain **Antonio Villalobos Ventura** from December 1942 until September 1943.

The following officers served under him:

Lieutenant **Blas de Frutos Miguel**	2nd Lieut. **Luis Pita Álvarez**

Soviet offensive, from 10 to 24 February 1943. Situation on the 24th.

V

The Artillery Duel

At 06:15 on 10 February, the part of the Ascarza Battlegroup located to the east of the Izhora River (the Spanish I Artillery Group and the 9th and 11th Batteries) opened fire on enemy deployment areas, followed almost immediately (at 06:20) by the other part of the battlegroup, III Group, emplaced on the western bank of the Izhora.

The Soviet artillery still remained silent. But for nearly an hour the front line troops had been clearly hearing the sound of engines, a telltale sign that enemy tanks were moving into position. It had been necessary to wait until the first light of day to identify their location with any degree of accuracy.

Orders from *Arko* were to open fire whenever a threatening enemy concentration became visible. It must be assumed that the German artillery groups already in the area (the 768th, the 910th, and the 928th) had the same orders, not just the Spanish batteries.

It would soon become clear that German firepower was inferior to what the Soviets were about to unleash; from 06:45 their batteries began to thunder. The aforementioned Captain De Andrés had experience of the toughest artillery duels of the Spanish Civil War and even he was shocked by what he saw:

"I don't remember who started the ruckus or how it started. All those artillery pieces we'd spotted and our own guns too started to spit out shrapnel and thunder along the entire width of the front. Not even in the capture of the heights of Cavalls during the Battle of the Ebro in our war do I remember experiencing anything similar. Everything was just noise, one continuous explosion, a permanent ebullition heard from inside a cooker. Everything was obscured with mud and slush. Houses, guripas:[1] everything flying, you couldn't see anything. Our house, with our telephone exchange, rabbit-ear binoculars, maps and our entire organization was shot to hell in just over ten minutes; I don't know how the radio transmitter survived; it still worked later. The gun which we had positioned in front of us for anti-tank protection a few days earlier received a direct hit and was put out of action. The guripas who did not die with Sergeant Jiménez[2] sheltered in the observation post. We had provided for a possible lack of connection with the gun line and, if this were to occur, Lieutenant [Justo Torres Torres] would on his own initiative lay down the defensive barrages that we had studied and communicated to the entire group. So that is what he did, although effectiveness was lost because it was like firing with your eyes shut".

It should be explained that "barrage fire" is a type of artillery fire intended to protect infantry, which is normally laid down after having reached agreements with the units to be protected so that the barrage can combine with the infantry's own heavy guns. It is laid down in front of the places which are assumed to be in the greatest danger, via an agreed signal or a direct order. This type of fire, which is carried out with the advantage of surprise and at a high rate of fire, tends to be highly demoralizing for the attacking enemy infantry.

Was De Andrés exaggerating when he compared Krasny Bor with the Battle of the Ebro? Not in the slightest. At the height of the battle, the attack on the heights of Cavalls by Nationalist Army troops, the principal artillery command of the Maestrazgo Army Corps attacked the Popular Front troops with 60 batteries for two hours and fired 10,000 rounds on the area chosen for the attack.[3] The Army Corps attacked at another two points that same day, consuming in the region of another 10,000 artillery rounds more. Readers need to bear these figures in mind.

The chaos was in fact worse than De Andrés himself was able to remember when, years later, he wrote his memoirs. Among the first victims of that terrifying bombardment were the men who were sent by Artillery Sergeant Julio García Ruiz to man the battery's two forward observation posts, which were located where the 5th and 6th Companies of the 262nd Regiment were deployed. And it was the front line infantry who were bearing the brunt of that hurricane of fire and shrapnel.

As early as 07:00 Colonel Wissmat, head of *Arko 138*, informed L Corps that the enemy had initiated a massive artillery attack with its *Schwerpunkt* in the area between the Izhora River to the Leningrad-Moscow railway line. Much more important was that the report was repeated, this time addressed to the General HQ of the 18th Army, at 08:45, once again reporting the enemy's tremendous firepower.

A clear indication of the ferocity of the artillery duel in progress was that Colonel Wissmat stated expressly in that dispatch that he had given orders for the heavy railway guns to open fire in order to strengthen the defence. It was extremely risky to use these guns in that tactical context since the enemy – with total air superiority – could locate and destroy them. Also, given the great mass of enemy batteries in action, Soviet counterbattery fire could have reached those railway guns, which were very powerful but extremely hard to move quickly, making them highly vulnerable. However, I repeat, Wissmat expressly states that he had decided to risk them due to the front line's apparently untenable defensive situation. In short, Wissmat reported that despite the strong reaction of the Spanish and German artillery, he was incapable of matching the enemy's *Trommelfeuer*.

Following on from Wissmat's report, the 18th Army's War Diary contains a report from the Volkhov Front, timed at 08:50. As the Germans had always expected, the Soviets intended to cut through the base of the Mga salient with a dual attack from the deep bulge into the German deployment that the Soviets had at Pogostye. But the dispatch from XXVIII Corps was no less revealing. The enemy was attacking the outskirts of Smierdinia but in terms of artillery they were using no more than 20 batteries and a few "Stalin's organs". Evidently that was not the focus of their main effort. News was still to come from the northernmost face of the Mga salient, where the Germans also expected the enemy to launch heavy attacks, in order to prevent the movement of reserves if nothing else.

In fact attacks were being made on the positions of all the "divisions" deployed to the north of the Sinyavino Heights. The inverted commas around divisions are because their strengths were no more than theoretical. Each was little more than a combat group with the strength of a regiment. The units that were being attacked were – from west to east – the 28th Light Infantry and the 21st, 11th and 61st Infantry Divisions. The troops of the latter division were being relieved by others of the 212th Division as from 8 February. But that was not where the Soviets were launching their main effort either.

That was what 18th Army command needed to know. The Soviet attack was as expected, but inevitably it had been necessary to wait for it to fully unfold before committing the scant available reserves. Now there was no doubt as to where the handful of available *Sturmgeschütz IIIs*, *Panzer IIIs,* and *Tigers* should be sent; to the Krasny Bor sector. At 00:30 on the 10th the *Sturmgeschütz IIIs* which had been requisitioned from the *Luftwaffe* Field Corps had begun to be loaded onto a railway train in the Oranienbaum area bound for Sablino. Now it was Group Hilpert which immediately had to hand over its meagre armoured force to L Corps, the order coming at 10:00.

The same decision affected artillery units, which were to be moved towards the Sablino area. Also at 10:00 the order was given to II Group of the 212th Artillery Regiment, en route from the Volkhov to Mga, to stop at Sablino in order to deploy wherever ordered to by *Arko 138*. III Group of the 3rd Rocket Launcher Regiment and II Group of the 70th Rocket Launcher Regiment were also ordered to go to Sablino.[4] At 10:30 similar orders were issued to IV Heavy Group of the 4th SS Division, which was held in reserve by Group Hilpert, and also to the 856th Heavy Group,[5] which unlike most artillery units was motorized, as were most of the *Heerestruppen* artillery units. Not for nothing did the artillery mass under the orders of *Arko 138* become known as the Sablino Battlegroup (*Gruppe Ssablino*), as already mentioned.

As we have been seeing, during the days before the battle German command had reinforced its artillery in the Krasny Bor sector as much as possible, and now that it was clear that that sector was in fact the *Schwerpunkt* of the Soviet offensive, it was to be reinforced even more. But those fresh units would take 12 hours at the very least to reach and be deployed in their new emplacements before they could take any part in the Battle of Krasny Bor. What was happening on the battlefield itself in the meantime?

At 07:45 the enemy infantry left their second line positions and prepared to attack. Their entry into action was inevitable since the Spanish infantry positions must have been severely mauled after an hour of being pounded by artillery. The battle entered a new phase, and at 08:00 the Spanish batteries – which had been firing at the highest rate of fire possible – reported that they were starting to run out of ammunition. They needed to be resupplied, and they thought it prudent to reduce their rate of fire since otherwise they might run out of ammunition entirely at a crucial moment of the battle.

The torrent of enemy fire had already affected the Spanish artillery in two ways. Firstly it had seriously damaged its transmission networks. Given the way in which an artillery battery is deployed and fights (with forward observers, a main observation post where captain in command was stationed, the gun line, and services further to the rear, where the baggage, draught animals, etc. were assembled) transmission networks are much more vital to the artillery than they are for an infantry company, whose captain can see how his men are deployed and communicate with them using runners.

But it is not only the "internal" transmissions of each battery that are important. For his guns to be useful in battle the commander of a battery needs not only to be in contact with his gun line, but he also needs to keep his lines of communication open with the upper echelons so as to receive orders from them. An infantry company can only fire on the sector they are manning, while an artillery battery can direct its fire wherever it is most needed and wherever command considers its fire will be most effective. And the first consequence of that torrent of shells had been the destruction of the communications network at many points. Links could be established only randomly and were mostly very limited.

Another matter which we need to highlight is that an artillery battery has no means of defending itself against an enemy attack. Its men are not grouped together but rather deployed over a great depth; from the forward observer hunkered down in the front line trenches to the men looking after the draught horses there was a distance of many kilometres, and many men – those responsible for transmissions – are in constant movement, laying or checking the wires. The only compact groups of men are those manning the gun line and those manning the main observation post, which is at the same time the unit's command post.

They also lacked the firepower required to repel an attack. In the Table of Organization and Equipment of the Blue Division referred to earlier in this book we see that each artillery battery was equipped with two machine guns. Although each gunner had his own weapons, the only weapons of any use in a battle of this scale were the machine guns. Two per battery was a totally insufficient number, especially bearing in mind that they tended not to be standard issue weapons but rather war booty guns, and that the gunners were not specialized in their use. It is therefore obvious that the artillery needed a protective screen of infantry. And on that fateful day it soon became clear that the Spanish infantry positions would be overrun by the enemy; hordes of them reached the observation posts and artillery command posts and, shortly afterwards, crashed through the gun line itself.

What happened to the Spanish infantry units deployed on the front line on 10 February 1943 is a story that has already been told[6] and here is not the place to repeat it. Our story concerns the fate that befell the main observation posts, command posts and gun lines of the Spanish batteries.

To summarize briefly, by 09:30 the Spanish infantry front line had been breached in various places (although pockets of resistance still remained), and the weak second line – comprising isolated pockets defended by sappers – was under enormous threat. The I/262nd Battalion, which had almost no depth to its deployment, had been ousted from its positions and the attempt by Captain Florencio Apellaniz Fernández, commander of the 4th/262nd Company, to improvise a second line to protect the two accompanying guns of the 13th/262nd

Company (under the command of Artillery Lieutenant Luis García-Ortega)[7] failed. Iturzaeta had provided steadfast support to his comrades of the I/262nd Battalion before finally running out of ammunition. The battalion was overrun.

The situation was a little different in the sector covered by the II/262nd Battalion. In this case there was a second line behind their front line, plus reserve units for counterattacking, and – what concerns us – several artillery command and observation posts. When the enemy broke through the lines of the 6th and the 5th Companies of the 262nd, the Soviet soldiers almost immediately fell on the 2nd Battery's observation/command post (Captain Eduardo Butler Pastor). They also overran the command posts of Lieutenant Colonel José Santos Ascarza (commander of the Artillery Battlegroup) and Major Guillermo Reinlein Calzada, commander of I Group.

Lieutenant Colonel Santos Ascarza was killed, along with nearly all the officers on his staff, Artillery Captain Pedro Lavín del Río, and Artillery Lieutenants Arturo Seguí Tomás, and Guillermo Hernánz Blanco;[8] Captain Luis Cámara Molina was seriously wounded.

Major Reinlein and the two officers and ten gunners of his staff were more fortunate; they managed to withdraw to the 2nd Battery's gun line, as did Captain Butler from his observation post. From there Reinlein and his group, together with Butler, continued in the direction of the command post of the sector commander and commander of the 262nd Regiment, Colonel Sagrado, to receive instructions and, in Reinlein's case, to try to give orders to what was left of his forces.

Another observation post that found itself in the midst of the enemy surge was that of the 1st Battery, which was shared with anti-tank commander Captain Felipe. Captain De Andrés recalls those moments:

"Our situation on a small hillock enabled us to see across the broad, seething front; not calmly, because we were in the eye of the storm, but clearly. With the exception of individual defence actions and hundreds of cases of heroism, which unfortunately did little to stem the mass advance, the line was overwhelmed and overrun almost from the River Izhora to the railway line (…). Our hillock split the advance of the attackers, who flowed around us like the water in a river, and they passed us by on both sides, but so close that in our role as defensive infantry – because we continued to be without any link with our guns – our best weapons were pistols and hand grenades. (…) By fiddling with our radio transmitter, which had not been damaged when the house fell in on us during the prelude to the attack, the radio section miraculously managed to establish a link with 3rd Battery's gun line, which was next to our gun line. Lieutenant [Guillermo] Gutiérrez Osuna was relieved to hear from me but told me in anguish that he didn't know where to fire and that the whole situation was one huge mess. Fearing that the radio link would be broken at any moment I told him that the front line had practically disappeared and that the defensive barrier that we had arranged was totally ineffective. I asked him to send a message to [Lieutenant Justo] Torres of my gun line telling him the same and that in order to be as

effective as possible he should fire on my own observation post and the area nearby as we were nearly surrounded by Russians, totally outflanked, and I had no time to be more specific (...). It was practically my only action as an artilleryman that morning".

Very close to the main road and much further away from the front line was the observation/command post of the 3rd Battery, whose commander, Captain Alejandro Mateos del Corral, had also lost direct contact with his guns from very early on. Fortunately for him his observation post did not come under any direct attack, and he tried everything he could to regain radio contact with his guns. He never succeeded in transmitting, but he did hear that his guns were receiving orders from Reinlein, who was adjusting his fire. He also found out that in the eastern sector of Krasny Bor the situation was more precarious than it was near his observation post, so he decided to abandon his post in order to be with his guns.

Around 10:00 General Esteban-Infantes ordered his men to counterattack and Colonel Sagrado himself with his staff and the men who had arrived at his command post were quick to respond. Major Reinlein pushed forward with his men in the direction of the 1st Battery gunline. When he arrived he found that Lieutenant Torres' morale was high and the visit from his commander only served to lift it higher; the order he received was to defend his position at all cost.

Reinlein, his Adjutant Lieutenant Gregorio Retenaga Valerdi, and Captain Butler then advanced towards the firing positions of the 2nd Battery. This battery had been the first to run out of ammunition, so it had been resupplied by the munitions service, which in the course of these dramatic hours had also been able to resupply the 1st and 3rd Batteries until the munitions dump for the sector itself ran out of rounds. Fortunately, from the relatively nearby command post of the Sapper Battalion another counterattack had been launched, and together they reached the 2nd Battery's gun emplacements, which were saved, at least for the moment. More importantly, the firepower of these guns was able to hold the enemy's tanks at bay, tanks which had held sway over Krasny Bor due to the fact that the Spanish lacked the weapons needed to take them out. The fighting around the 2nd Battery's guns was especially fierce, and it is no coincidence that the unit's three lieutenants, Pablo Arenas Reinosa, Mariano Martínez Viamonte, and Luis Enrique Villareal Miranda, were all wounded during the day.

Finally the group of gunners and anti-tankers who had been defending the 1st Battery's observation post was able to break out of their encirclement. Captain Felipe and his men fell back towards the Anti-Tank Group's command post, and from there on the direction of the main road, while De Andrés withdrew to his battery's gun lines. Just before he and the surviving members of his staff reached the line, Lieutenant Torres had been wounded and evacuated, which gave rise to a critical situation. The providential arrival of the captain would enable the 1st Battery's gunline to be turned into a veritable "hedgehog position", one of the pivots of the improvised defensive line that was being established in the southern area of Krasny Bor.

For quite some time the 2nd Battery's gun line would serve the same purpose. From this gun line to the east a defensive line was improvised, manned by the remains of infantry units, exploration squads, sappers, and also the gun lines of the 3rd and 11th Batteries, the latter situated at Popovka on the Leningrad-Moscow railway line.

When the last 150 mm rounds (it was a heavy battery) had been spent and given the likelihood that the enemy would eventually reach the guns, the battery's captain, Manuel López Alarcia, ordered the guns to be blown up to prevent them from falling into enemy hands. As from that moment his men served as riflemen under the orders of Major Bellod, commander of the Sapper Battalion.

As the day wore on the situation could not have been more dramatic. The heavy losses among officers and NCOs had left units without any command structure. Weapons and ammunition were in short supply, the number of dead and wounded among the men was extremely high and the survivors were physically exhausted, added to which there was scarcely no contact with the higher echelons. Ascarza Battlegroup's munitions dump, located in the extreme south of Krasny Bor, was one of the few points from where it was possible to communicate with the division's command post, so throughout the day a number of the officers who were improvising the new defensive line would pay it a visit. It also became a rallying point for men separated from their units.

Major Reinlein, in command of I Artillery Group, was tasked by Colonel Sagrado to command the left wing of the improvised line which had been established on the southernmost edge of Krasny Bor (Bellod was given command of the right wing). Meanwhile, the batteries were losing guns either by being hit by enemy shells or because, once they ran out of munition and were in danger of being overrun by the enemy, any guns still remaining were blown up. Of the batteries of I Group, the first to be put entirely out of action was the 2nd Battery, which the enemy had put under great pressure. The 3rd kept its guns firing for longer. But it was the 1st Battery which became the core of the defence. Although the men of López Alarcia's 11th Battery and some men of the 2nd and 3rd fell back towards Sablino with Bellod when the latter so ordered, the rest of the gunners who continued to fight in the sector ended up where the 1st Battery was emplaced. De Andrés recalled what happened at his battery's gun line:

"The emplacement became a hedgehog position. Linked to the rear by the corduroy road[9] which connected Krasny Bor with the main Leningrad-Moscow road. We collected all the stragglers who passed by the position and tried to organize a resistance, turning the position into the main defensive hub to try and halt the Russian advance.

"I have no very clear idea of how the time passed from 3 or 4 in the afternoon to 12 at night, which I suppose means that there was no real commotion. Several units or parts of them rallied there; my group's commander, Major Reinlein, turned up, accompanied by Lieutenant [Enrique] Gómez-Trenor and some guripas of his staff. Major [Joaquín de] La Cruz Lacaci [Anti-Tank Group commander], his captain, [Joaquín] Apestegui [Oses], and a fair

number of soldiers from the Anti-Tank Group also arrived. And Lieutenant Arenas from the 2nd Battery and Lieutenant [Máximo] Carretero [Gil] from the third. With those men and a number of disoriented stragglers who were passing by, the position was licked into shape".

These were not the only gunners who had distinguished themselves in the day's fighting. The men of the 13th Cannon Company of the 262nd Regiment were also an artillery unit. With the exception of the section that had deployed behind the I/262nd Battalion, the rest of the company had deployed in very forward positions, behind the 250th Mobile Reserve Battalion. The unit commander, Artillery Captain José Luis Gómez Díaz-Miranda, shared an observation post with the commander of the 8th Battery, Captain Víctor Castro San Martín, and from there he tried to direct the fire of the three sections of his company which were under his command.

When the enemy broke through the lines and neared the positions of his section of 150 mm guns he abandoned the observation post and moved back towards his guns with the idea of defending them. He improvised a new core of resistance, which would prove decisive in allowing other units to retreat to the bend in the River Izhora, where the Spanish would set up a new line of defence. His heroic sacrifice was seen by the captain of the 8th Battery, who would testify in favour of the award of the Individual Military Medal to this brave artillery officer, a medal he eventually would not be awarded.

This was not the only 13th Company in action that day. Albeit in a very modest manner (firing a total of 80 shots) we know that the 13th Cannon Company off the neighbouring 269th Regiment tried to do something to support their comrades of the 262nd Regiment, opening fire on the sectors of the 262nd which were within range of their guns. They even moved one of their sections – the one that fired most rounds – to the rear of the III/262nd Battalion.[10]

And since I have mentioned the 8th Battery, we must again remember that the three batteries which at that time formed III Group (the 7th and 8th light and the 12th heavy) had a day of frantic activity, although the fact that they did not have to sacrifice their last gun and fight as infantry may have taken the shine of their brilliant performance on that day. I shall be coming back to them later; now it is time to talk about the last of the batteries to the east of the Izhora, the 9th Battery.

Very recently, as has already been mentioned, Fontenla was able to recover a vital testimony, one which proved that this was the last Spanish unit to withdraw from Krasny Bor, since it remained there until the 13th.[11] The 9th Battery was the Spanish artillery unit which was situated furthest to the east, very far away from the rest of the Spanish batteries, a location which was due to its main purpose being to support the I/262nd Battalion. It was commanded by a captain whose name usually appears in documentation as José Andrada Vanderwilde (or Vanderville), although we now know that his full name was actually José María Andrada-Vanderwilde y de Barraute. For years we have assumed that his battery had been overwhelmed like all the other Spanish batteries, when the truth is that he led the longest defence by any Spanish unit at the Battle of Krasny Bor. As this publication is very recent I shall not be quoting extracts from it, since it can be easily found on the market.

I must say, however, that it was in fact mentioned in a few documents from that time, but they apparently failed to strike a chord. I shall be telling this battery's story in some detail. Scarcely was the Battle of Krasny Bor over when General Esteban-Infantes issued a dispatch on the battle which was sent to Madrid; this is the narrative that tends to be quoted in texts on this battle. It is even available on the web.[12]

But the truth is that a more detailed report, dated 16 February, was written. Totalling 20 folios, the wealth of information it contains is far greater. There is no copy in the Avila General Military Archive (or at least none has been found), but copies have been preserved in private archives. From one such archive comes the copy I have had the opportunity to read,[13] and that dispatch does mention the 9th Battery.

In fact the role of all the batteries is covered extensively, as is the role of Major Reinlein, to whom Esteban-Infantes had already awarded the Individual Military Medal (on 14 February) and appointed as his adjutant. References to the 9th Battery do not appear until page 17:

> "This account would not be complete without my giving the mention that their heroism deserves to a small unit which, separated from the rest of the forces whose intervention we have already recorded, resisted furiously until the morning of 13 February. I am referring to the 9th Battery, situated in the extreme east of the Division's sector and which should have been protected by infantry forces of the neighbouring German division. When our front collapsed, it was soon attacked by enemy infantry, which it stood up to with an indomitable spirit. With one gun out of action due to a direct hit during the [enemy's] preparation fire, the battery continued to fire with the other three guns whenever they were asked to. Captain Andrada,[14] who commanded the battery, fell back to his gun line and, attacked simultaneously from the north, the west and the south, he defended [his position] with such vigour, firing his cannons and accompanying machine guns, that he succeeded in keeping the enemy at bay, despite the number of casualties he was suffering, among whom was Lieutenant [Francisco] Álvarez Montes, killed, who had been defending the westernmost part of the position (the most difficult to defend and the most heavily attacked). This part was lost and regained numerous times. The battery formed a forward position on which rested the flanks of the German line, reinforcing the position with a 7.5 mm anti-tank gun and troops, who by then were in close camaraderie with the Spaniards. Despite both Captain Andrada and Lieutenant [Manuel] Valenzuela [Peralta], the only officers, being wounded, the position continued to be held. Its westernmost part was held by Spanish artillerymen plus a small core of men who, when the front was breached, were forced to withdraw towards the flank where the guns were, since the enemy had cut them off from their unit. The men continued to fight until they were given a categorical order to withdraw and rejoin the Division. This they did in the morning of the 13th; after the departure of the Spanish the line could be held for only a short time longer".

As we see, at the time the heroism of the 9th Battery, proposed for a Collective Military Medal (their captain was proposed for the Individual Military Medal), did not go unnoticed. In the first dispatch issued regarding the battle no mention could be made of the battery simply because the facts were not then known. But on the 16th the battery's feat of arms was duly recognized. However the truth is that those events were to a great extent erased from the Division's memory. For some reason of which I am unaware, and I mention it as an example, the recommendation papers for the Individual Military Medal for Captain Andrada-Vanderwilde have not been found by the researcher who made the greatest effort to search for them, the Blue Division veteran César Ibáñez Cagna.[15] But we should not be too surprised, since not only Andrada-Vanderwilde's medal denied him; many other requests for Individual Military Medals were also turned down after the Battle of Krasny Bor (six captains, as well as a number of lieutenants, 2nd lieutenants, NCOs and soldiers).

In short, the feat of arms of the 9th Battery has been overlooked for far too long, something which fortunately did not occur with the feats of those who mounted another heroic last ditch defence at the gun line of the 1st Battery. This is perhaps the time to point out that not so very far away from that gun line was deployed the heavy mortar section of I Group, which operated a 220 mm gun and was led by Lieutenant José María Michelena Castañeda, and the German 2nd/289th Coastal Battery temporarily attached to the 768th Heavy Motorized Group. And also the aforementioned munitions dump of the Ascarza Battlegroup. As happened to nearly all the artillery commanders, Michelena lost the link between his observation post and the guns under his command and had to improvise[16] until he received the direct order from Reinlein to go to the firing position of the 220 mm *Mörser*.

As we have seen, a core of resistance had been established at the 1st Battery's gun line. As the 10th drew to a close, the Spanish noticed that they were being heavily shelled... by the German artillery, which had assumed all that ground to have been lost to the Russians. There was nothing for it but to leave the area.

"Of my four little guns", recounted Captain De Andrés, "I already had two out of action. One had been damaged at the observation post shortly after starting its anti-tank duties: another was upended by Russian counterbattery fire. We set the charges that we had for situations like this on the other two and rendered them useless.

"And at 12 midnight on 10 February we embarked on the second withdrawal of the day, this time much more orderly and considerably sadder, provoked by force majeure (artillery fire from the Germans) but not pressed by enemy action (...) We travelled practically in two columns, one on either side of the road. One infantry column under the orders of Major La Cruz with Captain Apestegui at the head, made up of men belonging to anti-tank and other units, totalling around 150 soldiers. Another artillery column from I Group, commanded by Major Reinlein, with myself as captain, and lieutenants Sánchez Domingo of the 1st Battery, Pablito Arenas of the 2nd, Carretero of the 3rd,

Gómez Trenor, of Staff, and I don't know if there was anyone else. Most were from the 1st Battery, with around forty or fifty-something men. We were ordered to stop once we were past Krasny Bor Church (...) The commanders argued with a German lieutenant who I didn't know. The German was asking for protection and help to defend a position near where we were, arguing that he had very few men and that without our help he would have to destroy his 15.5 cm guns and retreat (...) We gunners turned around (...) And because the German position was close to the church and very close to where we were, all our gunners soon joined the German position."

This was the gun line of the German 2nd/289th Coastal Battery. Although by the 10th the enemy pressure would no longer be as great in the area, it continued to cause a large number of casualties. Of the gunners who had stayed with their German comrades-in-arms, Lieutenant Carretero was killed and the lieutenants Arenas and De La Vega were wounded (the latter, as mentioned previously, had been stationed at the munitions dump). Meanwhile, Lieutenant Michelena was able to evacuate his heavy gun thanks to German tow vehicles. The rest of the surviving gunners who had stayed with the German 2nd/289th Coastal Battery fell back towards Sablino between 12 and 13 February.

The fame enjoyed by the gunners of I Group for their epic resistance – doubtless well deserved – not only eclipsed the no less heroic resistance of the 9th Battery, but – and this is totally unjust – condemned the gunners of III Group to oblivion. In the dispatch reporting the battle this group is mentioned just once, saying that, together with I Group, it opened fire on enemy forces as soon as the first light of day revealed that they were in movement. It is true that they did not have to turn their gun lines into hedgehog positions and defend themselves like infantrymen, but that day they were totally effective in performing their mission as an artillery unit. The fact that the dispatch sent after the battle did not mention them among the forces in action throughout the entire day was a great injustice. And it contributed to distorting our understanding of the battle for a long time.

III Group had deployed its batteries specifically for this battle. The German and Spanish commanders expected the Red Army to make its main effort along the Leningrad-Moscow road. The previous Russian attack on the sector, when it was still being defended by the 4th SS Division, had been launched in this manner. The deployment adopted by III Group and by I Group was based on this assumption, and only the 9th and 11th Batteries were in a position to intervene in the railway line sector.

If III Group receives practically no mention in accounts of the fighting at Krasny Bor it is due to the fact that its men did not have to defend their gun lines in a fire fight with the enemy.

And it seems that even the veterans themselves have adopted the mindset that that fact places them in a position of inferiority. When I asked Captain Víctor Castro, commander of the 8th Battery,[17] for an account of his part in the battle he merely described how he had had to defend his observation post from the attack, but said nothing about the very heavy fire that his battery kept up. And the fact is that when a gunner is speaking, what we all expect to hear from him is how he used his guns.

So deep-rooted is this mindset that in a book the size of *...y lucharon en Krasny Bor* by Fernando Vadillo[18] no mention at all is made of III Group's activity in that epic battle. Activity that was constant throughout the 10th and also in the following days, when the Spanish established their new defensive line at the Izhora River.

Missing from the documents of the Division's commanders (i.e. in those documents to which we have access, because one day some documents that are now lost may reappear) and ignored by chroniclers and historians, the work of III Group needs to be reconstructed – at least for now – from other sources. For example, Captain Álvarez Lasarte's service record yields a great many clues. I have already quoted it in this book referring to the moments before the start of the Soviet attack. I shall return to it now:

> *"10th [of February] (...). At 6 hours and 40 minutes the enemy opened with preparation fire with a large number of batteries and about 25 "Stalin's organs" which lasted until 9:00. During this [barrage], the Group laid down two barrages of concentrated fire by order of Lieutenant Colonel, commander of the battlegroup, until communication with him was lost,[19] and also several barrages of concentrated fire on various targets selected previously in the outskirts of Yam Izhora and on roads used by the enemy. Once the line was broken we directed final protective fire on our own abandoned positions and [fired] barrages in the direction of the enemy attack, covering an area 200 metres to the north of the 8th Battery and southeast of this point. The Group constantly harassed the enemy forces, hampering their advance. The Group was resupplied with ammo in broad daylight with the enemy less than 400 metres away. During the night we fired in support of our own reconnaissance and directed interdiction fire on obligatory transit points.*
>
> *"11th, at dawn, the Group fired a large number of rounds on enemy infantry and tanks, succeeding in breaking the ice covering the River Izhora and sinking a number of the latter".*

Let us remember at this point that III Group also had a *Mörser* section and its gun also entered into action that day... and the following one. Although by the end of the day both the 8th Battery's gun line and that 220 mm *mörser* had become alarmingly close to the enemy infantry – with little more than the River Izhora between them – they were not moved to the rear for the time being.

We have found other documents confirming the words of Lasarte's service record, such as this recommendation for a medal signed by Colonel Bandín, regimental commander, dated 22 February. With regard to Álvarez Lasarte we can read:

> *"This captain accidentally commanded III Group (...) and also during the operations [of Krasny Bor] which are mentioned, forming a battlegroup with I Group under the command of Lieutenant Colonel Santos Ascarza,*

who died [during those operations]. Early on he obeyed the firing orders he received to perfection; later, with the lines of communication broken, not only did he provide effective support to the infantry, pounding the enemy effectively with the 7th, 8th and 12th Batteries and a 220 mm mortar under his orders, but he held his command post and guns in their positions, by bringing [to the fore] gunners from the second echelons of his batteries. And he held off the enemy, who were unable to cross the River Izhora, and did not move the emplacements [of his guns] until, several days later, he received orders from above, an operation that he had to undertake at night and under enemy fire".

These words of praise of Captain Álvarez Lasarte from his colonel once again evidences the prominent role played by III Group during the battle. And the same can be said of another interesting document,[20] the recommendation for an Iron Cross made in his favour by German Colonel Karl Koske who, as Artillery Commander 18 (*Arko 18*), had many dealings with this Spanish captain. I should start by mentioning that some time previously Álvarez Lasarte had been recommended for an Iron Cross 2nd Class, although one was not actually awarded to him until 20 April, 1943 (since they were awarded by the Germans, it was they who had to grant them and a great deal of time would often pass between the recommendation made by the Spanish and the German decision).

For Koske the recommendation was not a mere formality; he requested reports from Artillery Command 2 (*Arko 2*) of the XXXVIII Corps, with which the Blue Division had operated at the Volkhov. Lasarte's participation in operations in the Volkhov Pocket were therefore also taken into consideration in his report. Koske recalled how as commander of the Spanish 12th Battery, one of the few heavy batteries present, Lasarte had taken part in the operations whereby the pocket had been closed off, how he had taken over command of the Spanish IV Group after its commander became a casualty, and how – in short – he had been a very prominent commander of what he called the "Battlegroup North" of the Spanish artillery (the collection of Spanish artillery forces placed under German command for those operations): "*Artillery Command 2 – wrote Koske – which collaborated directly with the regimental Battlegroup North, fully recognizes the personal conduct and energy of Captain* [Álvarez] *Lasarte*".

However, what interests us in this book is how he assessed Álvarez Lasarte's role in the fighting at Krasny Bor:

"On the Leningrad Front, Captain [Álvarez] Lasarte once again had to abandon command of his battery [the 12th] in order to stand in for the group's commander. From around November 1942 he led III Group, to which his [12th] Battery was attached. In his role as the group's commander in the difficult days from 10 to 15 February, 1943, with III Group concentrated in the sector to the south and southeast of Federovskoye, he contributed effectively to containing the numerous Russian attacks and to halting with flanking fire the enemy which had burst into the right sector of the

Spanish Division, despite intense Soviet artillery fire on his command post, observation posts, and emplacements."

"At the right moment he reorganized his group in such a way that his firing rate was reduced only temporarily and to a minor extent and, once the new front had been established, he provided support for the infantry in [process of] reorganization from the new and well-chosen positions."

"For his exemplary conduct in these difficult situations he was congratulated by Spanish and German commanders alike, among which was Major Werner, the commander of the artillery group of the same name."

As in the case of Bandín, these words from German Colonel Koske not only refers to the officer in command of III Group but of III Group as a whole, whose role – I repeat – has been so unjustly overlooked.

But we are also sure that IV Group – at the time with a single heavy battery – and Group Werner – in practice attached to it – also took part in the firing that day at Krasny Bor. At the time of the famous ruse perpetrated by Spanish infantrymen and sappers in front of the positions of the 6th/262 Company in late December 1942 we know that not only did the light howitzers of Groups I and III intervene but also the heavy guns of the Group IV, the *Mörser* of Groups I and III, and those of the 1st Battery of Group Werner. Are we to believe that the guns of Group IV and Group Werner, which had taken part in actions in the Krasny Bor sector on earlier dates, would not do so on this occasion?

As unfortunately tends to happen the documentation preserved in military archives is always very lacking when it refers to days on which there are major battles. On those days nobody is in a position to keep a detailed record of what happened. The dispatch issued by the duty officer at the Division's staff at 14:00 on 10 February could not be less informative regarding the fierce battle being fought; he mentioned some clashes of patrols in the 263rd's sector, but regarding the sectors covered by the 269th and 262nd he stated that no communication was possible, while with regard to the artillery, his words were:

Artillery
Cannot communicate due to all units firing at full tilt.

In the news dispatch for 03:00 on 11 February made by the duty officer, where all the frenetic combat activity of the previous day should have been reported, once again we find information that is not only very limited but also ambiguous. Infantry activity is not reported; mention is made of a lack of communication. With regard to artillery we read:

Own activity
5th Battery.- 8 rounds onto zone 4856.
At 13:40: the 7th Battery [fired] 27 rounds.
At 13:40: the 6th Battery [fired] 86 rounds onto south Kolpino.
At 14:40: 45 rounds [from] the 7th Battery.

At 14:40: 60 rounds [from] the 6th Battery onto south Kolpino.
At 16:00: 6 mortar rounds from II Group.
At 16:30: 4 rounds from II Group.

Casualties
Group Werner: 1 dead, 8 wounded.
8th Battery: 1 sergeant seriously wounded, 8 soldiers wounded.
7th Battery: 3 wounded.
IV Group: 1 sergeant dead – 6 wounded, evacuated – 1 sergeant and 11 soldiers wounded, not evacuated.
At the time of this report we have no communication with I Group and the batteries under Lieutenant Colonel [Santos Ascarza].

For obvious reasons no information at all was given on the batteries to the east of the Izhora River. And the information on the units located to the west only allows us to surmise. Remember that II Group (at the time consisting of the 5th and 6th Batteries and two 220 mm *Mörser*) were the furthest away from the sector where the fighting was and, even so, it is reported how they tried to bombard Kolpino to help their fellow soldiers in the area under attack. But there is no information on the doubtless far more intense activity of IV Group (at that moment consisting of the 4th and 10th Batteries plus the Hessen Battery). And much the same can be said of III Group (barring the 7th Battery, about which there is some information, albeit minimal).

In the case of the 8th Battery, whose guns were now a stone's throw from the enemy infantry which had reached the Izhora, we can imagine the situation. There was simply nobody who had time to send any dispatches on artillery activity. But it was necessary to report on casualties, and thanks to this we can know that both IV Group and Group Werner reported casualties, evidence that on that day they had been subject to heavy bombardment at the very least. While it is true that this was not the intense drama being played out at the gun lines of the batteries to the east of the Izhora, for all the gunners to the west of the river that day was no picnic either. And yet their constant activity and casualties have been enveloped in a shroud of silence.

Even greater is the injustice committed by not mentioning the activity of the German batteries in the fierce artillery duel during that day. The first meticulously comprehensive book on the Battle of Krasny Bor was the work of Fernando Vadillo, … *y lucharon en Krasny Bor* which, despite its structure as a journalistic chronicle, is a work packed with facts and figures with an extensive documentary basis, including many valuable testimonies, chosen with good judgement.[21] And in this book we find only the scantest references to the German gunners. The first, very brief, is set in the early stages of the battle and describes a dispatch sent by Colonel Sagrado (commander of the 262nd Regiment and of the sector) in which he reports that L Corps' artillery had opened fire, and that in front of the lines of the 5th and 6th Companies of the 262nd Regiment three enemy tanks had been put out of action and ten more had been forced to withdraw.

The last reference to the German gunners attributes to General Esteban-Infantes some reflections on the inexplicable reasons why the Germans had not used its aviation and heavy artillery against the attackers for several days prior to and during the battle:[22] *"Why did they allow enemy infantry and tanks to attack [our] positions after heavy preparation fire, without using their large calibre guns and fighter planes to defend them?"* Words which are a damning indictment of the German commanders... an indictment which is not really sustainable.

The German documentation that I have been able to consult states that not only the Blue Division but also L Corps, the 18th Army and even Army Group North asked for the *Luftwaffe* to attack Kolpino before the 10th of the month, and on the day of the battle to have their aircraft ready to attack in the Krasny Bor sector precisely. But finally the *Luftwaffe* did not make an appearance on the battlefield until 15:00 on the 10th. The reason? Simply the very limited resources of the German air force.

What is surprising is that historians have consistently claimed that the German artillery took no part, neither on the 10th nor on the previous days. Just as we have seen that the Spanish artillery was kept extremely busy from before the day of the battle, we can be sure that the German batteries were equally busy. If not, why had they been sent there when there were other sectors equally under threat? What purpose other than directing heavy fire on the enemy could there be to explain the assignment of the Krasny Bor sector to a specific command, *Arko 138*? Even if *Arko 138* and each and every German gunner of the 910th and 928th Coastal Groups and the 768th Heavy Group hated the Spanish, they would have acted with the utmost energy that day against the Soviet attack, because to the right, left and rear of the Blue Division all were German units, for which a Soviet breakthrough would have caused terrible problems and placed them in grave danger. It is totally implausible to claim that they did not take part in the defence (and in any event there is documentary evidence proving otherwise).

Those of you who are familiar with the memoirs of military commanders will have already seen a common denominator of all of them; victories are always the result of the virtues of the winners' officers and soldiers, while defeats are always due to the overwhelming superiority of the enemy in material resources. Another constant is that if the war is waged in coalition, any misfortunes that may occur are always the fault of the ally.

The case of the Battle of Krasny Bor is no exception to these two narrative "traditions". The enemy's superiority in terms of artillery was obvious, unquestionable, but the margin is accentuated if we leave out of the account the action of III Group Spanish (direct) and that of IV Group (more indirect). And the account ends up entirely distorted if we ignore the activity of the German comrades-in-arms of the aforementioned German 910th and 928th Coastal Groups and the 768th Heavy Group, and the 1st/Werner Battery, all involved in the battle in the most direct way possible, and the activity of the 289th Coastal Group and the 2nd/Werner Battery, which intervene from further away.

Another example is provided by the activity of the *Flakkamftruppen* which were involved in the battle on the 10th. And there were three of them. These small but efficient anti-aircraft units must have been very effective when it came to holding off the terrible threat of the Soviet tanks that had penetrated among Spanish positions. No official Spanish document that I have been able to consult mentions their part in the battle and the relevant German documents are extremely vague. As I have explained, it is thanks to the collection of testimonies of Blue Division combatants that we have finally become aware that these German units actually took part in the fighting.

This phenomenon is not restricted to the artillery. A similar situation arises with the infantry. Before the end of the 10th, command over the segment between the Izhora River and the Leningrad-Moscow railway line was transferred to the German 212th Division. To the east of the railway the 4th SS Division was in command of the front.

More than one Spaniard has wondered why the 212th Division was not used earlier. In fact, the 212th Division was never deployed at Krasny Bor. This unit, as we have already mentioned, was on the march from the Volkhov Front to the Mga salient. On the 20th the only part in transit was the divisional staff together with one of its infantry regiments, the 316th. We saw earlier how weak the 390th Infantry Regiment was; well the 316th was also a weak unit, well below the full complement of a regiment. It had only two battalions, one with 360 and another with 330 men, which meant that its real strength was little more than that of a battalion. However, unlike the 390th, it was well equipped with machine guns and mortars. The commander of the 212th Division also had the 212th Exploration Group under his direct orders, a unit which was also in transit. And, in addition to his own infantry regiment, hc took tactical control over the 390th Regiment and other forces moved by the Army Corps towards the area under attack; two battalions of Estonian volunteers (which had been urgently sent, precisely to protect the gun emplacements of *Arko 168's* artillery groups, to be precise those of Wenner Staff)[23] and the 563rd Tank Destroyer Group.

Therefore the claim that there had been a German division-size unit which had been on the sidelines, unused while the Spanish suffered that tragic attack, is totally unfounded. The 212th Division was just an improvised battlegroup comprising forces of no great strength urgently cobbled together from various sources.

But in this book what we are interested in, I repeat, is the artillery. The 6th/215th Battery of the 215th Division which was accompanying the 390th Regiment on its march to Mga when the latter regiment was ordered to halt at Sablino to act as reserve in the event of an eventual attack on Krasny Bor, became the first operational reinforcement. It was assigned to the 928th Coastal Group, which was reinforcing the Spanish III Group to the west of the Izhora. Thanks to the decisions taken before the 10th, there were other units on the move throughout the day and by 20:15 *Arko 138* already had fresh units at its disposal: the 856th Heavy Group, Groups II and IV of the artillery regiment of the 212th Division, and III Group of the artillery regiment of the 4th SS Division. All these units were placed under the command of the 212th Artillery Regiment.

In fact none of these units was at full complement on that day and at that time. The 856th Heavy Group was about to deploy two of its batteries and took control of the 2nd/289th Coastal Battery, the same one that the Spanish gunners were still defending on the southern perimeter of Krasny Bor. Only two batteries of Group II/212th (the 4th and 5th) had arrived, with three 105 mm guns each. Group IV/212th now had the 10th and 11th Batteries of 150 mm guns, a total of 5 guns, but the unit was in no condition to fire. The 7th, 8th and 9th Batteries (i.e. III Group) of the artillery regiment of the 4th SS Division completed the regimental forces, while the arrival of 15 and 28 cm rocket launchers was imminent. III Group of the 3rd Rocket Launcher Regiment was considered to be operational late into the night, but before the close of the 10th, and its tactical control was also assigned to the 212th Artillery Regiment.

While this deployment of the 212th Artillery regiment was not planned (despite which it was carried out with remarkable speed),[24] the entry into line of the 4th SS Division, with its own artillery units,[25] had been planned since before the attack. However the Red Army's offensive began before this move could be completed, so most of the gunners of the 4th SS Artillery Regiment joined the fighting as infantrymen, while the remainder struggled to emplace the guns of Light Groups I and II and Heavy Group IV.

These were critical moments, because early in the morning of the 10th only the 910th Coastal Group was deployed behind the positions occupied by the I/262nd Battalion. And the sector where the Soviets were breaking through the most was precisely the one to the east of the railway. While between the Izhora and the railway the Soviets only succeeded in advancing their lines about 3 km southwards, to the east of that sector they were able to penetrate 6 km eastwards. This is unsurprising considering the very different densities of Spanish and German artillery units on the two parts of the line.

It was no mean feat to have positioned seven artillery groups and one rocket launcher group on the front line before the end of 10 February. Other forces were en route and two more independent heavy groups, the I/814th and the 809th,[26] would be emplaced on a second line very shortly. In fact, *Arko 138* now needed more than the Wenner Staff (previously Gronert Staff) to manage these units, so the 610th Regimental Staff was brought in from the area of III *Luftwaffe* Field Corps to take over the tactical control of these units.

The infantry forces which the Germans were able to deploy to replace the Spaniards and man the new defensive lines were smaller in number and, in some cases (the Estonian 658th and 659th Battalions, for example) poorly equipped. Conversely, the artillery units which were deployed to replace the five Spanish batteries which had been sacrificed in the Krasny Bor holocaust defending their front line positions, losing all their guns in the process, were numerically much stronger. On the 12th there were 20 batteries and on the 13th there were 25 batteries deployed on the front line in the sectors previously defended by the Spanish, and on the second line there were also considerable reinforcements. For a highly detailed description of the deployment on 14 February, see Appendix 3. The table below is a summarized version showing the efforts made by the German artillery to hold off the Soviet offensive:

Division type unit	Regiment type unit	No. of guns	
		26 January	14 February
215th Inf. Div.	215th Art. Reg.	32	35
2nd SS Brig. Inf.	110th Reg. Staff	45	44
Blue Div.	250th Art. Reg.	55	31
212 Inf. Div.	212th Art. Reg.	-	35 + 18 rocket launchers
4th SS-Police Div.	4th Art. Reg. SS	-	34 + 18 rocket launchers
Arko 18	Reg. Staff 802nd	37	28
	Other units	11	7
	Gronert Staff	20	-
Arko 138	Wenner Staff (*)	-	24
	610th Reg. Staff	-	21
		148	259 + 36 rocket launchers
Arko 18 initially; later split between Arko 18 and Arko 138 Railway guns		3	14
(*) Previously Gronert Staff, with Arko 18			

Readers who wish to know the breakdown by type of guns on the two dates should consult Appendix 4.

It is an undeniable fact that the offensive was halted and the *Wehrmacht* rebuilt their front in the Krasny Bor sector, despite the enemy throwing large infantry, artillery and tank forces into the battle. What did the *Wehrmacht* reply with? Documentation from L Corps dated 14 March evidences the paucity of the armoured resources which it managed to assemble in reply to the attack. The anti-tank force the *Wehrmacht* assembled was a little more respectable without being in any way impressive; two companies of self-propelled anti-tank guns and one towed, and 10 units of the *Flakkamftruppen* type (the anti-aircraft guns used for anti-tank warfare), none motorized. In comparison, the mass of artillery units deployed was truly impressive. A large percentage of L Corps' battle order, which does not include the organic artillery units of the various large units of the corps, is dedicated to the artillery forces of the *Heerestruppen* which were under the command of *Arko 18* and *Arko 138*. There may be no more graphic way to show the role that the artillery, including the Spanish gunners, had played in the battle.

And to conclude this chapter, I repeat once again what really ought to be obvious, but is not; the Spanish and the German artillery were never watertight compartments; they always worked closely together. While in the preceding paragraphs I have described the deployment of German units in support of the Spanish, now I wish to remind readers that the Spanish gunners also went to the aid of their German comrades-in-arms during these days. I refer once again to the unjustly overlooked III Group. With the segment of front between the Leningrad-Moscow road and railway line having been assigned to the 212th Division, one might expect the III Group to act only in defence of the Spanish troops which were now deployed at the Izhora River. But as well as doing that, they acted in support of the 212th Division time and time again.

Let us return to Captain Álvarez Lasarte's service record, for the day after the one where we last left it:

"12th [February]. Throughout the day and night interdiction fire was ceaseless and continued on the 13th and 14th. On the 15th, since the group had ended up on the right flank of the division, we cooperated with the artillery of the Army Corps in destruction and neutralization fire, and in the barrage fire of the neighbouring 212th Division, and during the night we laid harassment fire. On the 16th, just as the previous day, we laid harassment and concentrated fire with the artillery of the army corps. On the 17th (…) with the group we fired on "Stalin's organs" and enemy batteries, silencing the latter and forcing the former to withdraw. On the 18th we laid barrage fire in front of the neighbouring division, helping to repel an attack. The Group laid several concentrated barrages on the enemy's new positions and pounded truck columns on the road from Krasny Bor to Kolpino. On the 19th, in collaboration with Army Corps observation and location units, we silenced several batteries. The group hit trucks and tanks towed by tractors and also laid harassment fire.

"On the 20th the group directed concentrated fire on positions at Yam Izhora, destroyed positions at Staraia Mysa, and directed counterbattery fire. At nightfall on the 21st the group opened fire with defensive fire aimed at defending our positions from the enemy attack, which was repulsed, at the cost of many enemy casualties. Fire was directed on enemy positions and the Kolpino-Krasny Bor road, and harassment fire was laid during the night. On the 22nd the group kept up normal fire as part of this cycle of operations. For his conduct he [Lasarte] received a citation as Highly Distinguished from the general in command of the division and was recommended for the Iron Cross 1st Class. On the 23rd, as well as the normal fire, the group carried out the order to destroy wire fences and positions at Staraia Mysa. On the 24th counterbattery fire was directed in collaboration with the artillery battlegroup of the Army Corps. From the 25th to the 29th the group fired the normal barrages. 1 March was just like the previous day. And on the 2nd [Lasarte] handed over command to the titular commander and once again took charge of the 12th Battery".[27]

This was the normal state of things; the Spanish artillery worked together with the artillery of neighbouring German units, or with those of the Army Corps, just as the German artillery placed itself at the service of the Blue Division when necessary. Leaving this out of the historical accounts of the Blue Division, which had been the norm until now, has done more to cloud the history of this unit than shed light on it.

The Behemoths: Railway Artillery

In the course of this book the presence of railway-mounted artillery pieces in the Krasny Bor sector has been mentioned several times. These were unquestionably the most spectacular of all the arsenal of artillery pieces used by the Germans.[1] The professional soldiers who served with the Blue Division were fascinated by these weapons. In his very interesting book of campaign memoirs, José Díaz de Villegas Bustamante,[2] of the divisional staff, devoted a chapter to them entitled "The colonel's cannon". His choice of title was due to the fact that the Spanish volunteers who had come across guns of this type had fabricated an urban legend around them, to the effect that each gun was commanded by a colonel. As de Villegas points out, the reason why big railway guns were so useful during the siege of Leningrad was that there was a relatively dense railway network in the vicinity of this major city, which enabled a tactically flexible use of these super-calibre monsters.

Railway artillery is a weapon which people tend to associate with the First World War, and with good reason. Firstly because trench warfare encouraged the development of heavy artillery and there were motorized vehicles capable of towing them; they could only be moved and emplaced using railway lines. And secondly because military aviation had not yet reached the level of development that it would later attain.

The Treaty of Versailles obliged the Germans to destroy their entire arsenal of guns of this type and prohibited them from developing new ones. Nevertheless, as from 1933 they were manufacturing new guns, some of a very conventional type, directly inspired by those used in the First World War, and others of a more advanced design. In May 1940, when the French campaign began and it was thought that it might be necessary to attack the Maginot Line from the front, the German Army fielded 16 railway batteries with a total of 33 guns, with calibres ranging from 15 to 28 cm.[3] By June 1941 the number of batteries with these types of German made guns had risen to 20. And the Germans were also boosting their arsenal with a fair number of war booty guns captured from the French, with which they formed more batteries.

Although Army Group North had five railway batteries on its books on 10 February 1943, only four of them took part in the fighting (one only partially). When the attack began, the only active battery was the part of the 695th Railway Battery equipped with the captured *37 cm Haubitze (Eisenbahn) 711(f)* guns.[4] With the five captured pieces the Germans had created two batteries, one being the battery which concerns us, although the unit had later been completed with other German 280 mm guns. The French howitzers in question were capable of firing 516 kg shells a distance of 16,400 metres, or 710 kg shells a distance of 14,600 metres, with a maximum rate of fire of one shot every five minutes. As already mentioned, these guns were deployed near the Sablino railway station and entered into battle from the moment the Soviets unleashed their offensive until *Arko 138* ordered them to withdraw to the rear for reasons of safety (these guns were never emplaced near the front line). They must have been used quite intensively since reliable documentation has them being assigned to the reserve a few days later.

But, at the same time, the rest of the batteries in the 679th Railway Group under the orders of *Arko 18* entered into action, not as batteries but rather as individual guns, which fired a certain number of shots and then slipped away. Their size made them easy to locate and they could be attacked by enemy aircraft with a good chance of being hit. Hence, I repeat, unless they enjoyed total air superiority the normal tactic was to use individual guns for relatively short periods of time. Even used in such a limited manner their effect was terrible.

The other half of the 695th Battery was equipped with three German guns of the type *28 cm Kurze Bruno Kanone (Eisenbahn),* a type of which the Germans produced only eight pieces. It was capable of firing a 240 kg shell a distance of 29,500 metres with a rate of fire of one shot every 6 minutes. Until a very short time previously this half of the 695th Railway Battery had been at the service of Group Hilpert. In anticipation of the attack on Krasny Bor it had been transferred to L Corps, which placed it under the orders of *Arko 18*, along with the other large calibre railway guns. Although some of the units under the orders of *Arko 18* did not have the range to hit targets where the fighting was taking place, this was not the case of the railway guns and other super-calibre pieces. Of all *Arko 18's* railway batteries, we know that this one – part of the 695th Battery equipped with *Kurze Bruno* guns – was the one that fired most on 10 February.

The 688th was another "mixed" battery with German and French guns. It had two of the three *28 cm lange Bruno Kanone (Eisenbahn)* guns made, capable of firing a 302 kg shell a distance of 28,500 metres. The battery was completed by two examples of a French gun which in German nomenclature was known as *40 cm Haubitze (Eisenbahn) 752 (f),* a behemoth which could hurl a 900 kg shell over a distance of up to 15 km. The 693rd Battery was equipped with the same gun, although that battery had three such pieces (a total of eight guns were captured by the Germans).[5]

Major Guillermo Reinlein Calzada was the commander of I Group of the 250th Artillery Regiment at the Battle of Krasny Bor.

Above: A number of artillery officers in the cold winter of 1942-43. The third from the right is the then 2nd Lieutenant Joaquín Usunáriz Mocoroa.

Right: Gunner Julio Rodríguez Arce. He belonged to the 2nd Staff Battery of the 250th Regiment.

May 1943. Visit to the Russian Front of the then head of the Special Commission for War Materiel, Major-General Carlos Martínez de Campos, accompanied by his colleague Esteban Infantes. To the left, behind them, walks Colonel Bandín, commander of the 250th Artillery Regiment.

Artillery Captain Antonio De Andrés. Commander of the 1st Battery I/250. He took part in the Battle of Krasny Bor and returned to Spain in 1943 when he was relieved.

Gunner Antonio Galera García. He enlisted from the *Frente de Juventudes* (Youth Front), joining the Staff Battery of the II/250 Artillery Regiment in May 1942, although in November of that same year he was transferred to the Staff Battery of the I/250, where he remained until October 1943 when he was repatriated.

Emplacing work for a 15 cm gun of the kind used by the Blue Division.

Artillery Lieutenant Guillermo Hernanz Blanco. He belonged to the 11th Battery, situated at the eastern end of the town of Krasny Bor. He set off to liaise with Lieutenant Colonel Santos Ascarza in the centre of the town in the heat of the battle and nothing more was heard of him. Everything points to him having been killed while defending Ascarza's command post alongside the lieutenant colonel and members of his staff.

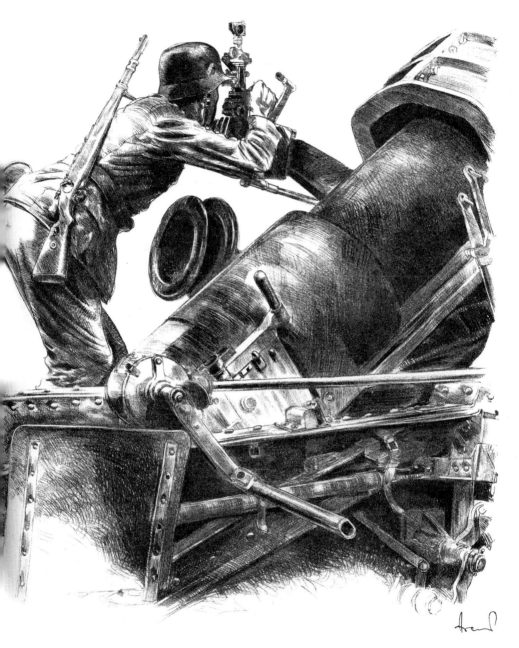

Aiming a heavy gun.

Gunner Juan Juan Marí, who took part in the fighting at Krasny Bor. He belonged to the Staff of I Artillery Group. (Courtesy of Juan Negreira)

Gunner Emilio Prieto Rodríguez. He served with the 5th Battery of the 250 Artillery Regiment. (Courtesy of Juan Negreira)

Horse-drawn 10.5 cm howitzer.

Sergeant Antonio Sánchez-Pascuala y Buendía, in charge of the radio equipment of IV Artillery Group and assigned to the staff of that group.

Palacio de Pushkin

Above and opposite: Various views of Catherine Palace in the Russian town of Pushkin, about 25 kilometres to the southeast of Leningrad. (Saint Petersburg)

Above and opposite: For many years this palace was the summer residence of the tzars of Russia. The Regimental Staff of the 250th Artillery set up their headquarters there.

Above, opposite and previous page: NCO Mariano Ysasi González, who served in the Staff of II Artillery Group. (Courtesy of Juan Negreira)

But the technological jewel in the crown was the *28 cm Kanone 5 (Eisenbahn)*, a sophisticated gun of which the Germans made a total of 25 pieces. It is without a doubt the best known of this type of weapon used in the Second World War. The 686th Battery had two, but Group Hilpert had another and there was only one in the Krasny Bor sector. While at 255 kg the weight of its shells was nothing to write home about, its range of 62,400 metres was extraordinary. Under normal conditions it could maintain a rate of fire of one shot every three minutes, when the normal firing rate for all these types of weapons was one round every 5 or 6 minutes. It became known when guns of this type were firing on the American beachhead at Anzio and one of them was captured and is now on show in a museum in Maryland, USA. But the first place these impressive guns were used was outside Leningrad.

In his book Díaz de Villegas provides a vivid account of the terrible effect that bombardments by this type of weapon caused and the panic they created among the Soviet troops. Although they were only able to fire a few rounds before having to make themselves scarce, the enemy suffered badly. German documentation evidences the fact that these guns were firing in the Krasny Bor sector on the 10th and also on the following days, with the effect on the rear of the attacking Soviet troops that can be imagined.

In the memoirs recovered by General Fontenla of Manuel Rodríguez Campano, one of the survivors of the 9th Battery Spanish, which as we have seen became completely cut off from the rest of the Blue Division, we read that on his way back to the Spanish lines on 14 February he passed through a place whose name he did not know where he noted that "*the Germans had mounted some enormous batteries on railway lines and some mortars whose shells we could see perfectly as they flew through the air"*. Indeed, those rail-mounted behemoths were firing from there, along with other super-calibre guns; the size of the projectiles combined with the mortars' low muzzle velocity meant that the trajectory of the shells could be followed with the naked eye.

I mentioned earlier the maxim that all military leaders attribute their victories to the virtues of their soldiers and their defeats to the superiority of their enemies' materiel. The Soviets are no exception and as I have already shown in my study of this battle, they blamed their defeat at Krasny Bor on *"the fierce opposition of large contingents of troops, [and] their enormous firepower"*,[6] a direct allusion to the courage of the Spanish infantry with whom they clashed, but also to the existence of Hispano-German artillery which they had never imagined could be as powerful and effective as it was. In the matter of "enormous firepower" of which the Soviets spoke, part of that must unquestionably be put down to those rail-mounted super-calibre guns. It was the first and only time Spanish soldiers fought alongside such singular weapons.

Incidentally, while at the beginning Spanish officers and soldiers rubbed their hands with glee when they knew that guns of this type were nearby, and when they heard them firing they imagined their devastating effect, this fascination soon wore off. In fact they came to fear the guns' activity; when the big guns fired the effects were as devastating as they had imagined, so the Red Army responded with a veritable deluge of fire all along the front. The soldiers of the front rank reached the conclusion that the effects this type of artillery fire had on the enemy gave them little direct relief, since the rounds were aimed well to the enemy's rear.

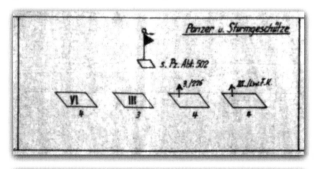

Order of Battle of L Corps. 14 February. Composition of the available Panzer and assault gun forces.

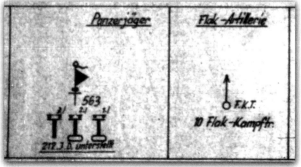

Heavy anti-tank forces available in the L Corps sector, as at 14 February.

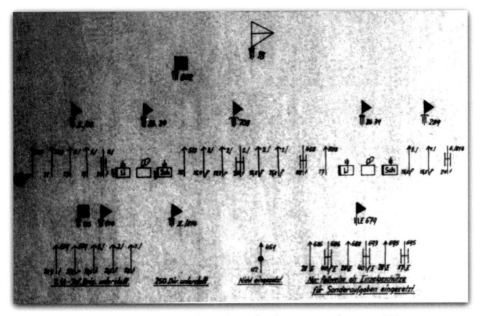

Heerestruppen artillery units under the orders of *Arko 18*, 14 February 1943.

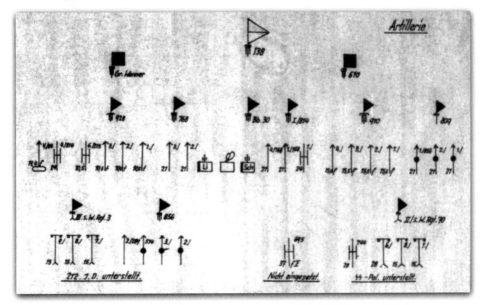

Heerestruppen artillery units under the orders of *Arko 138*, 14 February 1943.

Conversely, during the inevitable and massive Soviet response, the Spanish front line bore the brunt of the shelling. The rail-mounted super-calibre guns, which at first had been welcomed with such admiration and hope, would soon become viewed as a dangerous neighbour to have near you.

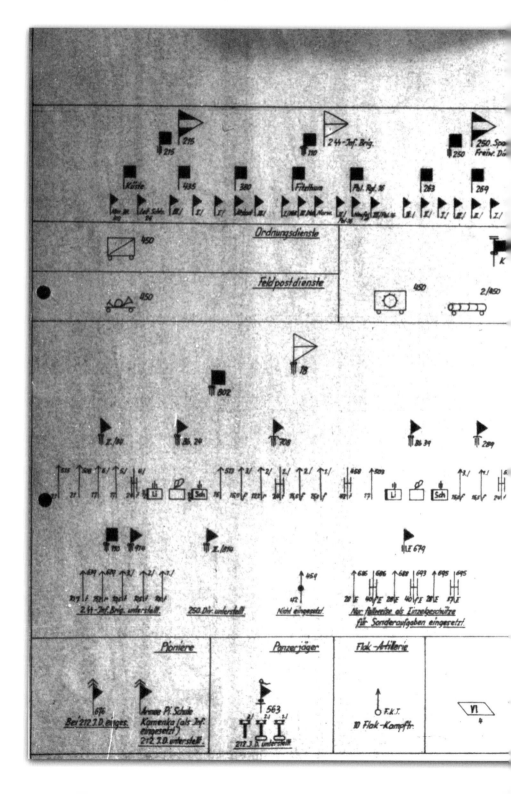

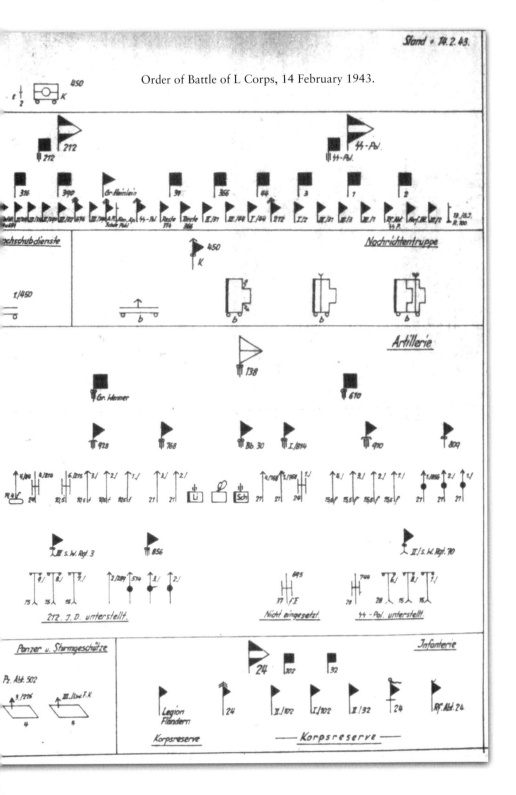

Order of Battle of L Corps, 14 February 1943.

VII

Analysing the Battle

If we analyse the Battle of Krasny Bor we reach an inevitable conclusion; the command of the German 18th Army achieved their objective; by gradually concentrating artillery forces in the last ten days of January 1943 in L Corps' sector, and more specifically in the Krasny Bor sector, they had brought together all the elements necessary to create a barrage of fire capable of effectively contributing to stemming the Soviet attack. This concentration of firepower could only be achieved by moving resources away from other sectors of the 18th Army, a tactic not without its risks, which left many divisions without any other cover than their own artillery, which was not always in the best of conditions. Readers interested in the details of this gradual concentration of the 18th Army's artillery forces in L Corps' sector (the one to which the Blue Division belonged) can follow the process by perusing the information provided in Appendix 5.

This shows just how absurd it is to claim, as many have done, that the Germans left the Blue Division without artillery cover. Quite the contrary; they reinforced it as much as they were able, given the strategic place the Blue Division was occupying on the front. Something which incidentally should give the lie to another claim, similarly repeated and equally absurd as the previous one, that during their presence on the Eastern Front, the Germans "parked" the Blue Division in unimportant sectors. In the allocation of artillery the Blue Division was treated well by the Germans. But this was by no means a case of "favouritism", but rather down to pure operational logic; they were defending the widest and most important sector, containing two clear approach routes for the Soviets, by road and by railway.

Unfortunately today we continue to be unaware to any degree of accuracy of the strength of the Soviet artillery which took part in the Battle of Krasny Bor, although German documentation gives a very approximate but reliable idea. And note that here we rely on that documentation. Unlike books of memoirs written after the event, which may contain an element of "justification", the documents we have consulted always reflect the reality of the situation, so that superior officers could have an accurate picture of the real situation on a tactical and strategic level and so assess future enemy plans and take the appropriate decisions to respond to them.

We also have Spanish reports which, however, in this case are less reliable. Let me make it clear that I am referring only to the part of those reports concerning the artillery deployed by the Red Army. This has a simple explanation; in order to assess the enemy's artillery, the Army Corps had access to highly reliable information collected by the observation and location units under the orders of the two *Arko* (18th and 138th) who, with the technical resources of sound ranging batteries, etc., were in a position to make scientifically based estimations. The Spanish commanders lacked any such resources and therefore their information is necessarily much less accurate. But we also need to take into account that automatically, we might say unconsciously, if we lack accurate data and try to work with estimates, we tend to exaggerate the power of the enemy's resources and belittle those of our own.

In the *Dispatch corresponding to the fighting on 10 February 1943 in the sector of the 262nd Grenadier Regiment*,[1] issued by divisional staff, we find these statements:

> "(…) Deployment of own forces.
> (…) Finally, the artillery was formed by Group I/250 with three batteries of 105 mm guns,
> strengthened by the Ninth [9th/250th] also 105 mm, and the Eleventh [11th/250] with three 150 mm 150 (…)
> THE ENEMY (…) Deployment (…)
> "Artillery deployment is unknown but is definitely very large, since in addition to the organic artillery of four divisions we are aware of the presence of the 12th Guard Artillery Regiment 289th and 690th Anti-Tank Regiments which, added to the infantry's accompanying batteries, is the army's artillery mass, from which we may logically assume that the total number of batteries is in excess of 150.
> "To this number we need to add the divisional mortar groups. We should note that as an indicator of the proportion used in the distribution of materiel that the 133rd Infantry Regiment [Soviet] were allocated six Stalin's organs just for the breakthrough. To sum up we can say that (…) were positioned (…) more than 150 batteries (…) and a large number of organs and heavy mortars".

The report dated the 16th (*Report on the battle fought in the Krasny Bor sector following an enemy attack initiated in the early hours of 10 February 1943*) adds little to what was said in the previous dispatch. After mentioning the five Spanish batteries deployed to the east of the Izhora the dispatch briefly adds that these batteries formed the "*Division's artillery, which also had the protection of artillery elements of the Army Corps*", something that was not mentioned in the previous report (however, once again the Spanish III Group was omitted).

It should be noted that the dispatch on the battle was immediately sent to Spain. News of the attack on Krasny Bor had arrived almost instantly, since the Soviets had boasted of having destroyed the Blue Division and the BBC immediately picked up this news and passed it on in their broadcasts in Spanish.

Finally, in his account of the Blue Division, Esteban-Infantes listed Soviet divisional and army corps artillery, anti-tank guns, mortars and rocket launchers, and reached a total of 187 batteries. Vadillo went into even further detail by stating that those 187 Soviet batteries were composed of 124 and 203 mm guns.[2]

We find ourselves here faced with a typical example of how a military commander will recount a battle inaccurately, perhaps due to lack of time, perhaps unconsciously, but in such a way that the relative strengths involved, in this case of field artillery, are described in a manner intended to try and justify, in this case, the result of the battle which, at the time, was considered to be very adverse. We remind readers that before the battle started the Blue Division could field 10 infantry battalions (nine forming parts of regiments plus the 250th Independent Reserve Battalion) and that after it finished only five remained what we might call intact. Of other forces which could be used as infantry, i.e. the Exploration Group and the Sapper Battalion, the former had been destroyed and the latter had been severely mauled. Of the artillery support units, the division's Anti-Tank Group had been almost totally destroyed and five of the division's 12 organic artillery batteries had lost all their guns. It was necessary to explain to the Spanish authorities, and quickly, how such a catastrophe had occurred. And, unsurprisingly, the commanders in the field sent back information which exaggerated the enemy's strength and diminished their own strength.

The problem is all the more complex because we need to clarify the definitions used. On the one hand, when speaking about their own artillery, Spanish reports are referring solely to field artillery. No consideration is given to the fact that the 262nd Regiment had its own cannon company, that Spanish infantry battalions had field mortars, and that there was a very strong presence of anti-tank units in the area, since the entire 250th Anti-Tank Group was deployed at Krasny Bor there was also the 14th/262nd, the anti-tank company of the regiment defending the area. And these guns are not taken into account. However, when speaking of enemy firepower reference is made to anti-tank cannons, mortars, etc.

Also, as I have pointed out repeatedly in this book, the activity of the three batteries forming part of the Spanish III Group. And the fact that the rest of the Spanish heavy artillery and the 1st Battery of the attached German Group Werner also took part in the battle; of this there can be no doubt whatsoever.

For too long the presence of German artillery in the area has been totally overlooked; at best only the battery which the Spanish helped defend is mentioned. Undoubtedly this apparent ignorance of the presence of German artillery was compounded by strict security regulations adhered to in the German Army, which established that each commander knew only what he needed to know. As the German batteries present in the area were not under Spanish orders but under the command of *Arko 138*, it is very possible that Esteban-Infantes and other Spanish officers did not have the complete and accurate picture of units they were.

We need to bear in mind that, rather than considering the German batteries as being assigned in support of the Blue Division, it would be more accurate to say that they were placed in their area of action. In other words, General Esteban-Infantes was never able to assign them firing missions or include their firing in his own defensive scheme (in fact quite the opposite occurred; the Spanish artillery was placed under the operational control of German *Arkos*). Therefore the Spanish commanders had no clear idea as to the role that the German artillery actually played in the battle.

An attack such as the one launched by the Soviets at Krasny Bor on 10 February should be debilitated at the so-called "Forward Edge of the Battle Area" through the application of a detailed plan which integrates the machine gun and mortar fire of infantry units deployed on the front line with the concentrations and barrages of the defending artillery. Due to their range, calibre and organic chain of command, the aforementioned German artillery units could not form part of this scheme (although ultimately they laid barrage fire in front of Spanish positions, repulsing one of the first tank attacks against the 5th and 6th Companies of the 262nd Regiment, as we have read earlier in this book), but were deployed to hit targets to the rear of the units of the first Soviet echelon. It is clear that their missions helped the Spanish Division – and considerably – but we must be aware that their activity was not perceived by either the Spanish infantry or their commanders. Neither the targets that these German batteries attacked, nor the priorities underlying their choice of targets were decided by the Spanish commanders, so it is understandable that they did not take much notice of the German units.

But – and let us make no mistake here – there can be no doubt that leaving these German artillery units out of accounts of the Battle of Krasny Bor has a great deal to do with the prevalent tendency in "military literature" to diminish the strength of one's own forces and exaggerate that of the enemy's. Because chroniclers must have been fully aware of the presence and actions of the Spanish III Group and yet this group also tends to be left out of accounts.

And as for the Soviet artillery forces, what did they actually consist of? We can get some idea of their magnitude due to the fact that, following their protocols, both *Arko 18* and *Arko 138* sent their ten-day reports to the commander of L Corps. Let us take a look at those that concern us. *Arko 18* issued a report for the period 29 January to 9 February, and another covering the period from 9 to 19 February. For their part *Arko 138*, which had just taken over the Krasny Bor sector, issued their first report for the commander of L Corps covering the period from 8 to 18 February. The first of *Arko 18*'s reports which covered up until the day before the attack, called attention to the fact that the enemy was reinforcing their artillery considerably in the Kolpino and surrounding area. The report also stated that the enemy had used their artillery especially against the storage areas and supply routes, but in the Blue Division's sector they seemed more intent on hitting the battery emplacements than anything else. Earlier the report quoted the numbers of own and enemy batteries that *Arko 18* estimated in their sector (at the time the entire L Corps). I will repeat the figures here, but this time comparing them with those in the reports issued by *Arko 18* and *Arko 138* – the two serving L Corps – after the Battle of Krasny Bor.

Soviet and own batteries deployed						
Author and date of reports	Red Army			Wehrmacht		
	Light	Heavy	Total	Light	Heavy	Total
Report from *Arko* 18, for 29 January to 9 February 1943	84	109	193	22	43	65
Report from *Arko* 138, for 8 to 18 February 1943	49	59	108	27	29	56
Report from *Arko* 18, for 9 to 19 February 1943	50	79	129	19	34	53
Totals in L Corps sector	99	138	237	46	63	109
Increase	(+15)	(+29)	(+44)	(+24)	(+20)	(+44)

The first thing we notice is that, as I have already pointed out, there is a notable increase in the number of Soviet batteries, unsurprisingly since they were going to launch an offensive. We need to bear in mind that these reports were issued at 18:00 at the end of the 10-day period, so the latest figures must refer to the morning of the 9th. After that date there is an increase in enemy deployment, but also in the deployment of Hispano-German batteries. In fact, in proportion to the figures of 9 February it is the German *Heer* which most boosts its artillery. While in terms of the absolute number of batteries the increase in the two sides runs neck and neck, if we compare the figures with those on 9 January, the Soviets "only" increased their artillery force by 23 per cent, while the Germans grew theirs by 67 per cent.

Having calculated the ratio between Soviet and Hispano-German batteries we find that the Germans reinforced L Corps' sector very considerably (and in particular at Krasny Bor), and while in purely quantitative terms the Soviets always maintained superiority, the superior qualitative level of the Hispano-German gunners (a matter to which I shall be returning later) actually balanced out the forces and, at this particular place and time, put an end to the overwhelming superiority normally enjoyed by the Red Army.

Ratio of number of batteries. For L Corps as a whole			
Closing date of report	Batteries	GERMAN	SOVIET
9 February	Light batteries	1	3.8
	Heavy batteries	1	2.5
	Total Batteries	1	2.9
18-19 February	Light batteries	1	2.1
	Heavy batteries	1	2.2
	Total Batteries	1	2.2
For *Arko* 138's sector (Krasny Bor and vicinity)			
18-19 February	Light batteries	1	1.8
	Heavy batteries	1	2
	Total Batteries	1	1.9

The report from *Arko 138* for 8 to 18 February 1943 is extremely important for us, since it expressly analyses the use that the Soviets made of artillery on the 10th. Of course the attacking divisions had their own artillery regiments and the infantry regiments each had a cannon company, which in practical terms we should consider as an additional battery and tally them as such. Therefore a division would normally field eight or nine 76.2 mm batteries and three 122 mm batteries.[3]

Based on the data provided by their location group, *Arko 138* calculated that the enemy had used 40 divisional artillery batteries of 76.2 mm guns (a figure consistent with having attacked with four divisions or, to be more precise, with the equivalent of four divisions), and 24 batteries of 122 mm pieces, which was equivalent to twice the artillery of this calibre that you would expect four divisions to have. It was clear that the enemy had reinforced its attacking forces with heavy guns brought in from other divisions.

However, this had not been the only artillery to take part, since the 55th Army – the major attacking enemy unit – had fielded another 13 heavy and superheavy batteries. The only field artillery unit which the Germans had been able to detect as forming part of the 55th Army was the 12th Guard Artillery Regiment, so in order to bring together that number of batteries it would seem clear the 55th had received units on loan from other armies.[4]

The mass of Soviet field artillery which opened fire on the Spanish positions on the 10th was – according to this report – therefore composed of 77 batteries, although the report admits to a possible margin of error and the actual figure could be anywhere between 70 and 80. The figure is impressive, but it is also true that it is a long way from the 150 batteries of which the Spanish dispatch speaks. This disparity of data may be due to various factors. The first is that the Spanish dispatch counted the guns of two anti-tank regiments which formed part of the attacking force. Their weapons, flat trajectory anti-tank cannons, were to be feared when they were pounding immobile targets such as fortifications (like those of the Spanish lines). But as each Soviet regiment of this type had only five batteries, the final figure (ten batteries) cannot explain the disparity between 77 and 150.

Neither would it be reasonable to assume that mortar units were confused with field artillery units. In the aforementioned Spanish report a clear distinction is made between the two weapons, and in the German report we are quoting, after setting out the data referring to the enemy's artillery, it says that "*from the start of the attack the enemy also directed intense mortar fire on our positions*". The same can be said about rocket launchers (Stalin's organs); the Spanish report does not include them in the number of batteries.

From where, then, does the figure of 150 batteries come? I fear that the only explanation is that the figure was reached at a time of great excitement in order to justify what was perceived as a major tragedy which had left the Blue Division very badly mauled. Without a doubt a desire to "justify" is behind the figure. But it is also true that it was very much an intuitive calculation, a very rough estimate. The Spanish artillery lacked the technological resources to make a calculation with any scientific basis (the sound ranging and flash ranging batteries were German) and the rate of fire received was so extraordinary, so much greater than anything experienced by the Spanish in Russia until then (or in the Civil War), that the number of batteries used was simply overestimated.

One important factor in the confusion must have been the huge volume of mortar fire received. Due to the type of trajectory of the shells, mortar fire tends to be more lethal than artillery fire for infantry. The Soviets' unusually large number of high quality mortars must have wreaked terrible havoc on the Spanish infantry, leading to their overestimating total enemy artillery fire.

If anyone believes that it was an attempt by the Spanish to exaggerate the Russian artillery fire after the event, they should forget that fairy tale. The mass of artillery fire was overwhelming. One author famed for his accuracy who always makes use of Soviet sources, the American historian Glantz, stresses that the Red Army's attack on 10 February at Krasny Bor was preceded by *"two hours of preparation fire from around 1,000 cannons and mortars"*.[5] In short, I am not attempting to diminish the importance of that deluge of artillery fire, but I only wish to establish as accurately as possible what part of it should be attributed to the enemy's field artillery. Of those 1,000 Soviet artillery pieces, around 270 must have been field artillery guns, between 20 and 30 multiple rocket launchers, between 80 and 100 anti-tank cannons, and between 600 and 650 medium and heavy calibre mortars.

While one thing is a field cannon and quite another a mortar, for the men on the receiving end of their shells the difference is largely irrelevant, and the fact is that the Soviet divisions were exceptionally well equipped with mortars, and excellent ones at that. Because while the 50 mm mortars in rifleman companies and the 80 mm in the heavy weapons companies of Soviet battalions were superior to and outnumbered those of their German counterparts, each regiment of the Red Army also had – in addition to the aforementioned cannon company – its own mortar company, equipped with superb 120 mm calibre pieces. These were so exceptional that the Germans ended up copying them.

The Soviets enjoyed a clear and unquestionable superiority in firepower and also in artillery, but in those terrible early hours of 10 February, the artillery forces that clashed head to head in the Krasny Bor area were not five Spanish against 150 Soviet batteries as has been repeated so often, but rather eight Spanish batteries and one German battery (1st/Werner) attached to the Spanish regiment, alongside 14 German batteries (reinforced up to a point by a number of more distant batteries, under the command of *Arko 18*) against an estimated 77 Soviet batteries.

As fortunately our knowledge of the history of the Blue Division never ceases to grow, today we have evidence that, even at the time, Spanish gunners had much more accurate information on the size of the enemy's artillery forces. For example, in the diary kept by Artillery Lieutenant Joaquín María Usunáriz Mocoroa there is a note written shortly after the battle to the effect that the enemy had used around 80 batteries and 20 multiple rocket launchers or Stalin's organs.[6]

The Soviets had no 30 to 1 advantage in field artillery batteries, which is the ratio suggested by the figures that historians have been repeating almost by force of habit. The ratio at the start of the battle was nearer three enemy batteries for every Hispano-German battery. The disproportion was still large enough for the glory that the Spanish and German gunners reaped by facing up to that hail of fire and shrapnel to remain entirely undiminished. But now we are moving closer to the truth, to reality. The highly effective use of those 23 Hispano-German batteries, and in particular the valiant resistance of the five Spanish batteries (plus the heroic cannon company of the 262nd Regiment!), who fought until the enemy reached their gun lines and forced them to spike their guns, won the time needed for fresh and powerful artillery forces to reach the area.

The report from *Arko 138* covering the 8th to the 18th included more important information. The data regarding ammunition consumption by the enemy is of remarkable value. According to their calculations, in the sector over which *Arko 138* had command, on the days prior to 10 February the enemy had a daily consumption of ammunition of between 200 and 500 rounds. When we say daily we mean the time elapsed between 18:00 of one day and 18:00 of the following day, as dictated by German protocol.

The artillery attack on the 10th was described as organized in two phases; between 06:45 and 09:30 there was *Trommelfeuer* in which the Soviet gunners fired 35,000 rounds. After a period of relative ceasefire during which only a limited use was made of artillery, between 14:00 and 24:00 the enemy guns roared again, using thousands of rounds in harassment fire (*Störungsfeuer*). Overall, in the sector defended by the Spanish, Soviet artillery fired around 40,000 rounds (a figure to which we should not forget to add mortar fire and the bombs dropped by enemy aircraft).

During the following days the Soviets were no longer in a position to maintain such a high rate of fire, although consumption of ammunition remained at levels higher than those before the 10th. While the sheer number of batteries firing was impressive, no less impressive was the Russians' remarkable ability to maintain such a high rate of fire, as evidenced by the amount of ammunition used by the Red Army each day, which was amazing.

The figures provided by *Arko 138* in the ten-day report were as follows:

Dates	No. of rounds fired
8 to 9 February	500
9 to 10	40,000
10 to 11	3 to 4,000
11 to 12	5 to 7,000
12 to 13	4,000
13 to 14	3,500
14 to 15	1,500
15 to 16	3,000
16 to 17	6,000
17 to 18	5,500
Approximate total	Between 74,500 and 77,500

Now is a good moment to return to Captain De Andres's comparison with the Battle of the Ebro mentioned earlier. The attack on the heights of Cavalls, the most ambitious artillery operation carried out by the Nationalist army in the entire Spanish Civil War, consumed 10,000 rounds. In a similar space and time frame, at Krasny Bor on 10 February the Red Army fired 40,000 field artillery rounds at the Blue Division. These figures speak for themselves; they are saying that the Blue Division volunteers who fought at Krasny Bor on that fateful day, 10 February, are the men who have suffered by far the worst deluge of fire and steel ever to have fallen on Spanish combatants.

The 10-day report from the other L Corps artillery command, *Arko 18*, issued on 19 February (9 to 19 February) also reported on the average amounts of ammunition consumed by the enemy in the sector which they now commanded.

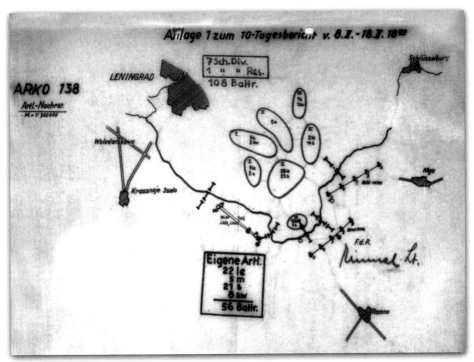

Enemy artillery deployment in front of *Arko* 138 and disposition of artillery ranging equipment.

Before the day of the attack there had been around 250 shots a day, but on 10 February the number of rounds peaked at 2,100 and during the following days the average was 1,300 shots a day. Meanwhile on the 10th alone, Spanish and German batteries had fired 900 rounds, which included 65 fired by superheavy and railway guns aimed at the attacking forces at Krasny Bor.

Seventy years on from the Battle of Krasny Bor our knowledge of the events that transpired there ought to be as accurate as it can possibly be. While I fear that there are still some documents not yet analysed and sources not yet exploited (especially Russian ones), I trust that this book which is now reaching its end has been able to shed some fresh light.

Some readers may come to the conclusion that, with so much German artillery in action, the role of the Spanish infantry in the Battle of Krasny Bor, which has always filled us with legitimate pride, has now been lessened to some extent. This would be an error on the part of any reader.

In the dispatch on the battle previously quoted we can read: "*The 5th Company* [of the 262nd Regiment] *has been completely destroyed by* [enemy] *action (…) and there is no one left to withstand the attack by tanks and flamethrowers that followed the* [artillery] *preparation.*"

Indeed, the volume of fire directed at the 5th Company of the 262nd Regiment, the one led by the legendary Captain Palacios, should have annihilated it. That is what the Soviets expected. And that is what the Spanish imagined. But the truth is that, although few in number, some Spanish soldiers were left alive. In strength they were the equivalent of a platoon which, led by some exceptional officers (Captain Palacios, 2nd Lieutenant Del Castillo, and Sergeant Salamanca, among others), held off the enemy attackers far longer than the Soviet commanders could ever have imagined or the commanders could ever have hoped for.

And the story of the 5th Company, which is told here because the company was assumed to have been completely wiped out, was repeated to a greater or lesser extent by the other companies of the I/262nd, II/262nd and Reserve 250th battalions; all of them put up more of a fight than the enemy had expected.

And when those companies were all overrun, the offensive came up against the pockets of resistance formed by Spanish sappers, who again halted them. And then the Russians had to deal with the counterattacks of squadrons of the 250th Exploration Group, before being halted again, now utterly exhausted, at the gun lines of the Spanish gunners.

The volume of artillery fire that the Soviets had directed against the Spanish infantry led them to suppose that any soldiers not wounded or dead would simply lose their will to fight, surrender, or run away. But that did not happen. Those whose bodies were not broken by shrapnel refused to let their spirit be broken.

And they were up against other infantrymen, the Soviets, who were also having to call on reserves of bravery in order to advance. Even before leaving their trenches that morning of 10 February they were already receiving much more artillery fire (Hispano-German) than they had expected. And once out of the trenches they came up against not only machine gun fire from the surviving Spaniards, but also barrage fire from Hispano-German batteries which, now that the Soviets were in open country, inflicted terrible casualties.

The surviving Soviet infantrymen eventually reached the gun lines of the Spanish artillerymen who were forced to sacrifice the howitzers of five of their batteries. But they would go no further since they had been terribly mauled and were exhausted. In the Krasny Bor sector, as we have read, they halted just in front of the positions of the 2nd/289th Battery (at the time forming part of the 768th Group).[7]

The courage shown by the Spanish gunners in the defence of their observation posts and gun lines was exceptional and their spirit of sacrifice and capacity to adapt to the changing scenarios of the battle can only be explained by their strong morale and the excellent leadership of their officers.

All it would have taken is for the Spanish infantry to have shown just a little weakness, and for the Spanish gunners, once they were out of ammunition, to have abandoned the battlefield, and the enemy infantry would have overrun the positions where the remaining men of the German 768th Group were deployed. From there they would have easily reached Sablino, a focal point to which all the German artillery units that had been placed on standby had been sent. Without the heroic resistance of the Spanish 9th Battery – together with gunners of the 4th SS Division who had come to their aid – the enemy would have rolled up the German 910th Group and placed the entire German Division in a very difficult situation.

If they had not been as weakened as they were, the Soviet infantry would have been in a position to cross the Izhora to put an end to the unceasing harassment they were receiving from the batteries of the Spanish Group III/250th and the German 928th Coastal Group. The gunners of the former group, and especially its 8th Battery, whose observation post became a pivotal point of defence and whose guns ended up occupying a very forward front line, were decisive in the creation of a new defensive structure.[8] Much the same can be said of the accompanying guns of the 13th/262nd.

The huge volume of Soviet artillery fire and the robust response from the Hispano-German artillery transformed a snowy landscape into a horrific sea of mud. Here the enemy forces preparing to exploit the bombardment (armoured vehicles, other motorized units, and skiers) would become trapped, an unexpected consequence of the tremendous artillery duel.

To sum up, the sacrifice of the Spanish infantrymen, sappers and gunners generated the time and preserved the space needed by the *Wehrmacht* to respond to this new challenge. A response that, as we have seen, was to a large extent artillery-based.

There has been a certain difficulty as to how to "classify" the battle on 10 February at Krasny Bor. Was it a defeat, but an honourable one? This is how it has been perceived for a long time, especially by Blue Division veterans. The sensation that despite everything it was a defeat may explain that need for "justification" of which I have spoken. But that way of seeing the result of the battle is based on a false premise: that of seeing the battle as a local Soviet offensive, aiming only to destroy the Spanish unit.

However, General Fontenla explains that the Battle of Krasny Bor can be best defined as a defensive victory. A battle when the enemy fails to breach what is known as the "Area of Resistance" may and should be defined as such. This "Area of Resistance" is not a purely linear concept – the trenches – but rather the area between the so-called "Forward Edge of the Battle Area" and the rear boundary. The German batteries to which we have been referring in this book were all situated forward of the rear boundary and, as has been explained, all but one succeeded in preserving their equipment and remaining in action; this is the most convincing proof that the enemy never reached that rear boundary, let alone broke through it. Without having reached the rear boundary of the area of resistance at Krasny Bor, the Soviets had nevertheless succeeded in advancing a handful of kilometres, but they had totally failed to achieve the objectives of their offensive. And this is what is really important. The attack on Krasny Bor was the first step in an ambitious operation which should have caused the equivalent of the Stalingrad encirclement for Army Group North (Operation Polar Star) and not, as the Spanish saw it for a very long time, a local Soviet offensive aimed at their destruction. Thus for the Blue Division the Battle of Krasny Bor was a victory, however paradoxical that may sound. The enemy's objective was not to grab a few kilometres of terrain and kill as many Spaniards as they could, but rather to reach the town of Tosno where they could link up with other Soviet forces from the Volkhov Front and so encircle the bulk of the 18th Army. That was the objective, one which – and I repeat – the Russians spectacularly failed to achieve. Therefore – and I repeat once again – the Battle of Krasny Bor can only be classified as a Hispano-German victory.

During the days following 10 February the role of the Spanish artillery would be much less important, as could be expected. Five field artillery batteries had been lost plus the accompanying guns of an infantry company, and only one of the 9th Battery's guns had survived. From German documentation we know that when the members of this unit were ordered to withdraw to the Spanish sector it was the 4th Battery of the Artillery Regiment of the 4th SS Division which took over the single remaining gun and continued to use it in the following days.

The men of the Blue Division who fell back on Sablino were immediately counted and the result entered in an *"Inventory of forces recovered after the Battle of Krasny Bor"*. It reports a total of 555 men for the I/262nd and II/262nd Battalions, the 250th Mobile Reserve Battalion, and the Ski Company; 293 for the Anti-Tank Group; 170 for the Exploration Group, and 150 for the Sapper Battalion. And 190 men belonging to the five artillery batteries which had been deployed to the east of the Izhora. A very low figure. However, fortunately, a hand-written note in the same document states that *"Not all the artillerymen are listed"*. And indeed that was the case; in the inventory no artillery commanders were listed in the column headed "Commanders" and yet Reinlein had survived. And only three captains are listed when in fact the five captains commanding the batteries to the east of the Izhora were also survivors. Losses among the gunners were terrible, but as can be imagined the long-suffering infantrymen came off considerably worse, both in absolute and percentage terms. In another book I have already listed the number of men of the 250th Artillery Regiment killed during the Russian campaign.[9] The table below shows the number of deaths attributable to the Battle of Krasny Bor:

Unit	Total deaths	Deaths at the Battle of Krasny Bor	Unit	Total deaths	Deaths at the Battle of Krasny Bor
I Group	56	17	IV Group	38	5
II Group	20	1	Other[1]	6	2
III Group	33	9	Unspecified unit	71	51
(1) Regimental Staff Battery, Munitions, *ad hoc* batteries					

Of the 225 Spanish gunners who died in Russia, 85 were killed at the Battle of Krasny Bor; 38 per cent of the total in barely one day's fighting.

Another way of assessing the conduct of the Spanish gunners in the battle is to see how many of them were cited as having shown Highly Distinguished (HD) or Distinguished (D) conduct in the reports compiled after the Battle of Krasny Bor. There were two different lists.

Appendix 6 of this book provides a detailed account of this aspect. But below readers can find a useful summary which shows us that 278 gunners (the figure includes those serving in the cannon company of the 262nd Regiment) displayed a conduct that could be classified as Highly Distinguished (HD) or Distinguished (D):

Unit		Comm-anders[1]	Captains	Officers[2]	NCOs[3]	Other off.[4]	Corporals	Priv/Gunn[5]	Total
13th/262nd	HD	-	1	-	1	-	-	-	2
	D	-	-	3	8	-	10	18	39
Reg 250	HD	1	-	-	-	-	-	-	1
	D	1	-	-	-	-	-	-	1
250th	HD	1	2	-	5	-	4	3	15
	D	-	1	11	18	1	14	37	82
th/50th	HD	-	1	-	3	-	2	2	8
	D	-	-	3	-	-	2	6	11
1th/50th	HD	-	1	-	2	-	-	3	6
	D	-	-	2	2	1	3	8	16
III/250th	HD	-	1	1	2	-	2	2	8
	D	-	3	8	9	3	10	37	70
IV/250th	HD	-	-	-	-	-	-	-	-
	D	1	2	5	2	-	3	-	13
Munitions	HD	-	-	-	-	-	-	-	-
	D	-	1	-	1	1	-	1	4
Totals		4	13	33	53	6	50	117	276

Total listed as Highly Distinguished: 40	Total listed as Distinguished: 238

1) Commander: Colonels, Lieutenant Colonels, and Majors
2) Officers: Lieutenants and 2nd Lieutenants
3) NCOs: All of those listed were Sergeants
4) Other officers. Includes: master fitters: 3; artificer: 1; medical officer: 1; chaplain: 1
5) Privates (in the 13th/262 and Munitions) and gunners (in the rest of the units).

It should be noted that while 185 of the gunners defined as "Distinguished" or "Highly Distinguished" were deployed to the east of the Izhora, the other 91 were serving on the western side of that oft-mentioned river. Nobody is cited as being "Distinguished" or "Highly Distinguished" in combat by being a mere spectator, which means we have further evidence that the Spanish artillery was more involved in the battle than we normally give credit for, since not only are there men from the so often overlooked III Group, but there are also men on the list from IV Group. Only II Group took no part in the battle.

If we make a comparison between units of a similar size – I and III Groups to be specific – we find there are 97 citations for the former group and 78 for the latter, further proof that the two groups fought with similar courage and determination during that epic day.

Unfortunately, save for very few cases, the lists of men whose conduct is classified as Distinguished or Highly Distinguished contain no explanation as to why they have been cited.

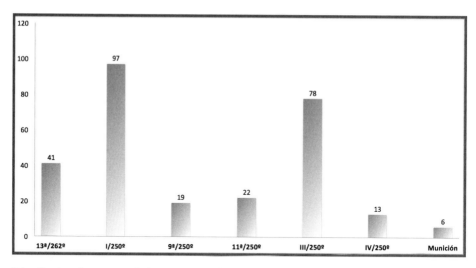

Distribution by units of the gunners of all ranks cited as distinguished and/or highly distinguished.

In the case of Major Guillermo Reinlein Calzada, who was awarded the Individual Military Medal almost on the battlefield itself, the reason for the citation is given. In the second of the two lists we can read:

"He showed great personal bravery, skill, and leadership qualities, instilling a feeling for Spain in the men under his orders brought together from scattered units. At Krasny Bor he withstood the enemy's attacks, held his position until he received the express order to withdraw, and then defended the position of a German battery which was held for a further 48 hours thanks to the reinforcement and morale boost provided by [his] forces. They withdrew from this last position three days after the sector had ceased to belong to the [Blue] Division, and were therefore the last troops to defend that ground".

The original list gave a more detailed description:

"He directed the [artillery] fire with accuracy, speed, and conspicuous effectiveness, until he lost his observation and command posts, destroyed by enemy artillery, and was left without a radio link with his batteries. He organized groups of scattered troops with whom, with the town invaded and the first and second batteries encircled, he broke out of the enemy encirclement and cleaned up the areas of those batteries. At the head of one of these groups he attacked enemy forces which had reached the C.P. [Command Post] of the 263rd Regiment and the hospital and were endangering the lives of the 120 wounded who were inside. He succeeded in wiping out most [of the enemy forces] and drove the rest out of the town. He stood up to the advance and fire of a red heavy tank that came within 20 metres of his position. In the

afternoon he made another sweep of scattered groups out of ammunition who were being chased by six or eight tanks that were patrolling the town, supplying them with the last ammunition available, and organized a defence close to the town, remaining in command of this centre of resistance until well into the night. On receiving orders at 21:00 to withdraw he conveyed the Germans' wishes that a group of Spaniards should stay to protect a German battery. He was authorized to do so, and did so until his duty was discharged".

Since Reinlein's role has already been covered in many books and he received the Individual Military Medal, it would seem unnecessary to dedicate more time to him. History did him justice some time ago. But his case has given rise to a familiar phenomenon; his light shone so brightly that he has put other cases of highly distinguished actions in the shade, if not in total darkness.

Those same documents also included a description of the conduct of Captain José María Andrada-Vanderwilde, for which he received a citation as Highly Distinguished. In the second of the lists we read:

"In his position he resisted enemy forces far superior in number to his own, and with no protection other than his gunners he defended the gun line with his own resources and continued to fire the only gun still serviceable. With most of his men either dead, wounded and missing, he received orders to change emplacement, which he did despite the difficult situation, during which operation he was wounded".

The first list contains a more comprehensive description of the fate of his men, and instead of the generic "dead, wounded and missing" we find these words:

"Of the 71 men holding the position, six were killed (1 lieutenant, 1 sergeant and four gunners), 28 were wounded, and 5 missing (1 sergeant and four gunners) probably taken prisoner".

As fortunately this officer and his valiant 9th Battery have already been duly acclaimed in Fontenla's book,[10] there is little I can add. So instead I want to focus on two commanders of the 13th Company of the 262nd Regiment (the infantry cannon company), who were also – in my opinion – unjustly treated when the medals were being given out. Both had been classified as Highly Distinguished in the documentation I have been referring to, and for both there is an account of what they did to be classified as such. Sergeant Fernando Rodríguez Menéndez belonged to the platoon of this company deployed behind the I/262nd Battalion. Of him it is said:

"He volunteered to blow up a gun before the enemy broke into the position, which he did with the help of a corporal, despite the closeness of the enemy which meant they had to enter with bayonets. Once he achieved his objective he withdrew, falling heroically dead as he did so".

Regarding the commander of the aforementioned cannon company, Artillery Captain José Luis Gómez-Díaz Miranda, it is said:

> "He demonstrated great spirit and courage; he volunteered to leave the observation post where he was in order to go and defend his guns, and at the head of a number of defenders he held off the enemy, inflicting a great many casualties. Unceasingly spurring on his men he was fatally wounded. Thanks to his determined attitude he won time for other forces to take up strategic positions".

I would have loved to have found more information about this sergeant but I was unable to. With the captain I was luckier, something that should come as no surprise because it is normally much easier to follow the trace of the history of an officer than of an NCO or a private. And thanks to a good friend[11] I was able to access the archive of one of Captain Gómez Díaz-Miranda's relatives who had religiously preserved his forebear's papers.

On 13 February 1943 the also Captain Víctor Castro submitted a recommendation for the award of the Individual Military Medal:

> "In the early hours of 10 February there was a heavy attack against the position of the Spanish Division to the east of the River Izhora. Despite intense artillery fire from the enemy, Captain Gómez Díaz [Miranda] remained at his observation post, personally directing the fire of the 4th Section [of 150 mm cannons] of his company, [firstly] firing on the enemy infantry's starting position, [then] laying down final protective fire when they began to advance. Once the front line itself had been penetrated the enemy advanced on the observation post at the same time as another group was outflanking him to the east and heading for the emplacement of his guns of the 4th Section. Faced with the risk that the enemy would reach them, Captain Gómez Díaz [Miranda] did not hesitate for one moment. He asked the commanding officer of the position[12] for permission to go and defend them. He said goodbye to the men he was leaving at the observation post, saying 'The time has come for each one of us to give everything we can for Spain' and, travelling cross country to save time, and ignoring the heavy fire he came under, he went to his emplacement. He arrived just as enemy groups were just 150 metres away and closing. He gave the order to blow up the guns while he confronted the enemy with his pistol in his hand, accompanied by a handful of soldiers whom he spurred on constantly. He killed a great many enemy soldiers and succeeded in holding them off until he was hit in the chest and fell, fatally wounded. Two sergeants were also killed and most of his soldiers were casualties, but his heroic conduct enabled a section of sappers from Lieutenant [Ramón] Corrochano [Gómez]'s platoon[13] to occupy a trench which dominated the gun emplacement, which pinned the enemy down and meant that the position was not taken by the enemy while Captain Gómez Díaz [Miranda]'s body was there".

The report from the commander of the 250th Artillery Regiment, Colonel Francisco Bandín, is also dated 13 February and is drafted in similar terms to the recommendation made by Captain Castro. Amongst other paragraphs we can read:

"He organized the defence of the position, whipped up his troops, and pistol in hand he kept up a heroic fight against the attacking forces, which outnumbered and outgunned us, inflicting a great many casualties and halting their advance (…) It was his heroic example that kept up the outstanding fighting spirit of the defenders".

For his part, General Esteban-Infantes, commander of the Division, issued his report dated 13 September 1943, which closed with these words:

"For such distinguished and conspicuous deeds, under current regulations I consider this captain to be worthy of the Individual Military Medal for which he has been recommended."

The General had signed these words in response to the information dossier that the awards section of his staff had submitted to him a few days earlier, on 9 September to be precise, in which we can read:

"This dossier originated from the recommendation report submitted by the captain of the 8th Battery of the 250th Artillery Regiment [Víctor Castro] (…) and which includes a favourable report from the commanding colonel of the regiment (…)

"In addition to the aforementioned report from the commanding colonel of the artillery regiment, a captain, a lieutenant, a 2nd lieutenant, and several sergeants, corporals and privates also declare in the dossier. All of them believe him to be deserving of a major award; some recommend the Individual Military Medal and Captain Castro says that the case is identical to others who were awarded the Laureate Cross of Saint Ferdinand and were subsequently admitted to the Gallery of Promotions of our Artillery Academy.

"The examining judge considers that his case is covered by Article 7 of the Awards Regulations and deserving of the award of an Individual Military Medal.

"The verifier states in his report that if all possible the pertinent procedures have been carried out and that the recommendation is ready to be sent to the Ministry of the Army for their final decision."

Everything appeared to indicate that Captain Gómez Díaz-Miranda would receive the Military Medal. And yet it would never be awarded to him. This man, who was an activist in the Falangist *Sindicato Español Universitario* (SEU or Spanish University Union) before the war[14] and a provisional officer during the Civil War, would thus be condemned to an unjust oblivion, from which it is now time to rescue him, since even the works dedicated to decorated Blue Division soldiers contain very little information about him.[15]

But of course it is not only a question of honouring him and him alone. Which is why in this book I have included a comprehensive list of all the gunners at the Battle of Krasny Bor who deserved to be considered as Highly Distinguished or Distinguished by their fellow soldiers. The vast majority of them are names that are totally unknown to the general public. Perhaps the only exception is Gunner Pedro Lazaga Sabater, a Catalonian volunteer who years later would become a famous film director. But I hope that the many scholars of the Blue Division, and also the relatives of those volunteers, will be proud that the heroism of those men is not allowed to be forgotten.

It is important to stress that the gunners who were serving in Russia at the time, were very aware of this heroism. Lieutenant Joaquín María Usunáriz, whose diary we have mentioned earlier, could not conceal his pride when he wrote in his diary shortly after the battle:

> *"Everything the artillery did was heroic. Reinlein is being given the [Individual] Military Medal. The gunners halted the attack. Andrada [9th Battery] especially by not allowing the red left wing to advance and Castro [8th battery] the right".*

It may not have been the most comprehensive and accurate description of the battle, but it was the most heartfelt expression of the pride and *"esprit de corps"* of a gunner!

Let us now return to the battlefield. In the aforementioned "Report on the battle…" dated 16 February, the final paragraph reads as follows:

> *"During that night [of the 10th] the heroic groups who had defended Krasny Bor rejoined the Division and, after a very necessary rest, the forces were reorganized. Taking advantage of the fact that for four days the enemy's exhaustion had prevented them from relaunching their attack, the combined force defending the flank on the River Izhora was restructured, and can now defend the flank effectively. The Division has an organized reserve of one battalion, one cycle squadron, two companies armed with rifles formed by the remnants of the anti-tank group, and two batteries created in the same way with the remains of the artillerymen manning the Krasny Bor garrison".*

Some time would pass before the Germans could replace their losses. Meanwhile, the gunners would serve in *"baterías pie a tierra"* which are what the Spanish army called units made up of gunners fighting as infantrymen. In his *Memorias de un soldado de la División Azul*, Gunner Blanch Sabench remembered the long months that he had had to serve as an infantryman:

> *"In the end all the guns had been put out of action and had been abandoned, so the gunners, now without artillery, were going to act as infantry. Which was how a small group of 15 men of which I formed part, led by a 2nd lieutenant, was to find itself on a piece of waste ground about 200 metres from the firing line in order to carry out infantry tasks. (…) To our right a bridge over a frozen*

stream led to a path which in turn led to a dugout in which we had a machine gun (...) we had orders not to fire and to keep this position concealed.

"We could only arrive without being seen at night (...) The two men who for periods of 24 hours were on guard duty with the machine gun could neither light a fire to warm themselves (we were at 30 degrees below zero) nor light a lamp (...) As we were so close to the enemy we had to sleep fully clothed, with our boots on and our rifle within reach (...)"

The first 105 mm howitzers delivered to the Spanish as replacement materiel arrived in March, but it was May before the deliveries were completed. The *Wehrmacht* was finding it increasingly difficult to replace lost materiel.

But if there were delays replacing the materiel it was because, as anyone familiar with the history of the Second World War will know, at that time the *Wehrmacht* was suffering terrible defeats (and the corresponding heavy losses of equipment) on the battlefields of southern Russia, as a result of the Battle of Stalingrad. Even if the Germans had wanted to replace the materiel lost by the Spanish on the following day, it would have been impossible.

However, what is unquestionable is that from the Battle of Krasny Bor to the end of the presence of the Spanish outside Leningrad, the Blue Division always had artillery cover which, while it may never have been able to match the increasingly abundant Soviet artillery, did in fact double the cover provided by divisional artillery, since German artillery units supplemented the Spanish ones. In his memoirs published some time ago, José Díaz de Villegas, the very competent officer who served with the Blue Division Staff as commander of the 2nd Section and also as overall commander, conveyed his impression that the Blue Division's sector had been well covered by artillery on the Leningrad Front. Thus, referring to the final months of the Spanish presence in Russia, he wrote:[16]

"Outside Leningrad our division ended up occupying 11 kilometres of front, representing a density of 1.2 men per metre. For each kilometre there were 72 automatic weapons, 4.5 anti-tank guns, and 2.5 infantry cannons. In addition to divisional artillery with calibres ranging between 10.5 and 15.5 [cm] plus the 2 [cm] mortars,[17] there was other artillery belonging to the army corps or the army, which in total, in the sector of the Blue Division's front, represented a density of one gun for every 70 or 80 metres of front. From time to time this artillery was augmented by rail-mounted super-calibre guns, cannons and howitzers, generally of 24 or 28 [cm], but sometimes 30 [cm]."

In another part of his book he was more precise, and in reference to an exact date (16 August 1943) and with regard to field artillery (i.e. not including either anti-tank guns or infantry cannons), Díaz de Villegas states[18] that the Spanish 250th Artillery Regiment had twelve batteries deployed in the Blue Division's sector:

- Nine batteries with 10.5 cm guns
- Two batteries with 15 cm guns
- One battery with 15.5 cm guns

In other words, one of the 150 mm heavy batteries had disappeared from the complement, but the Hessen Battery appeared to be at full strength. However, the most significant fact was that in the Blue Division's sector, which was 11 kilometres long according to Díaz de Villegas, a number of German batteries were deployed, as listed below:

- One of 24 cm howitzers (most likely *24 cm Haubitze 39* of Czech origin)
- One of 20.3 cm howitzers, which he points out were captured Russian guns (the Germans designated them *20.3 cm Haubitze 503 (r)*; there were three different versions depending on their traction system, one of which was tracked)
- One of three 21 cm "mortars" (we may assume these to be German *21 cm Mörser 18*)
- Three batteries of guns which he called "105 long barrel" (I imagine that these were *10.5 cm schwere Kanone 35* of Czech origin)

Also, *"on the immediate left"* (we have to assume these are artillery units of the neighbouring division – the 170th Infantry – capable of hitting targets in front of the Spanish sector), there were three batteries that he referred to as "105 mm light howitzers" (these must be the *10.5 cm leichte Feldhaubitze 18* of the groups forming part of divisional regiments). And *"on the right"* three batteries of 22 cm *"mortars"* (French *22 cm Mörser 531 (f)*) (at the time the 11th Infantry Division was on the right of the Spaniards, but batteries with these guns did not tend to belong to organic divisional artillery). Finally, Díaz de Villegas says *"to the rear"* (we have to assume he is referring to batteries located more deeply to the rear) one battery of 21 cm guns and another of which he is unable to give the calibre. In the first case he must be referring to a unit equipped with *21 cm Kanone 38*, which had an extremely long range. In short, on the 11 km of the segment of front occupied by the Spanish, according to this author 12 batteries with Spanish crews and 14 with German crews were able to fire. Bearing in mind that at that date – 16 August 1943 – what the Germans call the "Third Battle of Ladoga", a ferocious series of battles around the Mga salient, was at its height, it becomes even clearer that not even then was the Spanish sector left defenceless.

Scholars of military history will be familiar with the fact that a country's infantrymen normally sing the praises of enemy artillery (which they always tend to say is very good), while they are more reluctant to recognize the virtues of their own gunners, even to the point of making jokes about them. A common joke – among the infantry of course – is to say that the purpose of artillery is *"to fire on infantry, the enemy infantry if at all possible"*.

The Blue Division was no exception to this tradition. The Division's veterans have always expressed admiration for the effectiveness of the Soviet artillery, recognizing their virtues and exaggerating their capability.

However, studies by great analysts prove that there is a touch of myth in this assessment.[19] It has been revealed that while 90 per cent of German casualties on the Western Front were due to allied artillery, on the Eastern Front the percentage of German casualties attributable to Soviet artillery was 50 per cent, a much lower figure. And that although the Germans were nearly always outnumbered and outclassed in terms of their field artillery pieces, professionally the Germans were far superior to their Soviet opposite numbers, a statement that could be perfectly well extrapolated to include Spanish gunners. This was because the Soviets did not yet have a large population with advanced technical training, something essential for artillery. For this reason Soviet artillery tactics always erred on the side of rigidity and only achieved good results when guns were used in massive numbers.

In the case of my assessment of the qualities of the gunners, I would hazard to say that they may even have been superior to their German comrades-in-arms. I do not say this out of pride, but for the simple reason that the best artillery officers volunteered to join the Blue Division, while in the neighbouring German artillery units, formed by conscripts, there must have been some very good officers, others who were average, and a few who were poorly trained or plain incompetent.

While the exceptional fighting spirit shown by the Spanish gunners at Krasny Bor is undeniable, so is their high level of competence. This was demonstrated when, shortly after the battle began, the lines of communication between the observation posts and the gun lines were broken, and also when the command structure was truncated due to the entire staff of the Ascarza Battlegroup being killed or wounded. Thanks to the unity of doctrine among the batteries' officers, they continued to fire effectively and unceasingly.

I shall now return to the matter of the enemy artillery. In the case of Leningrad, it is true that the encircled city managed to concentrate a large number of heavy and superheavy guns, and it was no coincidence that a former artillery officer was in command of the besieged troops, but it is no less true that the garrison had difficulty achieving the extraordinarily dense concentrations of artillery that the Soviets assembled in other sectors. In his monograph on the battle for Leningrad, Glantz gives us many examples. When writing about the preparations for the breakthrough operation to the south of Lake Ladoga which began on 12 January and which opened up a corridor to the city, Glantz tells us that Soviet High Command made available to the Volkhov Front – which was attacking from outside the encirclement – a total of four artillery divisions, 10 mortar regiments, and two anti-aircraft regiments, drawn from general reserve units.

However, the Leningrad Front – which attacked from inside the encirclement – could only be reinforced with one artillery division, one artillery brigade, three artillery regiments, three mortar regiments, and five "mortars of the guard" groups (remember that "mortars of the guard" was the name the Russians gave to their rocket launcher units). To give readers a clearer idea of the significance of these figures I shall provide a few clues. An artillery division – a type of unit that no other army had – consisted of a large number of groups and regiments and had a total of 72 guns of calibre 76.2 mm, 108 of 120, 84 of 122, 68 of 152, and 24 of 203, all organized into six units called brigades which had a total of 11 units designated as regiments and eight designated as groups. Readers will see, therefore, that Soviet High Command understandably found it was easier to reinforce its troops deployed outside the encirclement from its general reserve than it was to reinforce its troops inside the encirclement. For this reason it was not until September 1943 that the Leningrad Counterbattery Artillery Corps was created, whose purpose was to counter the German heavy and superheavy batteries which were regularly pounding the city.

Once the euphoria of the first huge advances made in the summer of 1941 had passed and it had become clear that the Red Army was not about to collapse, the Germans increasingly put their faith in artillery firepower. They realized that only with artillery could they offset the huge advantage in human resources that the Soviets had over them. But, unfortunately for the Germans, the Soviets also constantly increased their artillery strength and improved the quality of their gunners. And they also finally gained air superiority, which meant that the Soviets were in an increasingly better position to cancel out the German artillery. When the Germans were forced to make major withdrawals (something which in Army Group North's area would not occur until January 1944), this would have catastrophic consequences for the artillery, since they lost a large number of guns.

This was inevitable because the vast majority of German artillery was horse-drawn or simply immovable. At the Battle of Krasny Bor we have already seen how the Spanish 250th Regiment lost five complete batteries; it had been simply impossible to withdraw them in the face of the enemy advance.

But in fact long before these catastrophic withdrawals forced the Germans to abandon so many guns, the problems caused by horse-drawn artillery were already very serious. The large number of horses needed to pull the guns and ammunition turned artillery regiments into "livestock" units which had to dedicate a significant percentage of their men and time to tending their horses. And mobility was so poor that it was impossible to concentrate guns with the required speed. Motorized artillery would have achieved better results with fewer guns, since the guns could have been concentrated more easily and redeployed faster, withdrawing them when they were at risk of being captured or destroyed. But as Germany had neither sufficient trucks or tractors nor enough fuel that option was never viable and the bulk of its artillery continued to be horse-drawn until the end of the war.

Other German artillery units, the heavy ones, were almost more difficult to move even if on paper they were motorized or rail-mounted. The state of the Russian road network meant that motorization was not always an advantage. When the Red Army finally succeeded in breaking out of the encirclement around Leningrad, forcing the Germans to make a rapid withdrawal, their greatest reward was to capture the guns that had tormented the city for years. Between 14 January 1944, the date of the breakthrough, and the end of the month, the Soviets captured 265 German guns, one third of which were heavy and superheavy calibre pieces. And nothing filled those Russian soldiers with more pride than to capture a gigantic 520 mm railway gun.[20]

Another serious problem experienced by the German artillery was that of ammunition supply. In the first stages of the Second World War, when months passed between campaign and campaign without any fighting, German industry was capable of building up large magazines, since for months consumption was minimal. Once the Russian campaign had started there was no respite and for months on end the fighting became increasingly more intense. However much the production of German factories was stepped up, it was never again able to fully meet the demand for artillery ammunition. Ammunition had to be rationed. The Spanish gunners of the Blue Division were always surprised by how sparingly the Germans supplied them with ammunition, and more than one suspected the Germans were acting out of bad faith or general tightfistedness. In fact it was just that they had an enormous difficulty manufacturing as much artillery ammunition as was needed.

If those limitations on consumption had not existed, during the days prior to the Soviet attack at Krasny Bor, the gunners and the Spanish could have flattened the enemy's jumping-off points, breaking up the offensive before it had even begun.

In short, the Blue Division artillery had all the virtues and defects that characterized their hosts, the *Wehrmacht* artillery, since the Spaniards were equipped with German weapons and equipment. For this reason, despite being outnumbered, it was able to fire on the Red Army and – reinforced by cooperating German units – contribute decisively to defending its lines. On the Army Group North's front this was possible at least until late 1943. And the Battle of Krasny Bor is a good example of this fact.

In this battle both the Spanish infantry and artillery admirably fulfilled their mission. The artillery pounded the enemy effectively since before the attack began, although they could not match the deluge of rounds fired by the Soviets. The infantry withstood that deluge stoically, without allowing themselves to be cowed by the artillery enemy and, when the attack was at its height, they broke the enemy's impetus and eventually halted them. This gave time for the German artillery to enter the battle.

But it was not only the capacity for resistance and sacrifice of the men of the Blue Division, the courage of the Spaniards, which halted the Soviet offensive, but the correct use of all available artillery firepower and the rapid concentration of fresh batteries were also fundamental factors.

As you might suppose, the enemy attack was not planned just for the 10th; it should have continued during the days that followed. The Red Army actually tried to continue, but they were unable to advance any further and the only territorial gains they made were on the 10th. That total halt was due to the tremendous attrition on the attackers on the 10th at the hands of the Spanish. As from that moment the Germans brought many infantry units to bear on the area but all of them were at such low strength that they could barely do anything other than defend and could certainly not counter-attack. The pathetically minuscule armoured forces that Army Group North could assemble were also brought to the area, but it was the artillery that was decisive in preventing any further advance of the Red Army.

To ignore the large scale presence of German artillery forces, both on 10 February 1943 and the following day, is a grave error of analysis, since it only helps to perpetuate a series of misapprehensions or myths regarding the Battle of Krasny Bor, which we need to bury:

- The Germans treated the Spanish like cannon fodder, without reinforcing them.
- The Spanish should have been used in an unimportant sector, since there was no artillery reinforcements available for their lines.
- The Soviet attack must not have been anything more than a local attack, since only Spanish artillery was used.

None of the above scenarios correspond to the truth, as we have been seeing throughout this book. What the Blue Division soldiers did on that fateful 10 February 1943 was to provide decisive help to cut off at its root a very ambitious enemy offensive. An offensive which was launched against them because they were deployed in a key sector and which could be halted with the inestimable support of the German gunners who fought alongside them. And the merit is not only due to I Group and the other two batteries which fought from positions to the east of the Izhora. III Group intervened decisively and IV Group contributed as much as it was able. Together with the heroes known to us for many decades now, the battle of Krasny Bor had other forgotten protagonists who need to be rescued from the unjust oblivion that their role in the battle has suffered for such a long time. I hope I have helped in that task.

When enough time has passed for us to have the necessary perspective, I believe that we all reach the conclusion that artillery was the decisive military arm for the whole of the 20th century, and if not, at least for the two World Wars. And yet it is surprising how absent it still is in the accounts provided by military historians. I also trust that this book will help to correct this absence. What we cannot do is carry on as we have done up until now, with artillery only being mentioned very sporadically (for example, when speaking of the amount of firepower unleashed when an offensive is initiated), without attempting to describe artillery deployments, movements, etc.

In the case of the Eastern Front around 1943, the importance of artillery was due, among other factors, to the depletion of the infantry. Accounts of military history continue to talk mainly about infantry divisions, and although seasoned readers will know each division's strength would be far below theoretical strength, I fear that they will still not be fully aware that divisions tended to be no more than regiment strength when they actually reached the battlefield.

What better than an example to illustrate what I am trying to say. On 21 February 1943, ten days after the attack against the Spanish at Krasny Bor, the commander of L Army Corps sent a report to the 18th Army on his *Gefechtsstärke*, the "combat strength" of the units of which he was in command. In this concept of *Gefechtsstärke* the Germans included the men in the units of each division which could be used as a front-line combatant; "in the trenches" we might say. It therefore included men in infantry battalions, exploration groups, and occasionally those in sapper battalions, and excluded units which provided fire support (artillery, anti-tank) or other types of support (radio, medical, transport, quartermaster, etc.). By then the 24th Infantry Division had joined the Corps, so in theory the Corps consisted of six large division-scale units. What was the real situation of these units? This table summarizes the actual strengths that could be fielded on the front line:

Gefechtsstärke of L Corps, to 21 February 1943						
Unit	215th Inf. D.	2nd SS Brig.	Blue Div.	212th Inf. D.	24th Inf. D.	4th SS Div.
Front line	2,092	1,610	3,049	1,508	1,574	1,987
Unit	215th Inf. D.	2nd SS Brig.	Blue Div.	212th Inf. D.	24th Inf. D.	4th SS Div.
Divisional reserve	97	456	800	57	45	120
Totals for the units	2,189	2,066	3,849	1,565	1,619	2,107
Army corps reserve			251		319	
Total for the Army Corps			13,965			

For comparison purposes, the *Gefechtsstärke* of the four division-scale units which were already operating in the sector on 1 January 1943 was: 215th Division: 2,529 men; 2nd SS Brigade: 1,670 men; Blue Division: 6,133 men; and 4th SS Division: 2,934 men. A sum total of scarcely 13,200 men to cover the arc extending from the Baltic coast to where the River Tosna empties into the River Neva.

This is the same arc which on 21 February was covered by what on paper were six divisions or similar formations. For a contact line that at the time was over 40 km long, L Corps had around 12,000 men deployed in the front-line trenches; i.e. one man every three and a half metres. It is true that divisional and Army Corps reserves accounted for another 2,000 men, but even if they were counted as already deployed, there would still be three metres of line for every man.

Let us look at the units, one by one (a detailed description with the exact numbers is to be found in Appendix 8). At the westernmost end of the deployment was the 215th Division, whose sector started on the shores of the Baltic. Its three infantry regiments (380th, 390th and 435th) had reduced their strengths from three to two battalions. One of the regiments, the 390th, had left the divisional sector and was the German unit that was acting in reserve in the Sablino area when the Soviets launched their attack against the Blue Division. We have already seen how weakened its strength was. The aforementioned L Corps report states that the 215th Division was going to send its III/435th Battalion to relieve III/390th, since the latter had virtually ceased to exist.

In order to beef up the front line the division had stripped its rearguard units and formed an alert battalion with men from those units to be used at the front. There was also a battalion formed by Latvians, recruited for police work in the rear, but who were now serving on the front line, and a unit of *"pie a tierra"* gunners, i.e. artillerymen fighting as infantrymen. The only reserve the division had was its exploration unit, which had been reduced to just one cycle squadron.

Their neighbour to the east was the 2nd SS Infantry Brigade, a unit that in principle, at this time, should have been made up of Dutch, Norwegian, and Flemish Belgian volunteer legions. As there were not enough to bring the unit up to strength, men from the police forces that should have been operating in the rear were attached. These included both German police and security forces recruited from Baltic countries, in this case a battalion from Latvia which, at that time, was being suitably armed for the front line.

These two units formed the western sector of L Corps and there was no other operational reserve available to the Corps.

In the central sector were the Blue Division and the 212th Division. The Spanish unit had suffered the most during the Russian offensive. Of its 262nd Regiment only its III Battalion had survived; I and II had both been destroyed. Both the 263rd Regiment and the 269th had sent battalions to take part in counter-attacks (the I/263rd and the II/269th) and neither battalion existed as such at that time. The 250th Reserve Battalion and the 250th Exploration (or Cycle) Group had also ceased to exist as such. With men from all the shattered units (equivalent to six battalions) new battlegroups had been improvised and deployed along the Izhora. The Spanish divisionary command was also trying to hurriedly rebuild an infantry battalion for the 262nd and the Sapper Battalion, by reorganizing and re-equipping those who had survived the battle.

To the left was what documents and maps refer to as the 212th Division. The Division had three regiments (316th, 320th and 423rd), by then already reduced to two battalions. But in fact only men from of one its regiments (the 316th) were present in the sector, together with a Rapid Group (a unit resulting from the merger of cycle and anti-tank groups) and men from the aforementioned 390th Regiment (of the 215th Division) and two battalions of Estonian volunteers.

For all this highly threatened central sector, L Corps had only two companies of Flemish Belgian volunteers acting in reserve.

The eastern sector was manned by the 4th SS-Police Division and the recently arrived 24th Infantry Division. This comprised three infantry regiments (31st, 32nd and 102nd), also of two battalions each. All were deployed in the sector, although two were with other units, so the 44th Infantry Regiment (a unit which organically belonged to another division, the 11th) had been attached to make up numbers. The sector occupied by the 24th Division was the one which, at that time, was suffering the most serious attacks, and the report expressly states how the strengths of its battalions had plunged alarmingly. The I/44th, which had arrived at the sector with 285 men, now had 110; the I/102nd had gone from 311 to just 66, and the II/102nd, from 302 to 105. The division was also using on the front line its exploration unit, the 24th Cycle Group, and, as an attached force, the Sapper School Battalion. The divisional reserve was a company of German gunners being used as infantry; they had already been present at the Battle of Krasny Bor alongside the Spanish.

And at the left-hand end, anchored on the Tosna River, was the 4th SS-Police Division. Only four of its original infantry battalions were still operational, and its Cycle Group and a battalion made up of men drawn from second line troops had to be used on the front line. Even so it was necessary to reinforce the division with infantry from neighbouring units. One of the battalions of the 24th Division acted as the reserve for the eastern sector.

Fourteen thousand men; that was the entire strength of an Army Corps of six divisions to occupy the front line. Of those 14,000, 47 per cent were not German, since in addition to the 3,849 Spanish there were 744 Latvians, 638 Dutch, 575 Estonians, 383 Norwegians, and 341 Flemish Belgians (the claim to be taking part in a European crusade against Stalinist communism was not mere propaganda, as we can see). It is clear that with such scant forces the front line alone could not withstand any serious attack. What was it, then, that gave the line its strength? The fact is that behind those hardworking and heroic front line combatants there were also some other important protagonists, protagonists that have been overlooked so many times. The gunners.

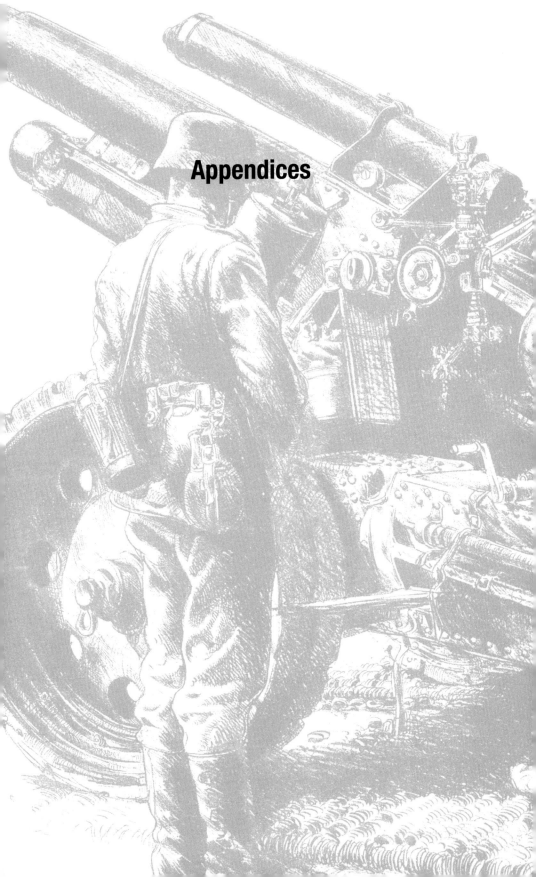

Appendices

Appendix 1. Comparison of the characteristics of the main artillery pieces mentioned (excluding railway and infantry cannons).

German designation	Country of origin	Combat weight (kg)	Projectile weight (kg)[(1)]	Maximum range (metres)[(2)]	Rate of fire (shots/ min)
7,62 cm Feldkanone-Haubitze 295 (r)	RUS	1,350	6.4	13,100	8
10.5 cm leichte Feldhaubitze 16	GER	1,525	14.8	9,200	4-5
10,5 cm leichte Feldhaubitze 18	GER	2,040	14.8	10,675	4-6
10,5 cm schwere Kanone 35 (t)	CZE	4,200	18	18,300	8
10,7 cm Kanone 352 (r)	RUS	2,380	17.2	16,500	5-6
12,2 cm Kanone 390/1 (r)	RUS	7,100	25	20,870	5-6
15 cm schwere Feldhaubitze 18	GER	5,512	43.5	13,325	4
15 cm Kanone 18	GER	12,460	43	24,825	2
15,2 cm Kanone-Haubitze 433/1 (r)	RUS	7,128	43.5	17,265	1
15,5 cm schwere Feldhaubitze 414 (f)	FRA	3,300	43.6	11,900	3
15,5 cm Kanone 416 (f)	FRA	8,956	43	17,300	1
17 cm Kanone 18	GER	17,510	68	28,000	1-2
19,4 cm Kanone i. Sfl. 485 (f)[(3)]	FRA	29,600	83.5	20,900	1
21 cm Kanone 38 and 39/40[(4)]	GER CZE	25,435 39,800	120 135	33,900 33,900	1 3 every 2 min
21 cm Mörser 18	GER	16,700	121	18,700	1
22 cm Mörser 531 (f)	FRA	2,810	100.5	10,800	2
24 cm Haubitze 39 (t)	CZE	29,900	166	18,150	1 every 2 min
28 cm Haubitze L/12	GER	37,000	350	11,400	1
42 cm Haubitze (t)	CZE	105,000	1,020	14,600	1 every 5 min

GER: Germany. RUS: Russia. FRA: France. CZE: Czechoslovakia. (1) All of these guns could fire more than one type of projectile. The one listed here was the heaviest. (2) The range depended on the type of ammunition used; here the range of the heaviest is quoted. (3) Sfl: self-propelled. (4) The documentation does not say which of the two types was used.

German designation	Feldhaubitze	Kanone	Mörser	Infanterie Geschutze	Panzerabwehr Kanone (PaK)	Flugzeugabwehr Kanone (Flak)	Werfe
Numerical criteria used by the Germans to classify the various types of artillery pieces							
Translation into English	Field howitzer	Cannon	Mortar	Infantry cannon	Anti-Tank cannon	Anti-Aircraft cannon	Rocke launche
Leicht (l) Light	Up to 12.9 cm	Up to 9.9 cm		Up to 7.5 cm	Up to 3.9 cm	Up to 3.6 cm	Up to 10.9 cn
Mitte (m) Medium	-	-	-	-	From 4 to 5.9 cm	From 3.7 to 5.9 cm	From 11 to 15.9 cn
Schwer (s) Heavy	From 13 to 20.9 cm	From 10 to 20.9 cm	From 21 to 24.9 cm	From 7.6 cm	From 6 to 8.9 cm	From 3.7 to 15.9 cm	From 16 to 21.9 cn
Schwerest (sw) Superheavy	From 21 cm	From 21 cm	From 25 cm		From 9	From 16 cm	From 22 cm

Appendix 2. Artillery of L Army Corps as at 26 January 1943.
Operational strengths of the various units.

Regiment	Group	Battery	Calibre	No. of guns	Range
215th Infantry Division					
Artillery regiment 215th	I/25	5015	22 f	2	10.8
		5016	22 f	1	10.8
		1/215	10.5	4	10.6
		2/215	10.5	3	10.6
		3/215	10.5	3	10.6
	IV/225	5017	22 f	2	10.8
		10/225	15.5 f (*)	3	11.9
		11/225	15.5 f	2	11.9
		12/225	15.5 f	3	11.9
	III/215	7/215	10.5	3	10.6
		8/215	10.5	3	10.6
		9/215	10.5	3	10.6

Note: 5th and 6th/215 Batteries were assigned to the *Luftwaffe* Field Corps at Oranienbaum
(*) The 15.5 cm assigned to the divisions were *schwere Feldhaubitze 414 (f)*

2nd SS Brigade					
Regiment	Group	Battery	Calibre	No. of guns	Range
110th Regimental Staff	SS Ausbildung (*)	I/SS Aus.	10.5	2	9.2
		2/SS Aus.	7.62 r	1	13.1
	II/215	4/215 Zug 1 (**)	10.5	3	10.6
		4/215 Zug 2	10.5	3	10.6
	914 Coast	1/914	10.5 t	4	18.3
		2/914	10.5 t	5	18.3
		3/914	10.5 t	4	18.3
		5003	22 f	2	10.8
		5009	22 f	2	10.8
		629	15.2 r	4	17.2
		639	10.7 r	4	16.5
	III/201	7/207	10.5	4	10.6
		8/207	10.5	3	10.6
		9/207	10.5	4	10.6
		Schlesien	15.5 f	0	11.9
(*) Instruction unit (**) Zug: Autonomous section					

Blue Division					
Regiment	Group	Battery	Calibre	No. of guns	Range
250th Artillery Regiment	I/250	1/250	10.5	4	10.6
		2/250	10.5	4	10.6
		3/250	10.5	4	10.6
		9/250	10.5	4	10.6
		Mort. Sect.	22 f	1	10.8
	II/250	4/250	10.5	4	10.6
		5/250	10.5	4	10.6
		6/250	10.5	4	10.6
		Mort. Sect.	22 f	2	10.8
	III/250	7/250	10.5	3	10.6
		8/250	10.5	4	10.6
		12/250	15	3	13.3
		Mort. Sect.	22 f	1	10.8
	IV/250	10/250	15	3	13.3
		11/250	15	3	13.3
		Hessen	15.5 f	1	11.9
		Mort. Sect.	22 f	1	10.8
	Werner (II/814)	1/Werner	22 f	3	10.8
		2/Werner	22 f	2	10.8

Artillery units of *Arko 18* (1st part)					
Regiment	Group	Battery	Calibre	No. of guns	Range
802nd Regimental Staff	II/84	4/84 Zug	10.5 t	4	18.3
		4/84 Zug	19,4 f	2	20.9
		5/84	17	2	28
		6/84	17	2	28
		508	21	1	33.9
		515	21	1	33.9
	708 Coast	1/708	15.5 f (*)	7	17.3
		2/708	15.5 f	1	17.3
			24 t	2	18.1
			12,2 r	6	20.8
		3/708	15.5 f	7	17.3
		513	15	2	24.8
(*) The 15.5 cm guns of the groups assigned to the Corps were *Kanone* 416 (f)					

Artillery units of *Arko 18* (2nd part). Under direct orders				
Group	Battery	Calibre	No. of guns	Range
289 Coast	1/289	15.5 f	5	17.3
	3/289	15.5 f	4	17.3
	503	17	2	28

Artillery units of *Arko 18* (3rd part)					
Regiment	Group	Battery	Calibre	No. of guns	Range
Gronert Regimental Staff	928 Coast	1/928	10.5 t	4	18.3
		2/928	10.5 t	4	18.3
		3/928	10.5 t	3	18.3
	768	2/768	21	2	33.9
		3/768	21	2	33.9
		2/289	15.5 f	5	17.3
	679 Railway	695 (*) Railway	37 f	3	16.4
(*) Half the battery					

Artillery units of *Arko 18* (4th part) in reserve							
Groups				Batteries			
Group	Calibre	No. of guns	Range	Battery	Calibre	No. of guns	Range
I/814	24 H t	3	18.1	458	42 H t	1	14.6
II/814	24 H t	5	18.1	459	42 H t	1	14.6

Appendix 3. Artillery of L Army Corps as at 14 February 1943.

Operational strengths of the various units

215th Infantry Division					
Regiment	Group	Battery	Calibre	No. of guns	Range
215th Artillery Regiment	I/25	5015	22 f	2	10.8
		5016	22 f	1	10.8
		1/215	10.5	4	10.6
		2/215	10.5	3	10.6
		3/215	10.5	3	10.6
	IV/225	5/215	10.5	3	10.6
		5017	22 f	2	10.8
		10/225	15.5 f	3	11.9
		11/225	15.5 f	2	11.9
		12/225	15.5 f	3	11.9
	III/215	7/215	10.5	3	10.6
		8/215	10.5	3	10.6
		9/215	10.5	3	10.6

2nd SS Brigade					
Regiment	Group	Battery	Calibre	No. of guns	Range
110th Regimental Staff	II/215	I/SS Aus	10.5	2	9.2
		4/215	10.5	3	10.6
	914 Coast	1/914	10.5 t	4	18.3
		2/914	10.5 t	5	18.3
		3/914	10.5 t	4	18.3
		5003	22 t	3	10.8
		5009	22 f	2	10.8
		2/SS Aus	7,62 r	1	13.1
		629	15,2 r	4	17.2
		639	10,7 r	4	16.5
	III/201	7/207	10.5	4	10.6
		8/207	10.5	3	10.6
		9/207	10.5	4	10.6
		Schlesien	15.5 f	1	11.9

Blue Division					
Regiment	Group	Battery	Calibre	No. of guns	Range
250th Artillery Regiment	I/250	1/250	10.5	0	10.6
		2/250	10.5	0	10.6
		3/250	10.5	0	10.6
		9/250	10.5	0	10.6
		11/250	14.9	0	13.3
		Mort. Sect.	22 f	0	10.8
	II/250	5/250	10.5	4	10.6
		6/250	10.5	4	10.6
		Mort. Sect.	22 f	1	10.8
	III/250	7/250	10.5	3	10.6
		8/250	10.5	4	10.6
		12/250	15	3	13.3
		Mort. Sect.	22 f	1	10.8
	IV/250	4/250	10.5	4	13.3
		10/250	15	2	13.3
		Hessen	15.5 f	1	11.9
		Mort. Sect.	22 f	1	10.8
	Werner	1/Werner	22 f	1	10.8
		2/Werner	22 f	2	10.8

Artillery units of *Arko 18* (1st part)					
Regiment	Group	Battery	Calibre	No. of guns	Range
802nd Regimental Staff	II/84	4/84 Z(*)	24 t	0	18.1
		5/84	17	2	28
		6/84	17	?	28
		508	21	1	33.9
		515	21	1	33.9
	708 Coastal	1/708	15.5 f	6	17.3
		2/708	15.5 f	0	17.3
			24 t	1	18.1
			12,2 r	6	20.8
		3/708	15.5 f	7	17.3
		513	15	2	24.8
(*) Zug: Section					

Artillery units of *Arko 18* (2nd part). Under direct orders				
Group	Battery	Calibre	No. of guns	Range
289 Coast	1/289	15.5 f	1	17.3
	3/289	15.5 f	3	17.3
	5/814	24 H t	1	18.1
Independent	458	42 H t	0	14.1
Independent	503	17	2	28

Artillery units of *Arko 18* (3rd part)								
Restricted use					In reserve			
Group	Battery	Calibre	No. of guns	Range	Battery	Calibre	No. of guns	Range
679 Railway	686 Rlwy (*)	28	1	62.4	459	42 H t	1	14.1
	688 Rlwy	40 f	2	15				
		28	2	28.5				
	693 Rlwy	40 f	3	15				
	695 Rlwy (*)	28	3	29.5				
(*) Half the battery								

212th Infantry Division					
Regiment	Group	Battery	Calibre	No. of guns	Range
212th Artillery Regiment	856	2/289	15.5 f	5	17.3
		514	21	2	18.7
		2/856	21	2	18.7
		3/856	21	2	18.7
	II/212	4/212	10.5	3	10.6
		5/212	10.5	3	10.6
		6/212	10.5	3	10.6
	III/4 SS	7/ SS	10.5	3	10.6
		8/ SS	10.5	3	10.6
		9/ SS	10.5	3	10.6
	IV/212	10/212	15	3	13.3
		11/212	15	1	13.3
		12/212	15	2	13.3
	III/W.3 (*)	7/W.3	15	6	6.1
		8/W.3	15	6	6.1
		9/W.3	15	6	6.1
(*) Rocket launcher unit (W: *Werfer*)					

4th SS-Police Division					
Regiment	Group	Battery	Calibre	No. of guns	Range
4th SS Artillery Regiment	II/212	1/212	10.5	3	10.6
		2/212	10.5	3	10.6
		3/212	10.5	3	10.6
	I/4 SS	I/4SS	10.5	3	10.6
		2/4SS	10.5	2	10.6
			15.5 f	1	11.9
	II/4 SS	3/4SS	10.5	2	10.6
		4/4SS	10.5	3	10.6
		5/4SS	10.5	2	10.6
		6/4SS	10.5	3	10.6
	IV/4 SS	10/4SS	15	2	13.3
		11/4SS	15	1	13.3
		12/4SS	12.2 r	2	8.9
			22 f	3	10.8
		744	28	1	11.4
	II/W.70 (*)	I/W.70	15	6	6.1
		8/W.70	15	6	6.1
		6/W.70	28	6	19
(*) Rocket launcher unit (W: Werfer)					

Artillery units of *Arko 138* (1st part)					
Regiment	Group	Battery	Calibre	No. of guns	Range
Wenner Regimental Staff (previously Gronert)	928 Coast	1/928	10.5 t	3	18.3
		2/928	10.5 t	2	18.3
		3/928	10.5 t	1	18.3
		6/215	10.5	3	10.6
	768	2/768	21	2	33.9
		3/768	21	2	33.9
	Independent	10/4SS	19.4 f	2	20.9
	Independent	I/W.70	24 H t	2	18.1
(*) Zug: Section					

Artillery units of *Arko 138* (2nd part)					
Regiment	Group	Battery	Calibre	No. of guns	Range
Regimental Staff 610th	1/814	1/814	24 t	3	18.1
		1/768	21	2	33.9
		4/768	21	2	33.9
	910 Coast	1/910	15.5 f	4	17.3
		2/910	15.5 f	4	17.3
		3/910	15.5 f	2	17.3
		4/910	15.5 f	3	17.3
	809	1/809	21	3	18.7
		2/809	21	3	18.7
		1/856	21	2	18.7

Artillery units of *Arko 138* (3rd part). In reserve			
Battery	Calibre	No. of guns	Range
695 Railway (*)	37 f	3	16.4
(*) Half the battery			

Appendix 4. Type and number of artillery pieces of L Corps, as at 26 January 1943.

Type of gun (German designation)	215th ID	2nd SS Brig.	Blue Div.	Arko 18	Totals
7,62 cm Feldkanone-Haubitze 295 (r)	-	1	-	-	1
10,5 cm leichte Feldhaubitze 16	-	2	-	-	2
10,5 cm leichte Feldhaubitze 18	19	17	35		71
10,5 cm schwere Kanone 35 (t)	-	13	-	15	28
10,7 cm Kanone 352 (r)	-	4	-	-	4
12,2 cm Kanone 390/1 (r)	-	-	-	6	6
15 cm schwere Feldhaubitze 18	-	-	9		9
15 cm Kanone 18	-	-	-	2	2
15,2 cm Kanone-Haubitze 433/1 (r)	-	4	-	-	4
15,5 cm schwere Feldhaubitze 414	8	0	1	-	9
15,5 cm Kanone 416 (f)	-	-	-	29	29
17 cm Kanone 18	-	-	-	6	6
19,4 cm Kanone i. Sfl. 485 (f)	-	-	-	2	2
21 cm Kanone 38 and 39/40	-	-	-	6	6
21 cm *Mörser* 18	-	-	-	-	0
22 cm *Mörser* 531 (f)	5	4	10	-	19
24 cm Haubitze 39 (t)	-	-	-	2	2
42 cm Haubitze (t)	-	-	-	-	-
	32	45	55	68	200

Appendix 5. Type and number of artillery pieces and multiple rocket launchers of L Corps, as at 14 February 1943.

Type of gun (German designation)	215th ID	2nd SS Brig.	Blue Div.	Arko 18	212th ID	4th SS Div.	Arko 138	Totals
7,62 cm Feldkanone-Haubitze 295 (r)	-	1	-	-	-	-	-	1
10,5 cm leichte Feldhaubitze 16	-	2	-	-	-	-	-	2
10,5 cm leichte Feldhaubitze 18	22	14	19	-	18	24	3	100
10,5 cm schwere Kanone 35 (t)	-	13	-	-	-	-	6	19
10,7 cm Kanone 352 (r)	-	4	-	-	-	-	-	4
12,2 cm Kanone 390/1 (r)	-	-	-	6	-	2	-	8
15 cm schwere Feldhaubitze 18	-	-	5	-	6	3	-	14
15 cm Kanone 18	-	-	-	2	-	-	-	2
15,2 cm Kanone-Haubitze 433/1 (r)	-	4	-	-	-	-	-	4
15,5 cm schwere Feldhaubitze 414	8	1	1	-	-	1	-	11
15,5 cm Kanone 416 (f)	-	-	-	17	5	-	13	35
17 cm Kanone 18	-	-	-	6	-	-	-	6
19,4 cm Kanone (f) i. Sfl.	-	-	-	-	-	-	2	2
21 cm Kanone 38 and 39/40	-	-	-	2	-	-	8	10
21 cm Mörser 18	-	-	-	-	6	-	8	14
22 cm Mörser 531 (f)	5	5	6	-	-	3	-	19
24 cm Haubitze 39 (t)	-	-	-	2	-	-	5	7
28 cm Haubitze L/12	-	-	-	-	-	1	-	1
42 cm Haubitze (t)	-	-	-	0	-	-	-	0
	35	44	31	35	35	34	45	259
Rocket launchers								
15 cm Werfer					18	12		30
28 cm Werfer						6		6

Appendix 6. Deployment of *Heerestruppen* artillery units in the various sectors of the 18th Army. Evolution from 1 January to 24 February.

I January	18th Army	III *Luftwaffe* Field Corps	L Corps	LIV Corps
Major Units		9 LFD, 10 LFD(1)	215 ID(2) 2 Br.(3) SS 100 Reg.(4) Mount. Light(5)	Blue Division, 4 SS Div., 5 D. Mount. Light
Artillery Commander	H *Arko* 303	-	*Arko* 18	*Arko* 138
Art. Rgt. Staff	802	610	110	49
Heavy Groups	II/84	-	I/814	II/814, 768
Heavy batteries	628	-	458, 626, 629, 639	459, 744
Coastal Art. Groups	708, 928	929	914	289 (-), 513, 910
Coastal Art. Batteries	508, 513, 515	-	503, 3/289	514
Railway batteries	686, 688, 693 (part)	-		695 (part)
Attached divisional artillery units(6)	-	II/121, II/215	-	-
I January (cont..)	**XXVI Corps**	**I Corps**	**XXVIII Corps**	**XXXVIII Corps**
Major Units	223 ID, 1 ID, 227 ID, 96 ID, 170 ID, Reg 374	28 Light D(7), 121 ID, 24 ID, Reg. 474	69 ID, 132 ID, 61 ID, 11 ID, 217 ID, 21 ID	212 ID, 1 LFD, Reg. 437
Artillery Commander	*Arko* 113	*Arko* 123	24	30
Art. Rgt. Staff	782, 818	-	-	785
Heavy Groups	II/*Lehr* 2(8) 624, 641,854, 856	II/37, 615 (bulk), 680, 850 (part)	153, 809	
Heavy batteries	1/615	-	-	-
Coastal Art. Groups	143	-	-	-
Coastal Art. Batteries	507	-	-	-
Railway batteries	691	-	-	-
Attached divisional artillery units	1/207	-	-	-

LFD: *Luftwaffe* Field Divisions; 2) ID: Infantry Division; 3) Br: Brigade; 4) Reg: Regiment; 5) Mount. Light: Mountain Light Infantry; 6) Belonging to divisional regiments but temporarily attached to other units; 7) Light: Light Infantry (not to be confused with Mount. Light); 8) *Lehr*: Demonstration Unit. German artillery had a number of "*Lehr*" regiments for evaluating new tactics and materiel and *Artillerie Lehr Regiment 2* was the one devoted to heavy artillery.

24 January	III *Luftwaffe* Corps	L Corps	Group Hilpert LIV Corps + XXVI Corps
Major Units	9 LFD, 10 LFD	215 ID, 2 Br. SS, Blue Division	5 D Mount. Light, 4 SS Div., 1 ID, 223 ID, Remains of Divs of XXVI AC[1]
Artillery Commander	-	Arko 18	H Arko 303[2], Arko 138, Arko 113
Art. Rgt. Staff	610	110, 802	49, 782, 818
Heavy Groups	-	II/84, I/814, II/814, 768 (part)	II/Lehr 2, II/37, 615, 809, 854, 856, 624, 641, 680 (bulk), 768 (part)
Heavy batteries	-	458, 459, 628, 629, 639	744
Coastal Art. Groups	-	289, 708, 914, 928	143, 531, 910, 929
Coastal Art. Batteries	-	513, 503, 508, 515	507, 514
Railway batteries	-	686 (part), 688, 693, 695 (part)	686 (part), 691, 695 (part)
Attached divisional artillery units	5/ and 6/215 Art. Regiment	-	-
24 January (cont.)	I Corps	XXVIII Corps	XXXVIII Corps
Major Units	121 ID, 24 ID, 13 LFD	69 ID, 132 ID, 11 ID, 217 ID, 21 ID	212 ID, 1 LFD, 81 ID
Artillery Commander	Arko 123	Arko 24	Arko 30
Art. Rgt. Staff	-	-	785
Heavy Groups	850 (part)	153	633, 850 (part), 815
Heavy batteries	626, 1 Batt. of the 680, 917 Sfl[3]	-	-

1) The divisions had virtually been reduced to battlegroups at regimental strength after the Soviet offensive of 12 January. 2) The 18th Army had assigned all the artillery units under its direct orders to the Army Corps and assigned its *Hoh. Arko* to the Group. 3) Sfl: self-propelled.

8 February	III *Luftwaffe* Corps	L Corps	Group Hilpert LIV Corps + XXVI Corps
Major Units	9 LFD, 10 LFD	215 ID, 2 Br. SS, Blue Division, 4 SS Div.	5 D Mount. Light, 1 ID, 223 ID, Remains of XXVI AC
Artillery Commander	-	*Arko* 18, *Arko* 138	H *Arko* 303, *Arko* 113,
Art. Rgt. Staff	610	110, 802	49, 788, 818
Heavy Groups	-	II/84, I/814, II/814, 768 (part)	II/*Lehr* 2, II/37, 615, 624, 641, 809, 854, 856, 680 (bulk), 768 (part)
Heavy batteries	-	458, 459, 628, 629, 639	744
Coastal Art. Groups	-	289, 708, 910, 914, 928	143, 531, 929
Coastal Art. Batteries	-	513, 503, 508, 515	507, 514
Railway batteries	-	686 (part), 688, 693, 695 (part)	686 (part), 691, 695 (part)

8 February (cont.)	I Corps	XXVIII Corps	XXXVIII Corps
Major Units	121 ID, 24 ID, 13 LFD	69 ID, 132 ID, 11 ID, 217 ID, 21 ID	212 ID, 1 LFD, 81 ID
Artillery Commander	*Arko* 123	*Arko* 24	*Arko* 30
Art. Rgt. Staff	-	-	785
Heavy Groups	850 (part)	153	633, 815, 850 (part)
Heavy batteries	626, 1 Batt. of the 680, 917 Sfl	-	-

24 February	III *Luftwaffe* Corps	L Corps	Group Hilpert LIV Corps + XXVI Corps
Major Units	9 LFD, 10 LFD	215 ID, 2 Br. SS, Blue Division, 4 SS Div., 212 ID, 24 ID	5 D Mount. Light, 1 ID, 223 ID, Remains of XXVI AC
Artillery Commander	-	*Arko* 18, *Arko* 138	H *Arko* 303, *Arko* 113,
Art. Rgt. Staff	-	110, 802, 610	49, 788, 818
Heavy Groups	-	II/84, I/814, II/814, 768, 856	II/*Lehr* 2, II/37, 854, 624, 641, 680 (part)
Heavy batteries	-	458, 459, 628, 629, 639, 744	-
Coastal Art. Groups	-	289, 708, 910, 914, 928	143, 531, 929
Coastal Art. Batteries	-	513, 503, 508, 515, 514	507
Railway batteries	-	686 (part), 688, 693, 695	686 (part), 691

24 February (cont.)	I Corps	XXVIII Corps	XXXVIII Corps
Major Units	227 ID, 13 LFD	69 ID, 121 ID, Gruppe Fehrenkampf[1], 12 LFD, 81 ID, 217 ID, 96 ID	23 ID, 1 LFD
Artillery Commander	Arko 123	Arko 24	Arko 30
Art. Rgt. Staff	-	-	785
Heavy Groups	850 (part)	153	633, 850 (part), 615, 815
Heavy batteries	626, 1 Batt. of 680, 917 Sfl	-	-
1) Tactical group with units drawn from various divisions.			

Appendix 7. List of names of artillery commanders, officers, NCOs and gunners who were cited as "Distinguished" in the fighting on 10 February 1943 in the Krasny Bor sector.

With a very similar title to the one heading this appendix there are in fact two documents which, when compared, show some significant differences. Although they are undated, one looks to be older than the other by a few days.

In terms of format, in the older version the "Highly Distinguished" men of all the artillery units are listed consecutively, followed by all the "Distinguished" gunners.

Another significant difference is that in the first list there are more men classified as "Highly Distinguished". In the second list most of them were downgraded to simply "Distinguished". There are only two cases of combatants who had been cited as "Distinguished" in the first list but were upgraded to "Highly Distinguished" in the second.

There are very few cases of men who appear in one list but not in the other. Some of these cases are striking. In the older list no mention is made of the commanding colonel of the regiment and yet there is a mention of a German interpreter. In the second list the German has disappeared and the colonel appears. There are one or two other very rare cases affecting other artillery units. But this situation occurs frequently in the case of the 13th Company of the 262nd Regiment, the infantry cannon company; in this unit the two lists vary greatly. For some reason the handling of this unit's data was chaotic, to the point that in the older list the name of the captain appears totally misspelled.

There are mistakes in the surnames and even in forenames, which I have tried to correct. When I have been unable to reach a conclusion as to which of the surnames is correct I have noted both possibilities.

The original lists were not in alphabetical order (not even within each unit). In my list I decided to order names alphabetically to make them easier to find.

In the two lists the units to which the men and officers belong are designated as follows:

- 13th Cannon Company of the 262nd Regiment. It appears in the documentation at the end of the lists for that regiment.
- Command of the 250th Artillery Regiment.
- I Group (including the 1st, 2nd and 3rd Batteries, plus the Staff Battery, but the lists do not differentiate between them).
- 9th Battery.
- 11th Battery.
- III Group (including the 7th, 8th and 12th Batteries and of course its own Staff Battery on the day of the Battle of Krasny Bor, but the lists only mention the group as a whole).
- IV Group (on 10 February 1943 it consisted of the 4th and 10th Batteries, the Hessen Battery and its Staff Battery, but the lists do not differentiate between them).
- Artillery Munitions Service.

However in this appendix in which the names are in alphabetical order, those classified as Highly Distinguished and Distinguished are mixed together regardless of their units and rank.

In the first column I have indicated the unit. Readers should bear in mind that it is the unit in which they were serving on the day of the battle. It may seem surprising, for example, to see a gunner known to be in the 12th Battery listed here in III Group. Under normal circumstances that battery belonged to IV Group, the "heavy" group, but on the day of the battle it was operating as part of III Group, in theory a "light" unit.

The second column shows the men's rank. Men (not officers) in the cannon company or munitions service are listed as "privates", while in artillery units they are listed as "gunners". All NCOs, officers and commanders belong to the artillery arm (even those in the cannon company or munitions). The master fitters and the artificers belong to what was known as CASE (Corps of Auxiliary Junior Army Officers).

After the names of the men there are two columns where we can see whether they appear in both lists (most do) or in only one. The column to the left corresponds to the older list.

In the last column a † sign indicates that the man in question was killed. These include those that are known to have died in the battle itself, those who died in the days after the battle from wounds received after having been evacuated, and those who were reported missing on that date but who were later assumed to be dead since nothing more was heard of them.

Unit	Rank	Surnames and forenames			
13th/262nd	Private	ABRUNEIRAS RIAL, José		D	
I/ 250th	Corporal	AGUADO MARTÍN, Pedro	HD	D	
III/250th	Gunner	AGUILAR LARA, Manuel	HD	D	
I/250th	Corporal	AGUIRRE BENGOA, Manuel (Forename: Miguel?)	D	D	†

Unit	Rank	Surnames and forenames			
11th/250th	Sergeant	AGUSTIN PALACIOS, Avelino	D	D	
IV/250th	Captain	AGUT MORALES, Severiano	HD	D	
I/250th	Gunner	ALBERT ALARCÓN, Juan	HD	D	
11th/250th	Gunner	ALCARAZ ESTEBAN, Vicente	D	D	
13th/262nd	Corporal	ALGARRA de CARLOS, Augusto	▓	D	
I/250th	Sergeant	ALONSO FERNÁNDEZ, José	HD	D	
13th/262nd	Sergeant	ALONSO GARCÍA, Manuel	▓	D	
I/250th	Gunner	ALONSO MANCHÓN, Demetrio	D	D	
III/250th	Gunner	ÁLVAREZ IGLESIAS, Luciano	HD	D	
13th/262nd	2nd Lieut.	ÁLVAREZ CONTI, Jorge	▓	D	
III/250th	Captain	ÁLVAREZ LASARTE, José Fernando	HD	HD	
9th/250th	Lieutenant	ÁLVAREZ MONTES, Manuel	HD	D	†
III/250th	Gunner	AMUNATEGUI ARROYO, Alejandro	D	D	
9th/250th	Captain	ANDRADA VANDERWILDE y BARRAUTE, José María	HD	HD	
I/250th	Captain	De ANDRÉS y ANDRÉS, Antonio	HD	HD	
13th/262nd	Private	ANDRÉS MARTÍNEZ, Álvaro	▓	D	
I/250th	2nd Lieut.	De ANDRÉS del CASTILLO, Eugenio	HD	D	
III/250th	Gunner	ARANDA SERRANO, Santiago	D	D	
III/250th	Gunner	ARDURA MOAR, Juan Antonio	HD	D	
I/250th	Lieutenant	ARENAS y de REINOSO, Pablo	HD	D	
III/250th	Lieutenant	ARGAMASILLA de la CERDA ELIO, Pedro Javier	D	D	
Munitions	Private	De ARMAS ACEBRERA, José (2nd surname: Cabrera?)	D	D	
III/250th	Gunner	ARRAZA ISOBA, Aquilino (1st surname: Obranza?)	HD	D	
11th/250th	Gunner	ARROYO FERNÁNDEZ, Miguel	D	D	
III/250th	Gunner	BAENA MENA, José	D	D	
250th	Colonel	BANDÍN DELGADO, Francisco	▓	D	
I/250th	Gunner	BARRAL LÓPEZ, Alfredo	D	D	
I/250th	Gunner	BARRÓN SÁNCHEZ, Gonzalo	HD	D	
III/250th	Sergeant	BEAMUD TROYANO, Alfonso	D	D	
11th/250th	Sergeant	BELLIDO de CASTRO, Pedro	HD	HD	
13th/262nd	Private	BELTRÁN MURO, Aurelio	▓	D	
I/250th	Corporal	BENITO GONZÁLEZ, Lesmes	D	D	
I/250th	Corporal	De BORBÓN y IRICH, Álvaro (2nd surname: Irión?)	HD	D	
11th/250th	Gunner	BOSCH ESCRIBANO, Pedro	D	D	

Unit	Rank	Surnames and forenames			
I/250th	Mast. Fitter	BUENO MINAYA, Manuel	HD	D	
III/250th	Sergeant	BUSTOS GIRALDEZ, Juan	HD	D	
I/250th	Captain	BUTLER PASTOR, Eduardo	HD	HD	
11th/250th	Corporal	CABANES QUINTANA, Gabriel	D	D	
III/250th	Sergeant	CABEZAS CORCHUELO, Manuel	HD	HD	
III/250th	Sergeant	CABRERA CABRERA, Ernesto	HD	D	
III/250th	Sergeant	CADARSO JIMENO, José	HD	D	
I/250th	Gunner	CALVO GONZÁLEZ, Moisés	HD	D	
III/250th	Gunner	CALVO MAESTRO, Manuel	HD	D	
IV/250th	Lieutenant	CAMPUZANO del HOYO, Juan Antonio	D	D	
11th/250th	Corporal	CANIVANO MARTÍN, Ángel	HD	D	
III/250th	Corporal	CANTERO LLOMPART, Silverio	HD	HD	
III/250th	Sergeant	CANTALLOPS SASTRE, Juan	HD	HD	
9th/250th	Gunner	CARBONELL GALLEGO, Luis	D	D	
III/250th	Lieutenant	CARDONA RODRÍGUEZ, Juan	D	D	
I/250th	Sergeant	CARNOTA RICO, Andrés	HD	D	
I/250th	Lieutenant	CARRETERO GIL, Máximo	HD	D	†
I/250th	Corporal	CASALOB ARANDA, Simeón (1st surname: Sasalot?)	D	D	
13th/262nd	Private	CASTRO, Venerando (2nd surname: ?)	D		
III/250th	Captain	CASTRO SANMARTÍN, Víctor María	HD	D	
I/250th	Sergeant	CAYÓN LOUDEIRO, Antonio	HD	HD	
I/250th	Sergeant	CHAO SANTAMARÍA, José	HD	D	
III/250th	Lieutenant	COLORADO y GUITIAN, Luis	HD	HD	
9th/250th	Corporal	CORNEJO CRIADO, Francisco	D	D	
III/250th	Gunner	CRUZ PÉREZ, Justo	HD	D	
I/250th	Sergeant	CUADRADO HERRERO, Cándido	D	D	
13th/262nd	Corporal	CUEVAS MATÉ, José		D	
III/250th	Gunner	DELARRA SALMÓN, Benjamín	HD	D	
I/250th	Gunner	DÍAZ MAJO, José	HD	D	
III/250th	Corporal	DÍAZ PALOMARES, Francisco	HD	D	
III/250th	Lieutenant	DOCAMPO PASCUAL, Emilio	D	D	
9th/250	Sergeant	DOPAZO BELTRÁN, Carlos	HD	HD	
13th/262nd	Sergeant	DURÁN RUIZ, Antonio	D		
I/250th	Gunner	ECHEVARRÍA MORENO, Antonio	HD	D	
III/250th	Gunner	ENGUIDANOS BUSTAMANTE, José	D	D	
III/250th	Sergeant	ENRÍQUEZ OTERO, Gerardo	HD	D	

Unit	Rank	Surnames and forenames			
III/250th	Gunner	ESCUDERO ESCOLAR, Máximo	HD	D	
I/250th	Sergeant	ESTEIRE PARDO, Moisés	HD	D	
III/250th	Gunner	EXPÓSITO FUENTES, Juan	D	D	
I/250th	Gunner	FARINAS ORTIZ, Manuel	D	D	
III/250th	Lieutenant	FARGE LÁZARO, Julio	D	D	
13th/262nd	Private	FERNÁNDEZ ENRIQUEZ, Antonio	D		
13th/262nd	Sergeant	FERNÁNDEZ GARCÍA, Florentino	D		
13th/262nd	Private	FERNÁNDEZ GONZÁLEZ, Manuel (Forename: Raimundo?)	D	D	
9th/250	Corporal	FERNÁNDEZ LÓPEZ, José	D	HD	
I/250th	Corporal	FERNÁNDEZ ORTIZ, Francisco	HD	HD	
9th/250th	Gunner	FERNÁNDEZ RIVERO, Arturo	D	D	
13th/262nd	Private	FERNÁNDEZ RODRÍGUEZ, Bautista	D	D	
I/250th	Gunner	FERNÁNDEZ RODRÍGUEZ, Manuel	HD	D	
9th/250	Gunner	FERNÁNDEZ RUIBAL, José Luis	HD	HD	†
III/250th	Lieutenant	FERRER GONZÁLEZ, Rafael	D	D	
11th/250th	Sergeant	FERRER OLIVER, Jerónimo	HD	HD	
13th/262nd	Sergeant	FLOGUERAS PÉREZ, Divino	D		
III/250th	Corporal	FUENTES LÓPEZ, Andrés	HD	D	
I/250th	Sergeant	FUERTES CASAS, Alfonso	D	D	
IV/250th	Sergeant	GABAS PRADES, Eusebio	D	D	
13th/262nd	Sergeant	GALERA SOLANO, Ramón		D	†
I/250th	Gunner	GALINDO GARCÍA, Julián	D	D	
9th/250th	Gunner	GARCÍA APARICIO, Rafael	D	D	
11th/250th	Gunner	GARCÍA BLANCO, Luciano	D	HD	
III/250th	Corporal	GARCÍA ESCUDERO, Vicente	HD	D	
13th/262nd	Corporal	GARCIA GACO, José		D	
13th/262nd	Private	GARCÍA GARCÍA, Antonio	D	D	
13th/262nd	Private	GARCIA GUTIÉRREZ, Félix		D	
9th/250	Sergeant	GARCÍA INFANTES, Antonio	D	HD	
I/250th	Gunner	GARCÍA PECES, Francisco	D	D	
III/250th	Corporal	GARCÍA ROCA, José	D	D	
I/250th	Corporal	GARCÍA RODRÍGUEZ, José María	HD	D	
I/250th	Sergeant	GARCÍA RUIZ, Julio	D	D	†
I/250th	Corporal	GARRIDO DOMÍNGUEZ, José (1st surname: Carrillo?)	D	D	
III/250th	Gunner	GARSO CARBONELL, Joaquín	HD	D	
III/250th	Lieutenant	GARZÓN LUIS, José	HD	D	

Unit	Rank	Surnames and forenames			
I/250th	Sergeant	GIL FERNÁNDEZ, Ángel	HD	D	†
13th/262nd	Corporal	GIL JIMÉNEZ, Ángel		D	
III/250th	Gunner	GIL LÓPEZ, Manuel	HD	D	
I/250th	Gunner	GIL MELIAN, Ildefonso	D	D	
I/250th	Sergeant	GIL PÉREZ, Gregorio	HD	D	
I/250th	Gunner	GOICOA MELÉNDEZ, Raúl María	HD	D	†
13th/262nd	Captain	GOMEZ DIEZ MIRANDA, José Luis	HD	HD	†
IIth/250th	Gunner	GÓMEZ del RIO, Maximiliano	D	D	
I/250th	Sergeant	GÓMEZ RUBIO, José	D	D	
III/250th	Gunner	GÓMEZ SANTOS, José	HD	D	
I/250th	Lieutenant	GÓMEZ TRENOR FOS, Enrique	HD	D	
III/250th	Sergeant	GONZÁLEZ ARTILES, Sebastián	D	D	
I/250th	Gunner	GONZÁLEZ CUERDA, Fructuoso	D	D	
I/250th	Gunner	GONZÁLEZ GARCÍA, Alberto	D	D	
13th/262nd	Sergeant	GONZÁLEZ PERERA, José		D	
III/250th	Gunner	GONZÁLEZ SALVADOR, Antonio	D	D	
Reg.250th	Interpreter	GOTTMANN, Helmut	HD		
I/250th	Lieutenant	GUTIÉRREZ de SALAMANCA y OSSUNA, Guillermo	HD	D	
13th/262nd	Private	GUZMAN CARRERO, Agustín	HD	D	
III/250th	Lieutenant	HERNÁNDEZ MIRANDA, Fernando	HD	D	†
III/250th	Gunner	HERNÁNDEZ MONTÓN, Luis	D	D	
I/250th	Gunner	HERNÁNDEZ PULIDO, Cándido	D	D	
III/250th	Gunner	HERNÁNDEZ RODRÍGUEZ, Modesto	HD	D	
IIth/250th	Lieutenant	HERNANZ BLANCO, Guillermo	HD	D	†
IV/250th	Corporal	HERRANZ ARRIBAS, Daciano	D	D	
I/250th	Gunner	HERRERA MUÑOZ, Manuel	HD	D	
I/250th	Corporal	HIGUERAS ARMERO, Vicente	HD	D	†
IV/250th	Lieutenant	IBAIBARRIAGA SUSO, Jesús	HD	D	
III/250th	Gunner	IGLESIAS ROLDÁN, Pedro Ángel	HD	D	
13th/262nd	Lieutenant	ITURZAETA GARCÍA ORTEGA, Luis		D	
III/250th	Gunner	IZQUIERDA MÁLAGA, Félix	HD	HD	
III/250th	Gunner	JIMÉNEZ CASTELLANOS, Jesús	D	D	
I/250th	Sergeant	JIMÉNEZ JIMÉNEZ, Emiliano	D	D	†
I/250th	Gunner	JIMÉNEZ NIEVA, Atilano	D	D	
I/250th	Gunner	JIMÉNEZ SANZ, Heraclio	HD	D	
I/250th	Sergeant	JOVER ROCA, Ángel	HD	HD	

Unit	Rank	Surnames and forenames			
I/250th	Corporal	JUAN MARÍN, Juan	D	D	
13th/262nd	Corporal	LARRATEGUI AYEZ, Pio	HD	D	
I/250th	Gunner	LAZAGA SABATER, Pedro	D	D	
III/250th	Gunner	LAZCANOTEGUI YANCES, Fermín	HD	D	
III/250th	Gunner	LIGHT JIMÉNEZ, Miguel	HD	D	
IV/250th	Lieutenant	LISSARRAGUE NOVOA, José María	D	D	
13th/262nd	Private	LISTA HERRANZ, Antonio		D	
I/250th	Corporal	LLANOS ALONSO, Julio	HD	D	
9th/250th	Sergeant	LLOMPART PERELLÓ, Nadal	HD	HD	†
I/250th	Gunner	LLUCH PASCUAL, Francisco	D	D	
IIth/250th	Captain	LÓPEZ ALARCIA, Manuel	HD	HD	
III/250th	Gunner	LÓPEZ ÁLVAREZ, Manuel	D	D	
I/250th	Gunner	LÓPEZ CAÑAVAL, Ernesto José	HD	HD	
III/250th	Corporal	LÓPEZ DELGADO, Zacarías	HD	D	
9th/250th	Gunner	LÓPEZ GONZÁLEZ, Elías	D	D	
IV/250th	Lieutenant	LÓPEZ ORIVE, José Luis	D	D	
9th/250th	Gunner	LÓPEZ PORRIÑO, Modesto	D	D	†
I/250th	Corporal	LÓPEZ RAVELO, Tomás	HD	D	
I/250th	Corporal	LÓPEZ SÁEZ, Juan	HD	HD	
I/250th	Gunner	LÓPEZ TERCERO, Manuel	HD	HD	
13th/262nd	Private	LÓPEZ TOMÁS, Pedro		D	†
III/250th	Gunner	LOZA MONTAÑÉS, Salvador	HD	D	
I/250th	Gunner	de LUCAS LÓPEZ, Modesto	HD	D	
I/250th	Sergeant	MAGARZO SANCHEZ, José	HD	HD	
13th/262nd	Private	MAGDALENA SANTIAGO, Luis		D	
III/250th	Corporal	MANUEL de VILLENA, Cosme	HD	D	
Munitions	Private	MAROTO RODRÍGUEZ, José	D	D	
IIth/250th	Corporal	MÁRQUEZ GARCÍA, Manuel	D	D	
III/250th	Gunner	MARTÍN de la CHICA, Cándido	D	D	
III/250th	Sergeant	MARTÍN del RÍO, Miguel	D	D	
III/250th	Corporal	MARTÍN SUÁREZ, Santiago	HD	HD	
IIth/250th	Mast. Fitter	MARTÍNEZ OSANTE, Ramiro	D	D	
I/250th	Lieutenant	MARTÍNEZ VIAMONTE, Mariano	HD	D	
13th/262nd	Private	MASCUNAN LUCAS, Tarsicio		D	
I/250th	Captain	MATEOS DEL CORRAL, Alejandro	HD	D	
III/250th	Gunner	MEDIAN de la FE, Emilio	HD	HD	
I/250th	Sergeant	MEDINA VÁZQUEZ, Isaac	HD	D	

Unit	Rank	Surnames and forenames			
13th/262nd	Corporal	MESA DOMINGO, Jaime		D	
I/250th	Lieutenant	MICHELENA CASTAÑEDA, José María	HD	D	
I/250th	Sergeant	MIRAMBEL ESBRI, Carlos	HD	D	
I/250th	Corporal	MONTERO ALBERT, José	D	D	
IV/250th	Sergeant	MONTERO GARCÍA, Emilio	D	D	
13th/262nd	Lieutenant	MONTOJO y MARTÍNEZ de HERVAS Ramón		D	
III/250th	Captain	MORENO AZNAR, Salvador	D	D	
11th/250th	Gunner	MORENO de la MONTAÑA, Francisco	D	HD	
III/250th	Captain	MUÑOZ ACERA, Fernando	D	D	
III/250th	Mast. Fitter	MUÑOZ BARRANCO, Alfonso	HD	D	
11th/250th	Sergeant	MUÑOZ MARTÍNEZ, Santos	D	D	
III/250th	Gunner	MURILLO MARTÍNEZ, Jacinto	D	D	
11th/250th	Lieutenant	MURO DURÁN, César	HD	D	
III/250th	Lieutenant	OCAÑA FÁBREGAS, Salvador	D	D	
Munitions	Sergeant	ORTEGA PÉREZ, José	D	D	
9th/250th	Gunner	ORTIZ VINADO, Manuel	D	D	
I/250th	Gunner	OSSORIO VALVERDE, Eugenio	D	D	
I/250th	Sergeant	OTERO GÓMEZ, Fidel	D	D	
III/250th	Gunner	OTERO GONZÁLEZ, Antonio	D	D	
I/250th	Sergeant	PACHECO MARTÍN, Esteban	HD	HD	
I/250th	Sergeant	PAN FERNÁNDEZ, Nicasio	HD	HD	
11th/250th	Gunner	PARRA LEÓN, Julián	D	D	
III/250th	Corporal	PASTOR VILLALOBOS, Benito	HD	D	
I/250th	Gunner	PEDRAZA PEDRAZA, Julio	HD	D	
9th/250th	Corporal	PÉREZ ALAYÓN, Juan José	D	D	
I/250th	Corporal	PÉREZ GÓMEZ, Justino	D	D	†
I/250th	Gunner	PÉREZ MEDIAALDEA, Antonio	HD	D	
11th/250th	Gunner	PÉREZ RUIZ, Guillermo	D	D	
IV/250th	2nd Lieut.	PITA ÁLVAREZ, Luis	D	D	
I/250th	Gunner	PLA MATAIX, Primitivo	HD	D	
9th/250	Gunner	PRIEGO RUIZ, Lázaro	D	HD	
I/250th	Sergeant	PRIETO PUERTAS, Vicente	D	D	
13th/262nd	Private	PULIDO DOBLADO, Antonio		D	
III/250th	Gunner	QUEVEDO FERNÁNDEZ, Manuel	HD	D	
I/250th	Gunner	QUINTO FERREIRO, Modesto	HD	D	
I/250th	Gunner	RAMOS PÉREZ, Rafael	HD	D	

Unit	Rank	Surnames and forenames			
III/250th	Gunner	RASTRERO GONZÁLEZ, José	D	D	
I/250th	Major	REINLEIN CALZADA, Guillermo	HD	HD	
I/250th	Lieutenant	RETENAGA VALERDI, Gregorio	HD	D	
III/250th	Gunner	del RIO CORRAL, Rafael	HD	D	
I/250th	Gunner	RIVERA ZAMBRANO, Juan (2nd surname: Manzano?)	HD	D	
13th/262nd	Sergeant	RODRIGUEZ MENENDEZ, Fernando	HD	HD	
IV/250th	Corporal	RODRÍGUEZ RODRÍGUEZ, Sebastián	D	D	
Munitions	Artificer	ROMERO GANGA, Enrique	D	D	
13th/262nd	Sergeant	ROMO GÓMEZ, Calixto		D	
III/250th	Sergeant	RUEDA PÉREZ, Rafael	HD	D	
I/250th	Sergeant	RUIZ GARCÍA, Gabino	D	D	
13th/262nd	Corporal	SALMERÓN RUIZ, José		D	
IIth/250th	Gunner	SÁNCHEZ BRUNETE, Claudio	D	D	
III/250th	Gunner	SÁNCHEZ CARDONA, Avelino	D	D	
I/250th	Lieutenant	SÁNCHEZ DOMINGO, José Luis		D	
III/250th	Sergeant	SÁNCHEZ de la NAVA, Luis	HD	D	
I/250th	Gunner	SÁNCHEZ PARDO, Francisco	HD	D	
13th/262nd	Corporal	SANTAELLA CRUZ, Agustín		D	†
IV/250th	Corporal	SANTIAGO HERNÁNDEZ, Jesús	D	D	
Reg.250	Lieut. Col.	SANTOS ASCARZA, José	HD	HD	†
I/250th	Sergeant	SANZ RODRÍGUEZ, Julio		D	†
13th/262nd	Corporal	SAVIN RODRIGUEZ, Albino		D	
I/250th	Gunner	SENEN AMORÓS, Vicente	D	D	
IIth/250th	Gunner	SENAO GÉNOVA, Teodoro	D	D	
9th/250th	Lieutenant	SIEIRO VILAR, Manuel	HD	D	
Munitions	Private	SIÓN GONZÁLEZ, Alfonso	D	D	
III/250th	Gunner	SUÁREZ ÁLVAREZ, José Antonio	HD	D	
III/250th	Gunner	SUÁREZ FERNÁNDEZ, Jesús	D	D	
I/250th	Gunner	SUÁREZ FERNÁNDEZ, José	D	D	
9th/250	Corporal	SUÁREZ GÓMEZ, Domingo	D	HD	
III/250th	Corporal	SUÁREZ MORENO, Julio (1st surname: Juárez?)	HD	D	
I/250th	Gunner	SUÁREZ PÉREZ, Santiago	HD	D	
13th/262nd	Private	TABARES PERERA, Juan (1st surname: Ybares?)	HD	D	
IIth/250th	Gunner	TENA SERRANO, Valero	D	HD	
I/250th	Lieutenant	TORRES TORRES, Justo	HD	D	

Unit	Rank	Surnames and forenames			
I/250th	Sergeant	TOSAR CANDO, José	D	D	
13th/262nd	Sergeant	TRANCHE PROENZA, Pedro		D	
I/250th	Gunner	TULLENQUE PUCH, Alfredo	HD	D	
III/250th	Corporal	TUÑÓN MARIANO, Remigio	HD	D	
13th/262nd	Private	VALDIVIA FLORES, Antonio	D	D	
9th/250th	Lieutenant	VALENZUELA PERALTA, Manuel	HD	D	
I/250th	Gunner	VALLÉS VALLÉS, José	HD	D	
13th/262nd	Private	VALMASEDA PORTU, José Luis		D	...
III/250th	Chaplain	VARGAS BLANCO, Marcelo	D	D	
IV/250th	Major	VÁZQUEZ GOLDARAZ, Camilo	HD	D	
13th/262nd	Corporal	VAZQUEZ REVUELTA, Antonio	D		
Munitions	Lieutenant	De La Vega VIGUERA, Enrique	HD	D	
I/250th	Corporal	VELASCO MÉNDEZ, Isidoro	D	HD	
I/250th	Corporal	VÉLEZ TABARRA, Armando	D	D	
III/250th	Gunner	VERACIERTO SORONDO, José Luis (1st surname: Beracierto?; 2nd surname: Seraudo? Lorondo?)	HD	D	†
I/250th	Corporal	VICUÑA BARRÓN, Heraclio	HD	HD	
I/250th	Gunner	VIDAL GARCÍA, Eduardo	HD	D	
III/250th	Gunner	VIDAL RODRÍGUEZ, Pedro	D	D	
III/250th	Med. Lieut.	VILLABASO MURGA, Manuel	D	D	
III/250th	Corporal	VILLAGRAS ZALLAS, Simeón	HD	D	
IV/250th	Captain	VILLALOBOS VENTURA, Antonio	HD	D	
I/250th	Gunner	VILLANUEVA MERCADAL, Domingo	HD	HD	(I)
I/250th	Lieutenant	VILLAREAL MIRANDA, Luis Enrique	HD	D	
III/250th	Gunner	VILLENA VERA, Emilio	HD	D	
I/250th	Gunner	ZAYAS GARCÍA, Manuel		D	

I) In the list of Blue Division casualties I Group gunner, Domingo Villanueva Rodríguez, figures as missing at the Battle of Krasny Bor. Given the frequent transcription errors in names and surnames, it is possible that he and the man listed are one and the same person.

Appendix 8. German tactical symbols applicable to the artillery.

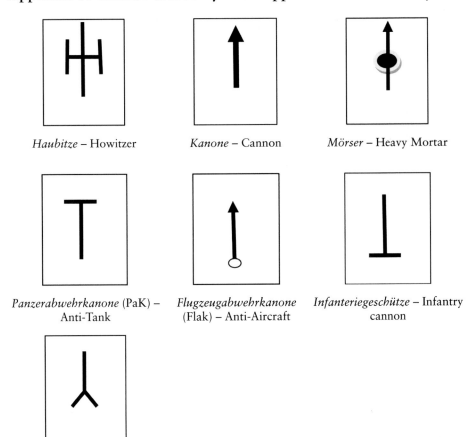

Haubitze – Howitzer   *Kanone* – Cannon   *Mörser* – Heavy Mortar

Panzerabwehrkanone (PaK) –   *Flugzeugabwehrkanone*   *Infanteriegeschütze* – Infantry
Anti-Tank   (Flak) – Anti-Aircraft   cannon

Werfer - Rocket launchers

The tactical symbols used for the command echelons are as follows:

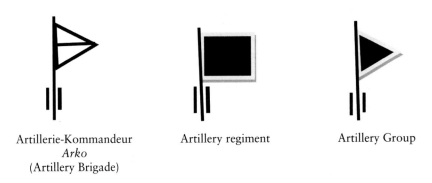

Artillerie-Kommandeur   Artillery regiment   Artillery Group
Arko
(Artillery Brigade)

We first need to know the symbols used to identify the type of weapon employed by the batteries/companies.

These basic symbols were combined with others to indicate degrees of mobility. Starting from the premise that the vast majority of artillery units were horse-drawn, symbols were used to identify which were motorized and which were static (such as the coastal artillery units mentioned in this book). A special symbol was used to indicate tracked artillery pieces.

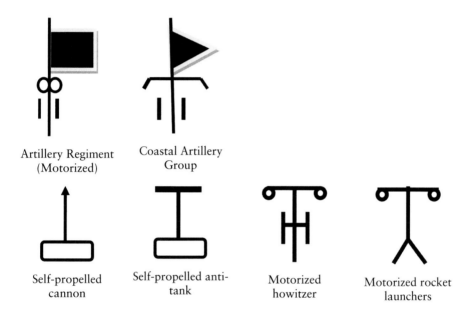

Artillery Regiment (Motorized)

Coastal Artillery Group

Self-propelled cannon

Self-propelled anti-tank

Motorized howitzer

Motorized rocket launchers

Numbers and letters were added to the above symbols.

Some served to identify the regiment, group or battery. Normally they were numbers; less frequently names. They were placed to the bottom right of the symbol in the case of regiments and groups, and to the top right in the case of batteries.

Continuing with batteries, other numbers identified the calibre. These were placed to the bottom left of the symbol. If the gun was not German, a letter indicating its origin (f for French: etc.) was placed opposite (bottom right). If the gun was rail-mounted this was indicated by an upper case E, also bottom right.

The observation groups had the initials "Bb" (for *Beobachtung*) before their identification number.

250th Artillery Regiment

693rd Railway Battery with French 40 cm guns

If batteries were operating within a regiment, only the number indicating which one it was in the regimental sequence appeared. This was also the case for independent groups rather than regiments. But if a battery was attached to a unit other than its own, the full designation would be shown, with the number of the battery and the number of the regiment or independent group separated by a slash.

Finally, other numbers might appear above and below. A number above (should there be one) indicated maximum range. A number below indicated the number of operational guns in the unit. There could be up to two numbers, one on top of the other. The uppermost number indicated the theoretical complement and the lower number the actual guns present.

Finally, with reference to batteries not using artillery pieces:

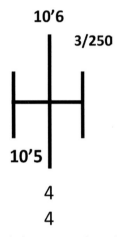

The symbols represent the 3rd Battery of the 250th Artillery Regiment, a horse-drawn unit equipped with four 10.5 cm *Feldhaubitze*, all operational and with a range of 10.6 km.

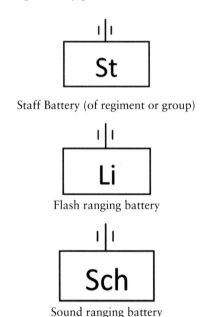

Staff Battery (of regiment or group)

Flash ranging battery

Sound ranging battery

Appendix 9. L Corps infantry as at 20 February 1943. Battalion strengths.

WESTERN SECTOR			
215th INFANTRY DIVISION			
Units deployed on the front line			
Organic units		Attached units	
Battalion I / 380th Reg.	317	303 *Kanonier Bataillon*[1]	220
Battalion III / 280th	321	24th *Shutzmannschaft Bataillon* (Latvian)[2]	368
Battalion I / 435th	329		
Battalion III / 435th	289		
Alarm Bataillon[3]	248		
Total men deployed on the front line			2,092
Divisional reserve		215th Cycle Squadron[4]	97
2nd SS INFANTRY BRIGADE			
Units deployed on the front line			
Battalion II / 16th Police Reg.[5]			278
Battalion III / 16th Police + 7th Company Dutch Legion			223
Battalion Neufeldt[6] + 3rd Company Dutch Legion			216
Battalion I / Dutch Legion + Brigade Ski Company			278
Battalion III / Dutch Legion			232
Norwegian Legion			383
Total men deployed on the front line			1,610
Divisional reserve		8th Company Dutch Legion	80
		16th *Shutzmannschaft Bataillon* (Latvian) Receiving equipment	376

1. This *Kanonier Bataillon* had been formed with men from artillery units under the direct orders of *Höherer Artillerie-Kommandeur 303*, specifically from the heavy units deployed to rear of the 215th Division.
2. The *Schutzmannschaft Bataillone* were battalions recruited from the local populace of territories occupied by the Soviet Union, and created by the German Police to take on security duties in the rear. The best, the battalions formed with men from Baltic countries, were sometimes used on the front line.
3. These *Alarm Bataillone* were created to use men taken out of second line divisional units (transport, logistic, medical, etc.) on the front line.
4. Exploration units were almost always listed as cycle units. In many cases in organization and strength they were effectively companies, but following the cavalry tradition they were called squadrons.
5. These German Police Regiments had been created for security duties in the rear.
6. This unit was an *Alarm Bataillon*.

CENTRAL SECTOR		
250th INFANTRY DIVISION (BLUE DIVISION)		
Units deployed on the front line		
Ad hoc units deployed on the Izhora		500 (approx.)
Battalion III / 262nd		367
Battalion II / 263rd		561
Battalion III / 263rd		570
Battalion I / 269th		527
Battalion III / 269th		524
Total men deployed on the front line		3,049
Divisional reserve	250th Sappers Battalion	200 (approx.)
	One infantry battalion receiving equipment	600 (approx.)
212th INFANTRY DIVISION		
Units deployed on the front line		

Organic units		Attached units	
Battalion II / 316th	155	Battalion II / 390th[1]	233
Battalion III / 316th	307	658th Ost Bataillon (Estonian)[2]	301
212th Schnell Abteilung[3]	238	659th Ost Bataillon (Estonian)	274
Total men deployed on the front line			1,508
Divisional reserve		III / 390th	57

ARMY CORPS RESERVE IN THE CENTRAL SECTOR	
Flemish Legion (less its 3rd Company)	251

1. The 390th Regiment belonged organically to the 215th Division.
2. The German Army had created the *Ost Bataillone* by recruiting men born in the Soviet Union to carry out security duties in the rear, in a manner similar to the *Schutzmannschaft Bataillone* created by the German Police. Also in this case the best men were those recruited in the Baltic countries and so they were sometimes used on the front line.
3. Many German divisions had grouped their two most highly motorized units, the Exploration Group and the Anti-Tank Group, into these so-called fast battalions when both had lost a large percentage of their strength.

EASTERN SECTOR			
24th INFANTRY DIVISION			
Units deployed on the front line			
Organic units		Attached units	
Battalion II / 31st	189	Battalion I / 44th[1]	110
Battalion II / 32nd	294	Battalion II / 44th	336
Battalion I / 102nd	66	Sapper School Battalion of Kamenka[2]	268
Battalion II / 102nd	105		
24th Cycle Group	206		
Total men deployed on the front line			1,574
Divisional reserve		Kanonier Kompanie 138[3]	45
4th SS-POLICE DIVISION OF INFANTRY			
Units deployed on the front line			
Organic units		Attached units	
Battalion III / 1st SS Police Reg.[4]	363	Battalion III / 31st[5]	197
Battalion I / 2nd SS Police Reg.	255	13th Company of the 100th Light Infantry Reg.[6]	75
Battalion III / 2nd SS Police Reg.	307		
Battalion III / 3rd SS Police Reg.	275		
4th Cycle Group SS	305		
Verfüngen Bataillon[7]	210		
Total men deployed on the front line			1,987
Divisional reserve		Alarm Kompanie	120
ARMY CORPS RESERVE IN THE EASTERN SECTOR			
Battalion III / 32nd			319

1. The 44th Regiment belonged organically to the 11th Infantry Division.
2. Instruction unit where men from all divisions of the 18th Army received training in anti-tank warfare. At times of crisis these types of units were used on the front line.
3. This was a unit of gunners used as infantry under the orders of *Arko 138*.
4. These SS Police Regiments were different from ordinary Police Regiments in that they had been conceived from the outset as front line combat units. Like all *Waffen SS* forces they were considered to be elite troops. After the reorganization of the division, these regiments would be redesignated as SS Infantry Regiments and numbered accordingly.
5. The 31st Regiment belonged organically to the 24th Division.
6. This unit belonged organically to the neighbouring 5th Mountain Light Infantry Division. Despite it being number 13, it was not a cannon company (as would have been the case if it had belonged to an infantry regiment), since Mountain Light Infantry battalions had five companies each, and therefore number 13 was an infantry company.
7. *Verfügung Bataillon* (Standby Battalion): another name for an *Alarm Bataillon*.

Endnotes

I. Introduction: The Overlooked Protagonists

1. CABALLERO JURADO, Carlos. *Morir en Rusia. La División Azul en la Batalla de Krasny Bor*. Quirón Ediciones, Valladolid, 2004. In later articles I made some additions to this original text: CABALLERO JURADO, Carlos. *10 de Febrero de 1943. La Batalla de Krasny Bor*; and CABALLERO JURADO, Carlos - TORRES GALLEGO, Gregorio. *La Artillería de la División Azul*: both are in *Aportes. Revista de Historia Contemporánea*, no. 61, year XXI, 2/2006, pages 51-85 and 147-173 respectively.

2. These are documents relating to Army Group North, the 18th Army, and L Corps (the three tiers of command to which the Blue Division was subordinate), among which are documents corresponding to the dates on which the battle was fought. German military documents were microfilmed by the US National Archives onto a huge collection of microfilm rolls. The ones used in this study were: roll T-311-56, containing the *Kriegstagebuch* (War Diary) of Army Group North between 1 and 28 February 1943; rolls T-312-856 and T-312-859, with the War Diary and other documents of the 18th Army; and rolls T-314-1235 and T-314 1239 with the War Diary and other documents of L Corps.

3. FONTENLA BALLESTA, Salvador. *Los combates de Krasny Bor*. Actas Editorial, Madrid, 2012.

4. See CABALLERO, C; FERNANDEZ NAVARRO DE LOS PAÑOS, L; GONZALEZ, O; SAGARRA, P; *La victoria de Krasny Bor. El ejército español humilla a Stalin*. Galland Books, Valladolid, 2013.

5. The first two will be quoted when we call on the testimony of these officers regarding the battle. Published a long time ago, they are now very hard to find on the market, which is why I have made use of long passages. This is not the case of the third, which I encourage you to buy and read: BLANCH SABENCH, José María. *Memorias de un soldado de la División Azul*. Galland Books, Valladolid, 2010.

6. ESPINOSA POVEDA, Arturo. *Artillero 2º en la Gloriosa División Azul*. Fundación División Azul, Madrid, 1992. See page 543.

7. MANRIQUE GARCÍA, José María. *Los cañones de la División Azul*. From the series *Estela. Monografías de Historia Militar de España. La División Azul (1941-1944)* Volume II: Published by Fajardo el Bravo, Lorca, 2013.

8. FONTENLA BALLESTA, Salvador. *Krasny Bor: el último reducto de la defensa. Las Memorias de Manuel Rodríguez Campano (9ª Batería)*. From the series *Estela. Monografías de Historia Militar de España. La División Azul (1941-1944)* Volume III: Published by Fajardo el Bravo, Lorca, 2014.

9. The *Archivo Militar General de Ávila* (AGMAV – Avila General Military Archive) houses the document collections relating to the Blue Division. According to its catalogue of documents, there was one entitled *Diario de Operaciones del Regimiento de Artillería 250* (War Diary of the 250th Artillery Regiment), for the period January to June 1943. But in fact it was a case of miscataloguing, since it was not the diary of the regiment but only of its II Group. This is just one of the examples which I might mention to evidence the limitations from which we still suffer with respect to documentation. New documents may appear, but this book has had to be written with the documentation currently available.

10. *Archivo Fundación División Azul. Carpeta I - Instrucciones División Azul* (Blue Division Foundation Archive. Folder 1 – Blue Division Instructions).

11. All instructions are also from the *Archivo Fundación División Azul. Carpeta I - Instrucciones División Azul*. Those in the first 1,000 series began to be issued when the Blue Division was already on German soil. Those of the 3,000 series were issued by the 3rd Section (Operations) of the Staff. Those of the 4,000 series were issued by the 4th Section - Services.

II. The Siege of Leningrad: Two Artilleries, Head to Head

1. Fortunately, Spanish readers now have access in their own language to an excellent general work on German artillery (previously readers had to consult works in other languages): VÁZQUEZ GARCÍA, Juan. *Artillería Alemana en la Segunda Guerra Mundial*. Ed. Tikal (from the collection: *La Máquina de Guerra de Hitler*), Madrid, 2013. The classic book on the subject is *German Artillery of World War Two* by HOGG, Ian V, Greenhill Books, London, 1997.

2. For example: PARDO MARTÍNEZ, Serafín. *Un año en la División Azul*. AF Editores, Valladolid, 2005. See pages 120-121.

3. Several German guns used in the Second World War were identified as "Model 18", a ruse to suggest that they had been developed in 1918, before the Treaty of Versailles (signed in 1919) had come into force. This treaty prohibited the Germans from developing their own artillery pieces.

4. CABALLERO JURADO, Carlos. *División Azul. Estructura de una fuerza de combate*. Galland Books, Valladolid, 2009. For artillery, see pages 61 and ff.

5. During a number of months in late 1941 and early 1942 at the Volkhov the 250th Artillery Regiment of the Blue Division created two of these batteries from materiel provided by the Germans, numbering them 13th and 14th in the regiment's organization chart. They were equipped with French 155 mm guns. Later both these guns would be passed on to the neighbouring German 126th Division.

6. The Germans use centimetres to express the calibre of guns, but in Spain they use millimetres; in this book we shall follow the Spanish tradition, except when referring to guns by their German designations.

7. Readers will find the criteria used by the Germans to classify the various types of guns in Appendix 1 of this book.

8. ENGELMANN, Joachim. *German Heavy Field Artillery in World War II.* Schiffer Military/Aviation History, Atglen (PA), 1995.

9. The information on the Order of Battle of the artillery units of the 18th Army was compiled on the basis of information provided on websites. For information relative to 22 June 1941 and 28 June 1942 the source was http://niehorster.orbat.com/011_germany/__ge_index.htm. For information relative to 1 January 1943 the source was http://www.lexikon-der-wehrmacht.de/.

10. It is extremely rare for these units to be mentioned in works on artillery. A notable exception is ENGELMANN, Joachim. *German Artillery in World War II, 1939-1945.* Schiffer Military/Aviation History, Atglen (PA), 1995.

11. When referring to Soviet artillery I have relied on an expert of the calibre of Zaloga. ZALOGA, Steven J. and NESS, Leland S. *Red Army Handbook, 1939-1945.* Sutton Publishing, Phoenix Mill (Gloucestershire), 1998.

III. The Two Blue Division Artillery Regiments

1. In my case, the mistakes I made referred to the 13th and 14th Batteries. Both had existed at the Volkhov front and, although now bereft of guns, there was reliable evidence that, as such, they had left the Volkhov front bound for Leningrad. On this front, there was evidence – also reliable – that the Spanish had 155 mm and 220 mm guns, and so I assumed that they formed part of the aforementioned batteries which I now know to have actually been dissolved as soon as the Blue Division reached Leningrad.

2. German Tables of Organization and Orders of Battle used very different tactical symbols from those commonly used in present day armies. See Appendix 7 for further information.

3. A comparative analysis of the two documents, the Table of Organization and Equipment and the Order of Battle, allows us to make some clarifications. In the TOE, one of the German Groups deployed in the Blue Division sector, the 768th, is said to have four batteries, when only two of them were actually deployed in the Spanish sector at that time.

4. For the purpose of comparison the main technical characteristics of these and other field artillery pieces mentioned in this book are set out in Appendix 1.

5. Among the authors who have provided some information, albeit vague, about this unit, is DIAZ DE VILLEGAS, José. *La División Azul en línea.* Acervo, Barcelona, 1967.

6. Daniel Burguete has documentary evidence that in August 1942 – when the Blue Division arrived at the Leningrad sector – this captain moved from II Group to command the Hessen Battery. But this is the only available information. We can surmise that the captain commanded the battery until his repatriation in July 1943, since there is no documentation suggesting that

he took up any other command. We are so far unaware of who took over from him at II Group.

7. The 814th Heavy Artillery Group had been created in March 1940 with four batteries. Just one month later it was split into the I/814th and II/814th Heavy Groups. Only the former was operational when the Western Campaign began, but as it proved unnecessary to attack the Maginot Line its role was unimportant. Both groups were sent to the Russian Front once the campaign against the USSR began. Their most noteworthy action had been during the Siege of Sevastopol. From there they had been transferred to the Leningrad Front. Due to depletion of materiel all operational guns were grouped into I/814th, leaving the men of II/814th gunless. However, by February 1943 the re-equipment of the two groups was in progress, during which the number of batteries increased from two to three.

8. The 215th was a division created just before the Second World War started. In December 1940 IV Group (the heavy one) of its artillery regiment had been transferred to a division in the process of being formed, and had not been reconstituted since the latter was a garrison division in France. When it was sent to the Russian Front in November 1941, a heavy group was attached taken from the 225th Division (IV/225th), not its own division. It was not until well into 1943 that this group was renamed the IV/215th.

9. The SS brigades were created to perform security duties in the rear of the Russian Front. When its men were sent to the front line, the German troops were incorporated into regular SS divisions. But the 2nd SS Brigade was kept to incorporate various "National Legions" of European volunteers serving in the *Waffen SS* which were at less than division strength, such as the Norwegian, Dutch, and Flemish Belgian. At the time there were also battalions of volunteers from Latvia. Due to having this non-standard structure, it had no artillery units of its own.

10. Two batteries of this Group II/215th were attached to the German forces deployed in front of the Oranienbaum bridgehead.

11. This coastal artillery group had been created in May 1941 with guns captured in Czechoslovakia, initially for use on the Baltic coast. As we have explained, several units of this type were attached to the 18th Army as early as June 1941, as is the case of this group, which was sent to the Leningrad Front as soon as the city was encircled.

12. The I/84th and II/84th heavy groups had initially been equipped with Czech 24 cm *Kanone*. Both took part in the Western Campaign and had for some time been used for coastal defence duties in France. For Operation Barbarossa they were assigned to Army Group North. In 1942 I/84th was sent to Army Group South and II/84th was re-equipped. Two of its batteries received 17 cm cannons and the other received a mixture of equipment; 10.5 cm cannons and some very eye-catching French 194 mm self-propelled guns, relics from the First World War.

13. The 708th Coastal Artillery Group had been created in August 1941 to be deployed on the Baltic coast. It was eventually used in the siege of Leningrad.

Its original complement of captured French guns was augmented by Czech and Russian pieces. Its batteries had an abnormally high number of cannons; in January 1943 it could field 22 operational guns.

14. Created in 1940, it was originally equipped with 210 mm guns and later grew from two batteries to four. Like all other heavy groups it was a motorized unit. While it started the Russian campaign with Army Group Centre, by August 1941 it had been transferred to Army Group North. Shortly after arriving at Leningrad it would take part in one of the most remarkable artillery duels in the area, in which it engaged the batteries of the Soviet heavy cruiser "*Petropavlovsk*" (which had previously belonged to the *Kriegsmarine* with the name "*Lützow*", but was sold to the Soviet navy under the terms of the Germano-Soviet Pact). The ship was put out of action, although the fact that it was anchored in the Port of Leningrad saved it from sinking entirely.

15. Created in April 1941 with Czech 105 mm guns to be deployed on the Baltic, it would finally be sent to the Leningrad Front. Like the group mentioned in the previous footnote, in 1942 it had joined the 18th Army.

16. In some cases, even in German documentation, it is incorrectly designated as II/289th or I/289th. The Army's 289th Coastal Artillery Group had been created in September 1941 and equipped with captured French 155 mm guns to serve on the Baltic. But it would be sent to the Leningrad Front where it was used as a land battery in 1942 and 1943, before being transferred to the Lake Ilmen area. In September 1943 it dropped the "Coastal" part of its name, as happened to all the units of this type serving with Army Group North.

17. There were already divisions whose artillery complements had fewer groups and/or fewer guns in each battery.

18. *Artillery is never held in reserve* gunners claim with pride. It is true that, while infantry tactics require a certain number of units always to be kept back from the fighting so they can join it when the time is ripe, artillery units are always "on duty". If the guns of these batteries were not used it was because they were not fit for the purpose at hand; they were too heavy and bulky. They were held back in reserve for when the assault on Leningrad was launched, when it was hoped that the *Luftwaffe* would have air superiority. Under "normal" conditions, deploying them near the front would have been too risky, because they could have been destroyed by counterbattery fire or enemy aircraft.

19. What the Spanish call artillery groups are known by the Germans as *Abteilungen;* the designation *Gruppe* in German artillery corresponds to what in Spanish is called an *agrupación* (translated into English in this book as *battlegroup*) – an ad hoc unit with a strength normally halfway between a group and a regiment.

20. The two batteries were equipped with 420 mm guns. Both had taken part in the Siege of Sevastopol.

21. Due to their particularity, railway artillery units are dealt with in a separate section of this book.

22. There is a copy in Burguete's archive.

IV. The Storm Closes In

1. The unusual designation of this unit was due to the fact that, while forming part of the *Waffen SS*, its members were all volunteers from German police forces.

2. Although these batteries of captured guns did not have their own means of transport and were static, this did not mean that German command did not redeploy them fairly often. In August 1942, L Corps which at the time included the troops deployed in front of the Soviet bridgehead at Oranienbaum and in the encirclement of Leningrad, right up to the sector held by the 121st Division, which was later to be relieved by the Spanish division. This corps had eight batteries, including the Hessen Battery, with a total of 24 French 155 mm guns (of which 18 were operational), and another seven batteries with French 220 mm *Mörser*. In September L Corps' front became shorter as the recently arrived Blue Division was incorporated into LIV Corps, another newcomer to the front, but the number of batteries equipped with *Mörser 531 (f)* grew from 7 to 22, making a total of 61 guns (although only 50 were operational). By then all of them were using the new 5000 series designation. As LIV Corps was to be the one to launch the assault on Leningrad and it was expedient to use standardized armament, that corps would transfer two more batteries of this type to L Corps, but shortly afterwards they had to hand over four batteries to XXXVIII Corps (which was operating on the Volkhov) and three to XXVI Corps (which occupied the corridor leading to Lake Ladoga). Therefore by November it was left with 17 batteries with 46 guns (33 of them operational). In December three batteries had to be dissolved to make up the numbers of the 14 remaining ones. And in January, when the Oranienbaum area became the responsibility of the *Luftwaffe* Field Corps, command was finally lost over the six batteries of this type deployed there. By the end of January 1943, after three more batteries were sent to XXVI Corps to make up for its losses in the battle to the south of Lake Ladoga, L Corps only had five 5000 series batteries left of the 24 which it had deployed at its peak.

3. These were the so-called *Artillerie-Kraftfahrzeug-Staffel*. The 18th Army had three of them.

4. I am grateful to Daniel Burguete for allowing me to consult this documentation.

5. The *Luftwaffe* field divisions and the army corps they formed part of were manned by air force personnel who had been diverted from ground services to serve as combat forces. Although they were used as infantry they continued to be part of the *Luftwaffe*.

6. Created in May 1941, it was incorporated in the 18th Army in June 1941. Its strength grew from three to four batteries.

7. This 182nd Anti-Aircraft Artillery Regiment formed part of the 2nd Anti-Aircraft Artillery Division, the *Luftwaffe Flak* unit covering the airspace around Leningrad. The Division's General HQ was in Krasnogardeisk.

8. One such episode is related in Francisco Torres's work on the volunteers from Murcia, thanks to extracts from the diary of a soldier from Murcia of the Spanish Anti-Tank Group, José Sandoval Caballero. He recounts how due to the ineffectiveness of the Spanish anti-tank guns, Sandoval and his fellow soldiers had to fall back and join one of these *Flakkampftruppen*. TORRES, Francisco. *Soldados de Hierro. Los Voluntarios de la División Azul*. Editorial Actas, Madrid, 2014. See pages 365-366.

9. The concept of *Schwerpunkt*, centre of gravity or main focus of effort, is characteristic of German tactics. In the case of artillery, units were expected to be able to concentrate their fire on these *Feuerschwerpunkte* or main focuses of effort for artillery fire.

10. These may be consulted at http://memoriablau.foros.ws/t6815/partes-de-operaciones-de-la-dev-en-krasny-bor/

11. Long after the event the then Lieutenant De La Vega wrote a history of the Blue Division. In it he provides a fairly detailed account of the part he played in the Battle of Krasny Bor: DE LA VEGA VIGUERA, Enrique. *Rusia no es cuestión de un día. Historia de la División Azul*. Ediciones Barbarossa, Madrid, 1999.

12. DUNNIGAN, James F. "*Organization of German Armed Forces*". In DUNNIGAN, J. and others, *The Russian Front. Germany's War in the East, 1941-1945*. Arms and Armour Press, London, 1978. These figures were split almost equally between the number of rounds with which the batteries were provided and the number that were transported by the columns of trucks of the Divisional Transport Group.

13. ESTEBAN-INFANTES, Emilio. *La División Azul (donde Asia empieza)*. Editorial AHR, Barcelona, 1956.

14. DE ANDRES Y ANDRES, Antonio. *Artillería en la División Azul. Krasny Bor*. Fundación División Azul – Fundación Don Rodrigo, Madrid, 2004.

15. One of the names given to the rocket launchers used by the Soviet artillery, which the Russians liked to call "Katyushas".

V. The Artillery Duel

1. The slang name given to Blue Division soldiers (broadly equivalent to *squaddie*).

2. Emiliano Jiménez Jiménez, Artillery Sergeant in charge of the gun assigned to tank killer duties in the 1st Battery, killed at this battle.

3. CASAS DE LA VEGA, Rafael. *Franco, militar*. Editorial Fénix, Madridejos (Toledo), 1995. See pages 471-472.

4. German rocket launchers are much less well known than their Soviet counterparts and yet they were the better weapon. Unusually they did not form part of the artillery but were incorporated in a separate corps. An introduction to the subject can be found in: ENGELMANN, Joachim. *German Rocket Launchers in World War Two*. Schiffer Military History, West Chester, Pennsylvania, 1990.

5. The 856th Heavy Group had been created in March 1941 and equipped with 21 cm *Mörser*. Although it started the Russian campaign with Army Group Centre, in October 1941 it was transferred to Army Group North.

6. See Caballero, 2004; and Fontenla, 2012.

7. It is worth repeating that, although in the German Army these accompanying gun companies and their commanders were part of the infantry, the Blue Division organized their companies with commanders and men from the artillery.

8. Surviving parts of this officer's diary have recently been published by relatives of his: HERNANZ BLANCO, Guillermo. *Diario de Guillermo en Rusia, 1942*. RH Ediciones, Madrid, 2013. This publication includes a letter that Lieutenant Muro, a fellow officer of the dead man, sent to his family. The letter tells that Hernanz did not die at his battery but at the battlegroup's command post, where he had gone in the line of duty for a purpose that is not clear, but was probably to liaise between the battlegroup's commanders and his battery.

9. Corduroy roads were roads made of birch logs tied together. They were used by *Wehrmacht* troops as communication axes during periods of mud and snow.

10. War Diary 269th Regiment, February 1943: *Archivo Militar General de Ávila* (AGMAV – Avila General Military Archive), C. 2016, Cp. 11, D 1/14.

11. Fontenla, 2014.

12. In fact there are at least two versions of this dispatch. The fuller version is the one written by the 3rd Section (Operations) of the Staff, which includes a fairly detailed description of the fighting and a list of officer casualties. The 2nd Section (Information) is limited to the part which evaluated the attacking force and how it had been left depleted after the battle.

13. This is not an exceptional case; in Fontenla's book *Los Combates de Krasny Bor* a large number of documents are reproduced of which there is no copy in the Avila Military Archive, but which had been preserved in private archives for reasons which do not concern us now. The copy of this detailed "*Report on the battle fought in the Krasny Bor sector due to an enemy attack in the early hours of 10 February 1943*", dated 16 February, which was recently placed at my disposal, was preserved in the archive of the former captain of the 5th/269th Company, Eduardo Blanco Rodríguez, who took part in the fighting. It was given to me by his brother, also a Blue Division veteran, Juan Eugenio Blanco Rodríguez, renowned for his book *Rusia no es cuestión de un día* (1954), which he had written with the aid of documentation provided by his brother Eduardo.

14. The surname was actually Andrada-Vanderwilde, but here we maintain the name as it appeared in the document.

15. In the *Blau Division* bulletin of the *Hermandad de la División Azul* (Blue Division Brotherhood) of Alicante, César Ibáñez Cagna published a detailed study over a series of articles of the divisionaries who had been decorated with the Laureate Cross of San Fernando or the Individual Military Medal, and also those who had been recommended for these

medals but did not finally receive one. In many cases the author found the relevant paperwork but in others not. One of these cases involved the captain in question. His case is set out in *Blau Division* no. 425. The captain was referred to as José María Andrada-Vanderwille because that was the name under which he appeared in the Blue Division General Order for 16 March 1943, which after identifying him as the commander of the 9th Battery, said: "*He stayed at his post against enemy forces far superior in number and with no other protection but that of his gunners, defended the gun line with the resources available to him, and continued to fire the only gun left serviceable. With most of those fighting alongside him either dead, wounded or missing, he was ordered to change emplacement, which he did, despite the difficult situation, and was wounded himself*". Ibáñez added to this text, the first step in the medal recommendation process, the following footnote: "*The recommendation for an Individual Military Medal was turned down. By way of compensation, on 23 February 1948 he was awarded a simple* Cruz de War *(War Cross)*".

16. See Fontenla, 2012, page 240.
17. See Caballero, 2004.
18. VADILLO ORTIZ DE GUZMAN, Fernando. *...y lucharon en Krasny Bor*. Ediciones Marte, Barcelona, 1975. 350 of its 550 pages dedicated to the Battle of Krasny Bor.
19. Due to the destruction of the battlegroup's command post and the death of Santos Ascarza and nearly all his fellow officers.
20. Both the documents referred to are from the archive of Daniel Burguete. Colonel Koske's document is dated 2 April.
21. This and other works by Vadillo were and continue to be monumental. Essential. Simply too good for the time in which he was writing. Nobody should read into my references to his works any criticism of Fernando Vadillo, who researched more than could reasonably be expected from one man. In truth it is a criticism of we historians who came after him, who are taking so long to take a fresh look at the history of the Blue Division.
22. VADILLO, *op. cit., cf.* pages 54 and 207.
23. As I have said, I shall be returning to this matter of the sending of infantry forces to protect certain German artillery units. It is strange that for a long time Spanish accounts of the Battle of Krasny Bor have referred to Spanish commanders as having "skilfully" taken Estonian battalions to cover positions on the front line, battalions which should have been deployed next to the German artillery pieces, and yet at the same time they have overlooked the existence of important emplacements of German artillery.
24. The regiment never deployed all its four groups at Krasny Bor. In order to assemble the three which finally participated in the sector it was necessary to call back units that were already in the Mga area and speed up the transfer of units that were en route from the Volkhov. Furthermore, while some of the men of the 212th Regiment remained under tactical control of the 4th SS

Artillery Regiment, the latter passed control of part of its men and equipment to the 212th Regiment.

25. There is a monographic book about this regiment, something which is not very usual: ROTTMAN, Gordon – ANDREW, Stephen. *SS Artillerie-Regiment 4. SS Polizei Division. A Study of German Artillery*. Concord Publications, Hong Kong, 2006.

26. The 809th Group had been created in June 1940 and equipped with 21 cm *Mörser*. From the start of the Russian campaign it was assigned to Army Group North.

27. Captain Álvarez Lasarte returned to Spain with a repatriation battalion in May 1943. His Iron Cross 1st Class was officially awarded to him when he was already back in Spain, on 18 July 1943. In November he was promoted to major.

VI. The Behemoths: Railway Artillery

1. By way of an introduction to the subject: ENGELMANN, Joachim. *German Railroad Guns in Action*. Squadron Signal Publications, Carrollton (Texas), 1976.

2. DIAZ DE VILLEGAS, 1967.

3. One battery with two 150 mm guns; two batteries with 170 mm guns (6 in total); one battery with a 210 mm gun; four batteries with 240 mm guns (7 guns in total); and eight batteries with a total of seventeen 280 mm guns.

4. *Eisenbahn*: railway.

5. These spectacular weapons have been the subject of a number of very specialized studies. See for example the following articles from the French expert on this subject, François Guy: "Les obusiers français de 400 mm", *Tank Zone. Blindés – Canons – Moteurs*, no. 9 (February-March 2010); "Les obusiers d'AVLF de 370 mm", *Tank Zone*, no. 14 (December 2010-February 2011); "Les canons de 28 cm "Bruno" de l'Eisenbahnartillerie (1917-1945)", *Tank Zone*, no. 15 (February-March 2011).

6. Caballero, 2004.

VII. Analysing the Battle

1. The dispatch is signed by Esteban-Infantes, is not dated at the foot of the last page, and consists of ten pages.

2. Vadillo, *op. cit.*, page 44.

3. For the Tables of Organization and Equipment of a Soviet division at that time, ZALOGA, Steven J – NESS, Leland S, *Red Army Handbook 1939-1945*, *op. cit.*

4. The eminent American military historian David M. Glantz, author of a now classic work on the battle for Leningrad, says that the core of the artillery troops of the 55th Army as at 1 January 1943 consisted of two regiments of field artillery (12th Guard and 126th), one anti-tank regiment (690th), one anti-aircraft regiment (474th), and one mortar regiment (531st). If this was so at the time of the attack on Krasny Bor, the 55th Army had not necessarily needed to resort on a large scale to artillery units from other Soviet armies in order to organize its attack. GLANTZ, David M., *The Battle for Leningrad, 1941-1944*, University Press of Kansas, Lawrence – Kansas – 2002.

5. Glantz, 2002, page 294.

6. Copy of the diary in the archive of Pablo Lope Sagarra Renedo, to whom I am grateful for the opportunity to consult it. The author of the diary did not take part in the battle, but that day and the next he anxiously sought information about it, since several of the dead and wounded officers were friends of his. There is a plan to publish this diary shortly.

7. Although according to Spanish accounts the 2nd/289th Battery had lost its guns, the fact is that it continued to be deployed on the front line. On 14 February it was serving with a group attached to the 212th Division, on the artillery front line, and according to German documentation it had five guns. But a detailed analysis of this documentation reveals that the other two batteries of the group to which it belonged organically, the 289th, had at that time five guns fewer than they had before the battle started. This leads us to suspect that the 2nd/289th Battery had lost all its guns, just as the Spanish had, but had received replacements from its sister batteries.

8. When writing my book *Morir en Rusia* on the Battle of Krasny Bor (Valladolid, 2004) I had the honour of having Captain Castro write a passage in it on the way in which his observation post and the gun line of his 8th Battery had been essential to the improvisation of a new defensive line on the Izhora.

9. CABALLERO JURADO, Carlos. *Atlas Ilustrado de la División Azul*. Susaeta Ediciones, Madrid, 2009. Page 242.

10. Fontenla, 2014.

11. The friend in question is Lorenzo Fernández-Navarro de los Paños y Álvarez de Miranda.

12. That commander was none other than Captain Víctor Castro.

13. He belonged to the Ski Company of the Sappers Battalion. He would be awarded the Iron Cross 2nd Class for his conduct at the Battle of Krasny Bor.

14. He is on the list of SEU founders which appears in JATO MIRANDA, David, *La rebelión de los estudiantes*, 2nd edition – expanded –, self-published, Madrid, 1967. See page 483.

15. GONZÁLEZ PINILLA, Ángel. *Héroes entre valientes. Los condecorados en la División Azul*. Ediciones Ágora, Madrid, 2013. See page 95.

16. Díaz de Villegas, *op. cit.*, page 138.

17. Remember that the writer is using the word "mortars" with its German meaning i.e. "heavy howitzer". From what he says it would appear that there continued to be such guns in his regiment right up until it was time to leave Russia.

18. Díaz de Villegas, *op. cit.*, page 228. On this occasion Díaz de Villegas uses centimetres rather than millimetres to express the calibre of guns. The writer also mentions a battery of 88 mm cannons, but as they were anti-aircraft guns I have not included them here.
19. Dunnigan, *op. cit.*
20. This is an example of the captured French gun which the Germans called *52 cm Haubitze (Eisenbahn) 871 (f)*. In fact the gun had been out of action since late 1941 when its barrel had burst while firing. But for the Soviet propagandists it was a golden opportunity to show the gun wrecked and abandoned, since everyone would assume that it had been Soviet artillery that had destroyed it and Russian infantry that had captured it.